EMPLOYMENT AND WORK RELATIONS IN CONTEXT SERIES

T0326215

Series Editors

Tony Elger and Peter Fairbrother

Centre for Comparative Labour Studies,

Department of Sociology,

University of Warwick

The aim of the Employment and Work Relations in Context series is to address questions relating to the evolving patterns of work, employment and industrial relations in specific workplaces, localities and regions. This focus arises primarily from a concern to trace out the ways in which wider policy-making, especially by national governments and transnational corporations, impinges upon specific workplaces, labour markets and localities in distinctive ways. A particular feature of the series is the consideration of forms of worker and citizen organization and mobilization in these circumstances. Thus the studies will address major analytical and policy issues through case-study and comparative research.

JAPANESE MANAGEMENT TECHNIQUES AND BRITISH WORKERS

Andy Danford

LONDON AND NEW YORK

First published in 1999 by Mansell Publishing Limited

This edition published 2013 by Routledge

Routledge   Routledge
Taylor & Francis Group   Taylor & Francis Group
2 Park Square, Milton Park   711 Third Avenue
Abingdon, Oxon OX14 4RN   New York, NY 10017

Routledge is an imprint of the Taylor & Francis Group, an informa business

British Library Cataloging in Publication Data
A catalogue record for this book is available from the British Library.
ISBN 0–7201–2368–2

Library of Congress Cataloging-in-Publication Data
Danford, Andy
    Japanese management techniques and British workers / Andy Danford.
        p.   cm. — (Employment and work relations in context)
    Includes bibliographical references and index.
    ISBN 0–7201–2368–2 (hardcover)
    1. Industrial management—Great Britain—Case studies.
    2. Industrial management—Japan.   I. Title II. Series.
    HD70.G7D36 1998
    658' .00941—dc21   97-52769
                                                                     CIP

Typeset by BookEns Ltd, Royston, Herts.

CONTENTS

TABLES

ABBREVIATIONS

ACTSS	Association of Clerical, Technical and Supervisory Staff
AEEU	Amalgamated Engineering and Electrical Union
APEX	Association of Professional Executive Clerical and Computer Staff
BAe	British Aerospace
BL	British Leyland
BMC	British Motor Corporation
BMH	British Motor Holdings
BS	British Standard
BSI	British Standards Institution
CAD	Computer-Aided Design
CAITS	Centre for Alternative Industrial and Technological Strategies
CBI	Confederation of British Industry
EEC	European Economic Community
EETPU	Electrical Electronic Telecommunication and Plumbing Union
EU	European Union
FDI	Foreign Direct Investment
GDP	Gross Domestic Product
GM	General Motors
GMB	General Municipal and Boilermakers' Union
HRM	Human Resource Management
IDS	Income Data Services
IRS	Industrial Relations Services
JIT	Just-In-Time
JSSC	Joint Shop Stewards' Committee
LRD	Labour Research Department
MDW	Measured Day Work

MNC   Multinational Company
MSF   Manufacturing Science and Finance Union
NVQ   National Vocational Qualification
OECD   Organization of Economic Cooperation and
          Development
PBR   Payment By Results
PCB   Printed Circuit Board
QC   Quality Circle
SMED   Single Minute Exchange of Dies
SPC   Statistical Process Control
SSP   Statutory Sick Pay
TEC   Training and Enterprise Council
TGWU   Transport and General Workers' Union
TNC   Transnational Corporation
TQM   Total Quality Management
TUC   Trades Union Congress
WDA   Welsh Development Agency

Introduction

My interest in the subject of so-called 'Japanization' – or, to be more precise, the introduction of 'Japanese-style' new management techniques into Western firms – began during the 1980s. Throughout that decade I served as a senior union representative at a large British Aerospace factory in Bristol and witnessed a series of quite dramatic changes at the workplace. The company became subject to what seemed like an incessant process of restructuring due to privatization, cuts in defence spending, recessions in civil aerospace and the introduction of such market mechanisms as competitive tendering. As a result, the site unions and their shop stewards found themselves continually fighting rearguard actions against rationalizations and job losses whilst periodically taking the initiative by publicly campaigning for new industrial strategies based on the principles of arms conversion and job creation in the civil manufacturing sector.

These developments met substantial media interest at the time. What received much less attention, however, were contemporaneous changes to the organization of work and the management of labour which, in many ways, had an equally acute impact on the factory's employees.

A short personal anecdote might be useful here. One day during the summer of 1987, I remember being called before one of our site directors, along with my colleagues on the Bristol Joint Union Committee. This particular director came from the traditional management school; he communicated by barking rather than soft-talking, he was burly, wore an old fashioned pin-stripe suit and smoked Churchillian-size cigars, continuously. I remember him standing up at the start of the meeting, placing a foot on the desk in front of him and announcing: 'Right lads listen to me. This site's in trouble. Our costs are too high, we don't produce enough and we don't produce on time. We're going to be "Japanized".' Amidst much vocal opposition, he proceeded to outline management's plans to establish plant-wide quality circles – and during the following months the site unions proceeded to block them. However, over subsequent years, despite union opposition and conflict, with the guidance of different teams of external consultants the management at Bristol and at many other plants in the aerospace industry introduced successive lean manning strategies, teamworking, greater labour flexibility, reductions in idle time, direct communications, individualization of pay, and new industrial relations policies seeking a marginalization of independent trade union activity. These were not negligible changes or mere continuations of previous managerial agendas. Neither did they engender a process of 'employee empowerment' as so many business writers might presume. Many people were sacked, whilst those lucky enough to keep their jobs suffered the effects of both labour intensification and continuing job insecurity coupled with a clear diminution in their ability to fight back, whether collectively or individually.

Towards the end of this period, during the winter of 1990, I was summoned before the site's new 'HRM-style' managing director and confidently advised that these were 'new times' for the unions and their activists: 'the company now employs a new breed of manager and worker – open-minded, committed and multi-skilled. There's no obvious role here for a traditional union anymore.' This manifestly individualistic ideology then became reified through a rapid informalization of industrial relations and the derecognition of trade unions in most bargaining areas within the diminishing Bristol site.

Although I was eventually made redundant in the summer of 1991, my exposure to the politics of production at one particular manufacturing enterprise, along with my wider role as a lay regional secretary with the MSF trade union, together induced a desire to gain a more thorough appreciation of the capitalist dynamic of workplace restructuring and its effect upon factory labour. This interest developed and became subject to the necessary academic rigour and debate during my subsequent under-graduate studies at the Department of Sociology, University of Bristol. At the same time, in the context of my own experience of the collective struggle to defend workers' interests, I became increasingly aware of the tendency of much recent sociology to effectively remove labour from the labour process, indeed, remove labour from society. I encountered many analyses of Japanese industry, Japanese management, the diffusion of Japanese management in the West, its implications for Western-based work organization, management and trade unions, but very few published studies of the impact of all this on the working lives of factory employees. I therefore attempted to help redress this imbalance by undertaking a PhD research project on Japanese management techniques and British workers in October 1993. The thesis was completed in September 1996 and this book is a revised version of it.

The book is divided into two unequal parts. The first comprises an introduction followed by two chapters which investigate the nature of work organization and employment relations in Japanese manufacturing transplants in South Wales. The second part comprises five chapters which together provide an in-depth case study analysis of the introduction of Japanese-style management techniques at a long-established British autocomponents factory – given the pseudonym 'CarPress' – based in South Wales.

Essentially, the original research upon which the analysis is based rests on a survey of 15 Japanese transplants in South Wales; interviews with trade union officials in the region; interviews with senior representatives of the Welsh Office, the Welsh Development Agency and different employers' organizations; two surveys of shop-floor and office workers at CarPress which required the analysis of 920 questionnaires; over 150 semi-structured interviews with CarPress workers and managers; and a process of observation of developments at the factory between December 1993 and November 1995. A summary of the research methodology employed is provided in the Appendix.

Chapter 1 provides a brief critical overview of the current 'Japanization' debate. The next two chapters establish the more salient aspects of Japanese management techniques which some British firms, including the case study, may be attempting to emulate. Chapter 2 focuses upon the organization of the labour process. Paying particular attention to the consumption of labour power in the different transplants, it investigates the nature of the work on the shop-floor; the skill levels required; the intensity of work; labour deployment practices such as flexibility and teamworking; the role of Japanese transplant workers in job design; and linked to this, the extent to which they participate in Total Quality Management practices such as kaizen. Chapter 3 addresses the different transplant human resource management policies and explores the connections between these and the disciplines of lean, mass production. Particular policies scrutinized are: recruitment, selection and equal opportunities; job security, including the flexibility practices which underpin this; employee involvement practices such as direct communications and single status; and finally, industrial relations strategies.

The remaining chapters focus on the British case study. The study is essentially an ethnography of one company's attempt to restructure the organization of work and management–labour relationships on the shop-floor. Chapter 4 introduces the case study firm and establishes the local and global contexts for the processes of change which unravel in subsequent chapters. Chapter 5 investigates the transformation of the firm's production control system and its intensifying effect on shop-floor labour processes. Chapter 6 chronicles the introduction of teamworking and kaizen. Drawing upon both qualitative and quantitative data, it analyses the different processes by which worker controls and defensive practices are undermined, work rates are intensified and certain groups of employees suffer deskilling. Importantly, this investigation does not just rely upon description of the impact of these developments on the shop-floor; it also traces the complex political strategies and conflicts which accompany the 'management of change' at work.

The conflict and struggle which remain immanent to the capitalist employment relationship come to the fore throughout Chapter 7 in vivid fashion. Here, the process of introducing Japanese-style production techniques is placed into the context of antagonistic labour relations. The chapter describes management's initial attempt to fashion a more 'consensual' style of industrial relations – something akin to business unionism – which eventually founders in the face of rank-and-file distrust to be replaced by a manifest coercion and victimization of workers. It ends with a discussion of the various structural factors which currently inhibit worker resistance to managerial intimidation.

Chapter 8 examines the impact of a package of new human resource management measures on the shop-floor. In particular, it critically addresses the assumption that socialization measures of the kind used by Japanese transplant managements succeed in engendering positive worker commitment and corporate loyalty. Following a similar path to Chapter 3, it focuses upon new employee recruitment and selection techniques; equal opportunity policy; labour retention and job security policies; and employee involvement measures such as more extensive employee communications and single-status policies. The chapter ends with an investigation of the effect on workers' values of the restructuring of work and employment relations. The concluding Chapter 9 draws together the research evidence and considers how our understanding of the new labour regulation practices may contribute to contemporary labour process theory on the nature of hegemonic regimes in advanced capitalism.

Finally, some acknowledgements. I owe a considerable debt to the managers and shop stewards at 'CarPress', to the participants in the survey of the Japanese transplants and to the different industrialists in South Wales who all agreed to give up their time to take part in this research. I am enormously endebted to the many CarPress workers who shared their hopes, concerns and fears with me during 1994 and 1995. The trade unionist I have called Ieuan Thomas in the text is first among these. I also wish to express my thanks to the Economic and Social Research Council for providing the grant which enabled me to complete the research.

I would like to express my gratitude to Professor Theo Nichols – my PhD supervisor – for his continual support, advice and academic stimulation. I am grateful to those other members of staff in the Department of Sociology, University of Bristol who offered different forms of practical support and to my fellow research students who provided friendship and debate, particularly, Erol, John, Maggie, Ian, Jae, Minghua, Steve, Barbara and Tony. I would also like to thank Dr Tony Elger for his help and advice and Dr Chris Smith for agreeing to read the draft manuscript. Finally, I owe my deepest debt to Eileen Danford for her unfailing encouragement and to our two daughters, Jess and Detta, just for being themselves.

Andy Danford

For Eileen, Jess and Detta

1 JAPANESE MANAGEMENT TECHNIQUES AND THE PARADOXICAL ABSENCE OF LABOUR

This book is about contemporary factory work. It investigates the different ways in which Japanese-influenced shifts in work organization and employment relations impact upon the working lives of factory employees. On one level, it seeks to build on our knowledge of the labour processes, the organization of technology, the employment of new working practices and the structure of industrial relations in Japanese manufacturing transplants in the UK. On another level – and the bulk of the book focuses on this – it explores the process of emulation of these facets of Japanese production by a long-established British manufacturing company. The enquiry examines the market-led influences and the underlying political forces which catalyse the diffusion of practices, it considers the various mechanisms of diffusion, and it considers managerial strategy and agency here as well. But above all, it systematically analyses the views and actions of factory workers; those who have the greatest stake in employment, but more often than not, the least say over the direction of change on the shop-floor of the 1990s.

The book asks a number of pertinent questions of the assumptions that prevail in much contemporary business analysis of the management of change on the shop-floor. For example, is there any substance to the fashionable maxim 'working smarter rather than harder', or to the idea of shop-floor 'empowerment', or to notions of a more democratic 'new industrial relations'? More specifically, what effect do Japanese-style new management techniques have on effort rates, on skills, on employee autonomy and on social relations between workers, their unions and management? To put this another way, does the restructuring of work and employment relations best seem to generate harmony and trust on the shop-floor? Or is it best understood to lie on a continuum of capitalist exploitation and subordination of labour accompanied by inherent processes of class struggle and resistance?

This agenda inevitably emphasizes processes at the point of production. However, the analysis is careful not to abstract these from wider political and economic influences. The imbalance of power between capital and labour over the past two decades has ensured that although workers enjoy little influence over events outside the factory gates, different employers and their principal guardian – the capitalist state – have had a profound influence over their working lives. The book, therefore, also investigates how factors such as changing product markets, depressed labour markets, new supplier–customer relations, the dominance of the customer over the producer and the state's role in shaping developments in industrial relations, have all impacted upon social action and the politics of production on the shop-floor.

During the 1980s, the salient position of Japanese manufacturers as increasingly powerful – and sometimes dominant – global competitors was noted with a mixture of interest and alarm by Western politicians, industrialists and trade union leaders. It also resulted in Japanese management methods acquiring a central place in a good many managerialist academic studies of developments in advanced capitalist commodity production. The influence of such studies has in turn contributed to a prevailing belief that as well as affording competitive advantage to employers, for those who labour in the contemporary locales of lean mass production, Japanese-style work organization can be an 'empowering', 'enriching' alternative to the alienation and degradation associated with conventional Taylorism.

One notable example of this assumption is provided by the authors of the International Motor Vehicle Programme of research into productivity and management practices in the car industry. Womack *et al.* (1990) present lean production as a pre-eminent, high-productivity manufacturing system which is now dominant in Japan and which, these authors argue, can and must be emulated by manufacturers in the West. They describe a model of lean production which, through the operation of such working practices as just-in-time, teamworking and continuous improvement, removes all slack, all human and material waste, from the manufacturing operation. Moreover – and it is this which has caught the attention of many contemporary industrial sociologists – by placing the 'dynamic work team' at the heart of the lean factory, they argue that shop-floor work in this highly stressed system somehow becomes 'enriched' and 'de-Taylorized' by incorporating new conceptual tasks and responsibilities:

> While the mass-production plant is often filled with mind-numbing stress, as workers struggle to assemble unmanufacturable products and have no way to improve their working environment, lean production offers a creative tension in which workers have many ways to address challenges. This creative tension involved in solving complex problems is precisely what has separated manual factory work from professional 'think' work in the age of mass production. (Womack et al., 1990, p. 101)

A similar line of argument permeates Kenney and Florida's (1993) more substantial analysis of the management of work and labour in Japanese transplant operations in the USA. In many respects, these authors exceed the evangelism of Womack et al. by insisting that not only is Western emulation of Japanese management necessary in terms of advancing industrial efficiency but it is also an *inevitable* outcome of the capitalist dynamic of technological and organizational progress. Drawing on Gramsci's exposition of Fordism as the most advanced system of production of its time – which, with or without the cultural supports of 'Americanism' was destined to penetrate the West as a distinctive mode of production organization (Gramsci, 1971) – Kenney and Florida argue that the diffusion of Japan's new management paradigm has the same inevitability about it.

In attempting to answer the question of why this should be, Kenney and Florida locate the advantages of lean production in the shifting social relations between intellectual and manual labour which are assumed to underlie Japanese technological and organizational efficiency. They conceptualize Japanese manufacturing practice within a framework of 'innovation-mediated production' characterized essentially by the integration and harnessing of the intelligence and knowledge of R&D staff, design engineers and shop-floor workers. Through the organizational mechanism of the multi-functional team, the shop-floor is transformed into a continuously innovative production laboratory. This creates advantages for both labour and capital:

> The new model has transformed ordinary workers' knowledge and intelligence into a source of value, created new methods of work, and established a very efficient system for turning the potential value embodied in

> innovations into mass-produced commodities that are the source of
> tremendous profit and capital accumulation. (Kenney and Florida, 1993, p. 9)

Described in this way – and with very little qualitative analysis of employee consciousness to substantiate the argument – Japanese work organization sounds an appealing and laudable alternative to the dehumanizing organizational principles of Taylorism. But to what extent do such interpretations reflect reality, or, by contrast, represent mere ideological constructions of industrial development (Stewart, 1996)? This is a problematic question because, in fact, we hear very little about the fundamental dictates and social dynamics of *capitalist* work organization in the above accounts; it is as if the factories of today are organized solely with social responsibility and welfare in mind rather than pumping ever more labour out of workers in the pursuit of profit. To be fair to Kenney and Florida, although it is only a secondary consideration, they do eventually turn their attention to the more negative consequences of the diffusion of Japanese management practices: labour intensification; health and injury risks; ideological control of workers; strict absence and attendance policies; the exploitation of temporary labour; unequal opportunities for black workers; and anti-trade-unionism.

This is a long list. Moreover, these admissions beg an important question. If Japanese 'innovation-mediated production' produces 'bads' as well as 'goods' then how do those human beings who labour under this system react to this? Are they so acquiescent and submissive that Japanese managements can literally raise the intensity of production with impunity? We are not told. The irony here is that in conceptualizing a manufacturing system that theoretically constitutes the anti-thesis of Braverman's (1974) imperative of direct management control under scientific management, the authors – and many others – effectively follow the latter writer's tendency to objectify labour and abstract the analysis of work from the concrete reality of continuing class struggle and resistance. In other words, in neglecting both the material condition and factory-based class consciousness of workers affected by the process of change, this living labour becomes conspicuously absent from the enquiry.

At least the implications of worker resistance take a more prominent position within Oliver and Wilkinson's (1992) influential study of the 'Japanization of British Industry'. These authors also deal in universalistic models. Their paradigm of Japanese manufacturing practices follows a similar pattern to the above American writers. It idealizes a system which completely synchronizes production with the demands of the market and which aims towards the complete elimination of waste in production. This is achieved through the application of a full repertoire of production practices which will be considered in some detail throughout this book: Total Quality Management (TQM) and continuous improvement (kaizen); production checks such as statistical process control (SPC); just-in-time production (JIT); labour flexibility; and multi-skilling through teamworking and job rotation. Oliver and Wilkinson argue that, cumulatively, these practices create a fragile production system which may be severely exposed to labour disruption. Consequently, the model incorporates supporting human resource management (HRM) practices which seek employee acquiescence and commitment; practices such as long-term job security for core workers, careful employee recruitment and selection techniques, performance-related pay, direct communications and enterprise unionism. Risk-avoidance also extends to buyers/assemblers maintaining long-term relationships with suppliers and close scrutiny of their manufacturing costs and employment policies. Thus, in theory at least, the high dependency strategies of Japanese production methods 'demand a set of social (and technical) relations to support the fragile production system. Under this system, strategies for living with uncertainty are swept away' (1992, p. 323).

On the basis of data accumulated from longitudinal survey techniques and a small number of limited case studies, Oliver and Wilkinson quantify an increase in the use of the above practices amongst both British employers and UK-based Japanese transplants. This leads them to assert that a 'Japanization of British industry' is in progress.

The problem with this rudimentary methodology is that it raises as many questions as it solves. Firstly, the analysis makes no attempt to explore variations in management practice between firms in different manufacturing sectors. For example, as Milkman (1991) discovered, rather than conforming to universalistic models, Japanese electronics assembly transplants in the USA were more influenced by the efficiency-based parameters of conventional production lines and the traditional social relations of the host country. In these conditions, fragmented assembly-line work, American anti-trade-unionism and limited employee involvement remained a simple, logical and effective method of labour control.

The authors' idealization of trust-building long-term customer–supplier relations raises further problems. Suppliers are supposed to gain here by enjoying such advantages as more predictable markets, help and advice from the customer, financial security, and so on, although they are also under constant pressure to produce the right quantities of goods on time. But this oft-quoted feature of 'stakeholder capitalism' (Hutton, 1995) rarely takes into consideration those who hold a stake in employment within supplier companies. Oliver and Wilkinson inform us that buyer/assemblers may often pre-empt disruption to JIT supplies by attacking traditional industrial relations practices at their supplying companies. If this is the case, then we need a more thorough investigation of the implications of such innovations for shop-floor social action in the many affected factories.

The same limitations to the authors' methodology raise a more fundamental criticism. The argument that the high-dependency nature of Japanese production methods operates within supportive HRM policies creating 'a functional fit between production methods and the social relations in which they are embedded' (1992, p. 323) constitutes the most original aspect of their thesis. They are not totally alone here. For example, Dohse *et al.* (1985) believe that 'only a comprehensive perspective that includes both the organization of the labour process and the organization of labour relations can adequately explain the functioning of the Japanese model' (1985, p. 134).[1] But if this is the case, then rather than rely on quantitative analysis to construct a facile functionalist fit between different sets of management practices we need to examine exactly how such innovations function on the shop-floor. In so doing, we might penetrate a further conundrum within Oliver and Wilkinson's argument. That is, if the new, 'Japanized' labour process really is characterized by more skill, more responsibility and more interest, to the extent that 'Japanese practices seem to hold out the opportunity for improved quality of life' (1992, p. 326), then why does this shop-floor empowerment require propping up by special ideological measures? Should we not expect worker commitment to emerge naturally from the enriched labour process? On the other hand, if, in reality, the labour process is low-skilled, multi-tasked, intensified and alienating then the 'cultural logic' of extensive employee involvement may also make little sense. These contradictions and ambiguities can only be resolved by moving away from the managerialist agenda and considering the standpoint of labour. If we wish to understand the real logic of the new HRM practices then we must turn our attention to their recipients, that is, we have to thoroughly investigate their concrete impact on the consciousness and social action of the *human* resource.

Despite some differences in detail, the above expositions share a common approach in their construction of a distinctive paradigm of Japanese work organization and employment relations. This is based on the general principles of flexible, low-waste production; enlarged and participatory labour processes; and cooperative employment relations. Although some authors may be critical of these principles, and others find them elusive in practice, the paradigmatic approach nevertheless dominates research in this area (see for example, Schonberger, 1982; Lincoln and Kalleberg, 1990; Milkman, 1991; Bratton, 1992; Jurgens *et al.*, 1993; Graham, 1994 and 1995; and Morris *et al.*, 1994). Moreover, rather than measure concrete practice in Japan against these ideal type constructions, many researchers either prescribe, or attempt to substantiate, a process of international convergence through Western emulation of the Japanese paradigm: a 'Japanization' of industry.

Before we consider particular case study evidence of this emulation process and its effect on factory labour, we need to take a more critical look at its underlying assumptions. Some writers deny the Japanese any influence over contemporary workplace restructuring. For example, de-emphasizing investigation into changes within organizations, Ackroyd *et al.* (1988) shift the enquiry towards the national economic structure. They argue that fundamental differences between an integrated Japanese economy – characterized by high levels of coordination between banking, manufacturing and traditional capital – and a highly fragmented British economy, present decisive limits on any attempts by British firms to respond to the Japanese challenge through emulation. However, the problem with this approach is that although changes at the organizational level *are* mediated by the structural features of the political economy, as they are by structural *changes* in product markets, labour markets, state industrial policies and so on, this does not mean that investigations at this level must necessarily become secondary. If we wish to investigate the hypothesis that Japanese work organization and labour performance may be having a significant global impact, then whether or not we call this 'Japanization', our first port of call must be the workplace. And if corporate aims to raise labour productivity and profitability constitute the dynamic behind attempted emulation, then developments in the process of extracting surplus value at the point of production must surely be our prime, though not sole, focus of investigation.

This clarifies the level of analysis employed in this book but it does not deny external structural influences on work organization. Serious questions do need to be asked of the paradigmatic approach. Can we accurately speak of a universalistic Japanese model to which competing Western manufacturers aspire? Do not the concrete ramifications of different sectoral practices, different technologies, product markets, labour markets, national state policies, industrial relations traditions, and indeed, distinctive single corporate cultures and logics, together undermine notions of universalism and convergence? If, as Elger and Smith (1994b) observe in their conceptualization of 'Disaggregated Japanization', Japanese transnational corporations are equivalent in intent to their Western counterparts in that, 'Japanese firms take advantage of different regions of the globe for market and cost reasons, and selectively adjust their factory regimes to fit into these local conditions' (1994b, p. 38), does this eliminate any organizational distinctiveness? Moreover, if, as the same authors suggest, emulating firms mobilize fears of the Japanese 'competitive threat' more as an ideological component in their attempts to reinforce traditional management prerogatives, whilst merely borrowing certain elements of the Japanese model in piecemeal fashion, does this render the concept of 'Japanization' completely redundant?

These questions should certainly alert us to the fact that it would be wrong to 'overinterpret what are certainly significant innovations, to read them uncritically as the precursors of a wholesale transformation of work and employment relations, and thus to gloss over substantial continuities, real variations and persistent sources of conflict in the contemporary restructuring of work and employment' (Elger and Smith, 1994a, p. 5). But it might also be a mistake to assume that the influence of the Japanese is therefore restricted to the realm of managerial ideology, that particular Japanese-style management innovations have had minimal concrete impact on the lives of British factory workers.

On the basis of the personal experience outlined in the Introduction, this author came to doubt the suspicion that management's understanding of Japanese manufacturing performance and new working practices was passed on to subordinates solely in ideological terms. Even if companies rarely implement complete 'Japanese packages' in paradigmatic fashion, the ensuing, more fragmented changes can still significantly undermine rank-and-file power on the shop-floor with detrimental consequences for thousands of workers. When Japanese managements set up their manufacturing transplants abroad, they may often maintain the organizational and industrial relations traditions of both their particular sector and the host country, but they are also careful to sweep away those particular traditions which are hostile to their intensive capital accumulation strategies. For example, there is hardly a Japanese transplant operating on a greenfield site in the UK which tolerates such shop-floor traditions as seniority and informal rank-and-file controls over the labour process, or union regulation of skill and task demarcations, or union influence over effort rates and labour deployment.

The important point then becomes, to what extent, in the distinctive economic and political conditions of the 1990s, are British firms on brownfield sites emulating the managerial strategies of these transplants by implementing the same labour regulation policies and attacking their own shop-floor traditions? And is the social organization of production that is distinctive within Japanese methods likely to cause a significant change in British shop-floor attitudes towards work and working practices (Turnbull, 1986), or, is the process of 'Japanization' characterized by inherent worker resistance and conflict? These are the concerns of this book, and it is in connection with the above relationship, that is, between managerial innovations in UK-based Japanese transplants and the impact of such innovations within emulating British firms, that the contested expression 'Japanization' is occasionally employed.

Case Studies of Japanese Management Techniques

Comprehensive studies of the impact of Japanese management innovations on factory labour are few and far between. Whether managerialist in intention or not, too many research designs rely on different types of managers as key informants, occasionally accompanied by a small number of perfunctory interviews with shop stewards and members of the trade union bureaucracy to convey a sense of balance. As a result, whenever the standpoint of the rank and file on the shop-floor is considered, the ensuing account relies upon, at best, empathetic understanding and, at worst, pure speculation, rather than any systematic, in-depth analysis of workers' views. Of course, managers do provide crucial information on contemporary corporate strategies governing marketing and sales, product design, quality assurance and production. And as agents of capitalist control, they are key informants on questions of labour regulation. But accumulating data primarily from those representing the management side of the capital–labour relationship can sometimes result merely in a reproduction of managerial ideology as Trevor's (1988) interpretive account of the restructuring of Toshiba's electronics plant in Plymouth exemplifies.[2]

Moreover, many of the more radical exposures of managerial ideology and practice in Japanese production provide only a limited picture of the various ways in which worker resistance constrains the exercise of managerial prerogatives. Theoretical ideal types of management control become reified on a shop-floor devoid of politics. Delbridge et al.'s (1992) examination of management control and labour intensification under JIT/ TQM regimes provides a case in point. These authors provide a compelling account of the ways in which the acceptance of new responsibilities and tasks under teamworking forces workers to become more accountable both to management and each to other for their individual performance. The natural visibility of the production process and worker performance in a highly synchronized JIT factory offers management a simple means of direct control over the labour process. More subtly, the application of peer pressure in a 'market environment', where assembly line colleagues suddenly take on the role of customers cajoling each other to maintain performance, provides a more corrupting form of labour control. These regimes are presented as systems of efficient capital accumulation which more completely subordinate labour to capital by denying employees any space to exercise counter-controls over the pace of work and task execution (1992, p. 98).

The problem with this type of approach is its tendency to both over-emphasize the effect of individualizing processes in the workplace and suggest an omnipotent management system (Stewart, 1996) which is itself partly a function of the imbalance between the accumulation of factory managers' and workers' viewpoints in research designs. And even where this is not the case, such as in Delbridge's (1995) participatory observation-based study of the stress and intensity of assembly line work in a Japanese electronics transplant, preconceptions of absolute management control lead the author to conclude that:

> The experiences of workers under JIT and TQM reflect an increasingly effective pressure from management toward the processes of accommodation and adaptation by workers with the reduction in effective counter-control and resistance. In effect, workers are forced toward surviving rather than resisting their exploitation. (Delbridge, 1995, p. 814)

Here again we have no exploration of exactly why the expected resistance is curtailed. Why do these transplant workers not unambiguously oppose their conditions of intense exploitation? Why do they turn on each other rather than management when the level of intensity is increased? Why is it a question of survival; why don't they just leave? These crucial questions remain unanswered because the analysis fails to procure the views of those who – if they are lucky – may spend all of their working lives 'surviving' the exigencies of assembly line work.

Of course, it might be argued that this represents a primitive line of enquiry based on the supposition that the intensity of Japanese transplant production remains embedded in Western social values of instrumentalism. In traditional mass-production factories, workers would be expected to reject managerial attempts to heighten levels of exploitation because dominant instrumentalist values permit them to think and act for themselves. As Graham puts it, 'workers are free to hate their work openly. Their attitudes are their own. The bargain they strike with the company is simple and straightforward: make quota and you get your pay' (1995, p. 133). In contrast to this, much of the literature on Japanization emphasizes those ideological and socialization components of Japanese production methods which attempt to colonize the worker's psyche in order to control his or her labour power.

In their study of Nissan's car assembly transplant in Sunderland, Garrahan and Stewart (1992) provide an influential analysis of this process; of managerial endeavours to control and subordinate the workforce by mobilizing an ideology built on the appealing principles of consensus and participation. The essential claim of these authors is that despite the highly exploitative nature of the production system – a highly stressed system of labour intensification through low skill job enlargement – Nissan's workers come to support and identify with the objectives of their employer. They display a 'corporate consciousness'. Garrahan and Stewart assert that in the absence of any effective means to articulate their collective identities and interests, such as an independent trade union, Nissan's workers become attracted to a seductive corporate ideology which advocates a collective spirit of teamwork and consensus. The idea of a dichotomy of opposing management and worker interests has no place here. An ideology of consent operates on two levels. Firstly, through specific social forms such as kaizen, and teamworking, which depends 'precisely upon self-subordination for it shifts the locus of control onto individuals, who perceive themselves as guardians of quality and flexibility' (1992, p. 94). And secondly, through a wider organizational framework which ensures that Nissan's one-sided vision of a classless factory can be reproduced on the shop-floor each day:

> What we are witnessing at Nissan is not only an organization which depends upon and promotes consensus-building structures for quality products. The flip-side of this is an organizational hierarchy of constraint, one that allows only those views of work which are commensurate with its own. (Garrahan and Stewart, 1992, p. 111)

Once again, we are presented – even though this is most certainly not what these authors desire to see – with a picture of complete worker subordination, of total management control. Is there any substance in this? Although we must acknowledge the significant influence of mass unemployment and the lack of effective collective representation on worker consciousness, nevertheless, can we really expect individuals labouring under these regimes to display total commitment and even to participate in the intensification of their own exploitation? Different case studies of Japanese auto transplants in the USA suggest not. For example, Fucini and Fucini (1990), Rinehart et al. (1994) and Graham (1995) discovered that although shop-floor workers may display an initial enthusiasm for the process of kaizen as a means of improving working conditions and health and safety, they soon become disillusioned with managements' sole interest in reducing waste and idle time. As a result, this process of 'mass employee participation' eventually becomes the property of managers, engineers and just a sprinkling of token workers. This contrasting evidence exposes the fact that we have no real evidence of the extent to which Nissan has won the 'battle of hearts and minds' with its Sunderland workforce. Although Garrahan and Stewart raise many important conceptual points concerning labour exploitation under Japanese management regimes, this particular study is again undermined by a deficiency of views from the factory floor.

Distinctive corporate ideologies constitute just one example of capital's repertoire of labour control mechanisms. Technological development is another. The spatial reconfiguration of existing technology, such as a Japanese-style conversion of traditional clusters of single-function machines into a multi-functional cellular organization (Schonberger, 1986), can effect efficiency savings and significant shifts in shop-floor social relations. If new computer technologies are then incorporated into this reorganization of technology, then labour regulation may be further enhanced. Bratton's (1992) study of what might be termed, 'computer-aided teamwork', found that this type of technological change, in small-batch skilled production work at least, provided a degree of shop-floor autonomy whilst simultaneously enhancing overall managerial control. Here we have a kind of technologically mediated 'responsible autonomy' (Friedman, 1977). Bratton's operators enjoyed some discretion and new skills in the process of self-management of teams, but senior management surveillance through computerized production control systems ensured the extension of overall managerial control over the labour process.

However, Bratton's case study analysis contains certain shortcomings. Ostensibly concerned with the process of 'Japanization at Work' it centres almost exclusively on changes in technology. He fails to operationalize the full range of measures aimed at restructuring work organization and employee relations with which we identify the Japanese. The thesis is therefore incomplete. Moreover, its more salient points apply only to changes within small-batch craft production – an area of work which is important and interesting in itself – but, notwithstanding the quixotic ideas of flexible specialization theorists such as Piore and Sabel (1984), this overlooks the fact that the dynamic of change associated with Japanese production techniques is located elsewhere, in capitalist mass-production.

We must turn again to the USA for a more thorough examination of 'bases of control and resistance' at the point of production under a Japanese management regime. In her ethnography of shop-floor work at a Subaru-Isuzu Automotive (SIA) transplant – which utilized covert participant observation techniques – Graham (1995) provides a rich personal account of the day-to-day stress and conflict that accompanies life on a Japanese assembly line. Drawing explicitly on Burawoy's (1985) conceptualization of the hegemonic factory regime, Graham argues that the success of the Japanese production system depends upon 'management's ability to fashion an environment which appears free of coercion, giving no impetus for resistance. Instead of management devoting time and energy to controlling the workforce directly, workers control themselves' (1995, p. 97). She provides seven particular components of a multi-dimensional framework of compliance which together form, in Weberian fashion, an 'iron cage of control': sophisticated recruitment techniques; scrupulous employee induction programmes (both of these are eventually displaced by the practice of employing and monitoring temporary workers); the team concept and the disciplinary influence of peer pressure; a philosophy of kaizen; shaping shop-floor culture from the top down; a computerized assembly line; and just-in-time production.

Graham usefully explores the contradictions between what is, in abstract terms, a sophisticated model of compliance and the harsher reality of working on an assembly line. For example, the increasing intensity of a labour process characterized by rapid and repetitive limb movements caused 25 per cent of the workforce to suffer periodically from carpel tunnel syndrome and other disabilities after just a few months of employment. Yet, although the management tried hard to alleviate the symptoms of this labour intensification by offering different medications, it could not modify the driving logic of its system of lean mass-production:

> The repetition and speed of assembly line work was inherently harmful to workers. Any solutions that would reduce the work intensity created by repetition and line speed would threaten production quotas – something team members believed the company would never consider ... Providing a truly safe workplace is beyond their [the company's] control in a competitive environment where the priority is quotas rather than safety first. (Graham, 1995, p. 93)

And predictably, even in their non-union environment, Graham's workers do oppose this exploitation. She provides different instances of individual forms of resistance, for example, workers maintaining a silent protest during team briefings and more effective collective forms, such as team members surreptitiously stopping the line in order to gain a breather.

Graham's methodology does have certain drawbacks, however, in that by concentrating on the more mundane, everyday events which unfold on a transplant assembly line it loses sight of the wider picture. Covert participant observation prevents the researcher from seeking answers to awkward questions from all actors involved in the politics of production, that is, different managers, shop stewards and a reasonable cross-section of factory workers. Moreover, her highly focused ethnography excludes any historical analysis of the development of management–labour relations in the auto industry. Consequently, we are led to believe that, on the basis of surface appearances, the Japanese production model merely represents an extension of the 1970s job-redesign/human-relations movement and its attendant concerns with the consequences of worker alienation. The alternative possibility, that many of the new management techniques may have the more fundamental objective of appropriating traditional worker controls on the shop-floor, is ignored, as is the influence on this process of external agencies such as the customer and the state.

Notwithstanding these criticisms, this particular study succeeds in switching our attention away from managerial systems and simplistic abstract conceptualizations of 'total management control' by elevating worker actions and consciousness to a pivotal point in its investigation. In so doing, it underscores the essential contradiction between contemporary Japanese managerial ideology and the demands of capital accumulation: 'the Japanese model is not equipped to deliver on its promises to workers. During a corporation's quest to maximize profits, workers simply become expendable. Work intensification and safety, issues traditionally addressed by unions, are the first areas to be sacrificed for profit' (Graham, 1995, p. 154). And if this contradiction is embodied in certain forms of worker resistance on a non-union, greenfield site, where management could more readily fashion a pro-company culture, we should expect an intensified conflict on the battle-scarred terrain of the conventional brownfield shop-floor.

Unfortunately, up-to-date empirical evidence on brownfield sites is somewhat scarce. However, the small number of case studies which investigated work organizational change and accompanying conflict during the 1980s do confirm this expectation. For example, in Britain's food processing industry, Scott (1994) discovered that the introduction of teamworking – ostensibly to develop fulfilling work routines and open relationships between workers and supervisors – could not disguise the inherently alienating nature of the assembly line labour process. Neither could it conceal management's demand for a tougher unilateral approach to discipline and effort. In his case study of the reorganization of work at a strongly unionized frozen-food works, shop stewards were initially able to exploit the self-management of teamworking in order to maintain control over effort rates, labour deployment and job rotation. When management then decided to claw back its prerogatives, increase production and raise standards of discipline, it was forced to jettison the 'soft' participative approach and defeat rank-and-file opposition by provoking, and eventually defeating, an all-out strike.

Other case studies of British manufacturing plants attempting to emulate Japanese working practices in the 1980s found that, despite the distinctive free-market economic and political environment of the time, and despite occasional management coercion, shop-floor resistance and trade union organization continued to place limits on the exercise of managerial prerogatives (Turnbull, 1986; Starkey and McKinlay, 1989; Taylor *et al.*, 1994). Indeed, where the economic and political environment does act to enforce cooperative relations these are unlikely to be permanent. At Taylor *et al.*'s 'Central Rebuild' electronics plant for example, 'the orchestration of a qualified cooperation depended heavily on a sense of the continuing precariousness of the whole factory against a background of marked sectoral and regional recession' (1994, p. 222). Thus, we cannot assume that the restructuring of work organization along Japanese lines and the promulgation of new, consensual corporate ideologies must necessarily, in mechanical fashion, engender a dynamic of Japanization in employment relations characterized by the emergence of durable worker loyalty and commitment.

In contrast to the currently fashionable conceptions of the 'conflict-free' factory, these latter studies suggest that capital's attempts to restructure the organization of work and the employment relationship are not unproblematic. They raise the possibility that despite managerial intimidation, despite the cumulatively pernicious impact of anti-trade-union legislation, despite the apparent demise of the strike weapon, despite the continuing rationalization of jobs in manufacturing, and despite the crippling stranglehold of consumer debt to building societies and other financial institutions, workers still have a propensity to oppose managerial prerogatives. Why might this be?

Earlier in this introductory chapter, the author posed a series of rudimentary questions to challenge some of the dominant assumptions which influence our understanding of contemporary change at the workplace. Questions such as what is the impact of the new management techniques on effort rates? their impact on skills? on worker autonomy? and on workplace democracy and labour relations? These are all raised at various points in the coming chapters. But a central theme of the book – and one which is absent from much of the current literature – is that the implementation and unfolding of the new Japanese-style management practices in established factories is a long drawn out and complex political process which is propelled by a dynamic of tension, conflict and struggle between capital and labour. It cannot be presented merely as the unproblematic substitution of one model of work organization for another, as a clean rupture from Taylorism or Fordism for example. Managers and workers have conflicting class interests. For most factory workers, life on a production line remains arduous, monotonous and alienating. The slow, uneven development of formal and informal rank-and-file influence over the pace of work, job content, labour deployment and so forth was not the result of inherently cantankerous work attitudes but instead the outcome of a long, fragmented, collective struggle for at least a limited sense of dignity and autonomy at work. Contemporary management attempts to undermine these gains and secure its own prerogatives in the name of 'progress', 'efficiency', 'empowerment' and even 'company survival', are likely to be subject to different forms of working-class opposition. The efficacy of this opposition will also be contingent upon the prevailing balance of power between capital and labour at the point of production and in the wider political economy. These are the realities which govern the perspective of this book; realities which provide an awareness that 'Japanization' at the workplace is both a function and outcome of the immanent process of class struggle in advanced capitalist societies.

Notes

1   In posing the question of why Japanese workers seem to accept the labour intensity and stress which is inherent to their model of Japanese work organization, Dohse et al. (1985) emphasize different functional aspects of the social relations which accompany the highly exploitative production methods. That is, the system of lifelong employment induces worker dependence on single corporations; the individualized *satei* wage system – which is similar in many respects to performance-related pay – constitutes a decisive factor in the 'committed worker syndrome' since it induces worker dependence on the arbitrary judgements of supervisors; and the absence of independent trade-unionism militates against the collective articulation and representation of Japanese workers' interests, which forces workers to turn against each other (in the form of peer pressure) rather than against their employer.

2   Trevor's (1988) 250-page investigation draws on qualitative analysis, spread over seven chapters, of interviews with a small number of senior managers at Toshiba along with just one trade union official – an evangelical, 'new realist' national officer of the EEPTU (now AEEU). On this somewhat uneven empirical basis, we are informed that such innovations as careful employee selection and induction, total labour flexibility, single status, management-controlled direct communications, management-controlled company councils and no-strike agreements provide employees greater job satisfaction and security. Significantly, the one chapter which considers the shop-floor's standpoint by analysis of an employee attitude questionnaire survey, provides little evidence to substantiate this.

2 JAPANESE LEAN PRODUCTION IN SOUTH WALES

In contrast to elsewhere in the UK, manufacturing industry in Wales enjoyed a significant revival during the 1980s. Between 1985 and 1990, manufacturing output rose by 32.9 per cent, 14.5 percentage points higher than the UK figure for the period; the long-term decline of manufacturing share of total GDP was reversed – an unparalleled development in the OECD countries; and investment per manufacturing employee amounted to 167 per cent of the UK average, the highest figure for any UK region (Price *et al.*, 1994, pp. 10–11).

Price *et al.* argue that recent inward investment in the region contributed substantially both to this superior economic performance and to the restructuring of Welsh manufacturing in favour of such light engineering sectors as automotive components, office equipment and consumer electronics. In fact, the 'Welsh renaissance' goes back further than this. The diversification and growth of the manufacturing sector took hold nearly three decades earlier and, just as today, was led by non-indigenous businesses including a high proportion of branch plants of international firms (Lovering, 1983; Morris, 1987). Many of these employers operated purely as low-skill assembly units rather than centres of R&D and administration. Consequently, the process of job creation was accompanied by a qualitative erosion of job content and remuneration: 'the net result was an overall decline in the total of well-paid (male, skilled) jobs, and a rise in lower-paid (female, unskilled) employment' (Lovering, 1983, p. 61).

This restructuring process has continued unabated over recent years. During the 1980s, Japanese multinationals accelerated their search for overseas investments in response to a number of politico-economic pressures: the need to recycle Japan's trade surpluses; increasing protectionism in world markets; the appreciation of the yen; the increased prices of Japanese real estate and stocks which acted to push investment out; and the globalization of these firms' trade and corporate structures (Elger and Smith, 1994a, p. 20). Coincidentally, Japanese investment in Britain was actively encouraged by successive Conservative governments both to rejuvenate the country's declining manufacturing base and to undermine the traditions of free collective bargaining between employers and independent trade unions.

As a result, between 1986 and 1990, Japanese investment increased sevenfold in the UK. Wales was a major recipient of this; indeed, between 1979 and 1991, the region accounted for 14.2 per cent of all Britain's foreign direct investment (Price et al., 1994, p. 12). Many companies arrived in Wales because its restructured labour markets offered certain distinctive advantages. Of course, the factors which determine the specific location of foreign direct investment are many. However, as Morris and Hill (1991) point out, relative unit labour costs and labour adaptability constitute the most important considerations for Japanese companies. In Wales, the decline of coal, steel and older manufacturing industries created large pools of malleable, dependent labour along the southern valleys and in the old industrial towns. This deindustrialization also established the Welsh labour force as the lowest paid in the UK.[1]

The presence of Japanese capital in Wales, therefore, is partly a function of these advantageous economic conditions. By 1992, the region contained the highest number of Japanese-owned manufacturing transplants in the UK: 34 factories which together employed 13,000 workers out of a total of 50,800 for the UK as a whole (Anglo-Japanese Journal, 1992). These transplants operate in the consumer electronics, electronic components, autocomponents, office equipment and plastics and chemicals sectors. Many are concentrated in South Wales.

The purpose of this chapter, and the next, is to explore the salient features of Japanese management practice in the South Wales region. Drawing on quantitative and qualitative data accumulated through a survey of the region's Japanese manufacturing transplants, the analysis seeks to establish exactly what, if anything, is distinctive about Japanese work organization and employment relations in this region and how this impacts upon the interests of shop-floor labour.

This chapter investigates those features of management practice most commonly associated with the 'Japanese production model': the reskilled labour process; lean production control; flexibility, teamworking and other aspects of labour utilization; and total quality management (TQM) practices such as kaizen.

Table 2.1 *Participating firms by sector and size*

Company	Manufacturing sector	Total employees
Calsonic	Autocomponents	701
AIWA	Consumer electronics	980
Matsushita Electric	Consumer electronics	1650
Sony	Consumer electronics	2750
Hitachi	Consumer electronics	800
Star Micronics	Consumer electronics	206
Gooding Sanken	Electronic components	233
Electronic Harnesses	Electronic components	150
Yuasa Batteries	Electronic components	640
Matsushita Electronic Components	Electronic components	251
Matsushita Electronic Magnetrons	Electronic components	40
Sekisui	Chemicals and plastics	80
Dynic	Chemicals and plastics	40
Diaplastics	Chemicals and plastics	205
Takiron	Chemicals and plastics	72

At the time of the survey, in 1994, there were 17 fully Japanese-owned manufacturing transplants based in the South Wales region.[2] Many of these are concentrated in the consumer electronics and electronics component sectors, although firms operating in the autocomponents and chemicals and plastics sectors are also present. Of these 17 firms, 15 agreed to participate in the survey and all of the above sectors were represented (see Table 2.1 and Appendix).[3]

Work Organization and the Labour Process

Most of the transplants organized their production on the principle of continuous-flow assembly lines involving repetitive and monotonous task routines. These lines would be automated where batch size or standardized components made this feasible; otherwise, production relied principally upon labour-intensive manual work. The nature of the labour processes in the different transplants will now be examined, sector by sector.

Autocomponents

Calsonic is the only wholly-owned Japanese subsidiary operating in the auto sector in South Wales. The factory manufactures different types of heat exchanger units with a customer base spread across the European vehicle assembly industry. Unlike the other transplants in the survey, Calsonic is not a classic Japanese greenfield operation. Its Llanelli factory was formerly an old British Leyland/Rover plant which underwent a management–employee buy-out in advance of the Rover privatization in 1988. The Calsonic Group subsequently purchased the plant in 1989. However, despite this brownfield status – and the legacy of shop-floor control over the labour process which accompanied it – the combination of competitive market pressures and the emergence of a more compliant trade union organization[4] weakened by almost continual threats of redundancy since 1988, facilitated a significant restructuring of work organization involving the implementation of just-in-time production control techniques and teamworking.

Looked at purely in technological terms of 'efficiency' and 'flexibility', this restructuring could be described as the substitution of continuous-flow, cellular production for the more inflexible, dedicated machine layouts associated with conventional Fordist techniques. The Calsonic management inherited an orthodox form of work organization based on the separation of machines and workstations into discrete functional areas or 'clusters' (Schonberger, 1986). Gradually, cell-based teamworking replaced this arrangement allowing different machines and tasks to be grouped together by product family rather than single function. The different teamworkers also became more personally responsible for the quality of their work and more responsive to the just-in-time supply requirements of the customer.

However, these changes also had a major political dimension. Rather than introduce quixotic notions of 'ownership', 'self-management', or, as one writer has put it, 'the creation of little factories within a factory' (Turnbull, 1986), the reorganization was aimed primarily at intensifying work rates and re-imposing managerial prerogatives. In particular, it resulted in the rationalization of jobs, the removal of both formal and informal job demarcations and the dismantling of those production buffers which gave operators occasional breaks from the incessant intensity of production. Using classic work-measurement techniques, teams of industrial engineers set about reorganizing workstations, reducing the number of non-profitable process tasks, removing waiting times in stores and transit, removing factory-floor pallet areas for temporary workstation storage and removing the stores themselves. What appears, ostensibly, as a series of quite mundane organizational changes had more profound implications for shop-floor operators. One shop-floor manager commented:

> Our style of working on the shop-floor has undergone quite a radical change as a result of all this. We've virtually got rid of all the old buffers which literally used to pile up shoulder high at every workstation. No longer do our operators work stop-go, stop-go, sometimes going flat out, sometimes taking a rest. It's now bell to bell, steady, continuous working – with the machines and technology driving the men rather than the other way around. It might not sound like much of a change but it's a big change for us I can assure you.

The introduction of teamworking did little to enrich the operators' work. During the processes of assembling, clinching and brazing the different metal rods, tubes and gills that comprise a radiator assembly, operators in the labour-intensive manual areas might rotate from one narrow task to another. But their work remained essentially fragmented and low-skilled.

The factory also contained high-volume automated areas, where assembly and brazing operations were performed by dedicated robotic-based technology. In these areas, although the different teams of operators enjoyed higher status because they were employed on 'state of the art' technology, they also suffered de-skilling. In effect, they were converted into unskilled 'line feeders' (Jurgens et al., 1993) with the sole responsibility of loading materials and parts into machine silos, magazines and fixtures.

This segmentation of production tasks had a significant gender dimension. A rationalization of jobs in the labour-intensive production teams resulted in many women leaving the factory over recent years. At the same time, operators working in the automated areas enjoyed relative job security. The fact that the latter were all men was no coincidence. Stereotypical assumptions concerning 'natural' men's and women's skills contributed to a gradual gendering of the work process (Cockburn, 1985). The management at this plant, like many interviewed elsewhere, believed unquestioningly that women in manufacturing were only suitable for light, repetitive assembly work. Anything beyond this represented entryism into traditional male territory.

Consumer Electronics

A similar dichotomy between capital-intensive, automated component insertion and labour-intensive manual assembly characterized the organization of production in the large electronic assembly transplants. The technological logic of this has been described in some detail by Taylor *et al.* (1991; 1994) and Delbridge (1995). Without exception, predominantly male operators were deployed in the automated areas, feeding and monitoring computerized component insert equipment used for mounting standardized electronic components into printed circuit boards. Female operators were then employed along conventional assembly lines for the more numerous and complex manual assembly operations which go into the manufacture of domestic videos, TVs and the like.

Patriarchal assumptions governing distinctions between 'men's work' and 'women's work' informed this division of labour as well. However, this was not the only factor. The mass exploitation of large pools of low-waged female labour from the ex-mining communities of South Wales provided major advantages to these different capitals in terms of minimizing wage costs and enlarging surplus value. Matsushita Electric apart, where union organization was relatively strong and occasionally militant, most of the electronics plants in the survey participated in informal wage-setting arrangements.[5] As a result, most women employed as bottom-grade assembly line workers earned a 'going rate' of around £140 per week gross compared to the £155–£170 plus shift premia received by their higher-graded male colleagues.

In the automated areas, although the technology itself was complex, the male operators were again effectively reduced to little more than line feeders. Their daily tasks comprised loading basic printed circuit boards, component ribbons and cassettes to machines; multi-machine minding; picking up and reloading dropped components; and feeding off finished work. Equipment breakdowns were the responsibility of skilled maintenance teams or local contractors. The work was both monotonous and degrading.

The same adjectives can be used to describe work in the main manual areas except that this was also marked by its exceptional speed and intensity. The basic labour processes were no different to those encountered in Cavendish's (1982) ethnography of life on an assembly line. Operators sitting at discrete positions along a conventional production line carried out a small number of repetitive manual operations at rapid speed. Whether the task was component insertion, dry joint probing, mechanical assembly, final packaging, or whatever, the basic skills were the same: rapid component handling and perfect hand coordination.

Many operators appeared to the observer as highly charged automatons. At Matsushita Electric in Cardiff for example, experienced component inserters were expected to complete their operations on ten boards per minute. Most cycles comprised fitting eight components to a board. Thus, most of these operators were fitting 80 components per minute, more than one per second. And they did this continuously. The key difference between the labour process in these plants and traditional British practice – as outlined by Cavendish for example – is that bell-to-bell working means what it implies. The process allows no potential for creating individual buffers and informal breaks; talking on the line is a disciplinary issue; all tasks are value-added only so that extras, such as stopping work in order to change a component box, are allocated to line side feeders; and operators enjoy no short breaks during machine downtime, they immediately move on to alternative lines. Workers are expected to squeeze 60 minutes labour power into every hour. As a shop steward complained:

> Mind you, if the targets are constantly missed then the operative is taken to the desk. You get warnings from your supervisor and you're told that, 'you're too busy talking', or, 'you're looking around you too much and not concentrating'. But sackings are rare; 95 per cent of the poor performers are transferred to an easier department if there is such a bloody thing. So, the system is if you're caught talking and dreaming you're generally given a first formal warning and then you're moved. It's harsh isn't it? Some of the departments on the shop floor work under tremendous pressure. On the insertion lines and the control block lines you just haven't got time to blink.

Electronic Components

The organization of work in this sector followed no set pattern, although, like all other transplants in the survey, these Japanese electronic component suppliers displayed an invariable work intensity and sense of discipline on the shop-floor.

The diversity of job design and manufacturing technique was a function of quite different product and process technologies and specific market characteristics and traditions. At Gooding Sanken's new Welsh Development

Agency greenfield site, for example, the shop-floor was again divided into automated component insertion and manual assembly areas. Here, however, fixed workbenches arranged as long assembly lines, but without expensive conveyor-belt technology, sufficed for the plant's low-volume market requirements. The operators' labour processes again comprised repetitive manual assembly tasks whilst the intensity of work was dictated by fixed cycle times and tightly policed by shop-floor supervisors. Distractions from the task in hand, such as talking to workmates on the line, were a common occasion for reprimand and disciplinary threat.

By comparison, both Yuasa Batteries and Matsushita Electronic Magnetrons exploited more capital-intensive work processes. Since it was established in 1982, successive investments in automated process technology enabled Yuasa Batteries to manufacture around 5 million sealed lead acid batteries of different designs each year. Although this technology furnished the plant's 30 in-house maintenance staff with a number of new skills, the 450 process operators employed on the shop-floor were again reduced to mere machine feeders and minders. Indeed, the minimal skills required here allowed the company to recruit most of its workforce straight from local secondary schools.

Similarly, Matsushita's Electronic Magnetrons Cwmbran plant presented itself as a hi-tech 'factory of the future' on the basis of its total automation and integration of the manufacturing process. The factory employed just 19 direct operators who each day produced 7,500 magnetrons for the domestic microwave industry. The operators' labour processes were organized around five robotic workstations located along one line and each linked by a sophisticated enclosed conveyor system. Put crudely, operators fed the required materials and components onto conveyors at each workstation; robotic equipment performed different press, clench and assembly operations; and on this cumulative assembly basis, every minute, twenty completed magnetrons appeared at the other end of the factory, ready for despatch.

Maintaining the same inverse relationship between automated production technology and operator skill observed elsewhere, the work was rudimentary, sometimes intense, but always demanding in the sense that workers had to survive a monotonous and lifeless working day, week in, week out. Japanese managerial efficiency, combined with the exploitation of sophisticated new technology of a type that would enthral our contemporary business writers, had created a degrading, no-skill labour process. As one manager put it when questioned on labour flexibility:

In fact, we rotate our operatives every one to two hours. This is not a requirement of the production process, it's purely for 'job enrichment'. The problem here is that the work is very boring on the line and if we leave an operative at a single workstation for more than a couple of hours then the work becomes so monotonous that mistakes can be made. In truth, without being disrespectful, we could train monkeys to do these jobs. The only skill involved is the use of a bit of aptitude when things go wrong.

Chemicals and Plastics

The managers in these suppliers of different types of foams, plastic mouldings and PVC products again emphasized both the importance of securing control over labour deployment and maintaining the daily discipline and intensity of production unfettered by union intervention. However, they emphasized the lack of anything distinctively 'Japanese' about the way work and technology were organized.

The manufacturing systems in these factories mainly incorporated different types of unitary extrusion machines on large-batch, continuous processes. The operators' routine, low-skill shop-floor tasks were also standard for this type of industry: feeding in raw materials, machine setting, multi-machine minding and feeding off the finished product. Thus, in this sector the deployment of capital and labour corresponded with the traditions and technological parameters of the indigenous industry.

The chapter's remaining sections investigate particular management practices which govern the intensity of production, the deployment of labour and worker participation. However, the significant preliminary point to emerge from the analysis thus far is that the basic shop-floor labour processes in these South Wales manufacturing transplants were not 'enriched' by the implementation of some novel Japanese work organizational paradigm. Without exception, production operators were employed on a variety of low-skill, monotonous and repetitive tasks in the interests of efficient capital accumulation.[6]

Lean Production Control

Although the processes of just-in-time production control (JIT) are rarely researched in any empirical depth, the concept remains central to managerialist presentations of efficient, waste-free Japanese production practice. Schonberger (1982) places JIT at the heart of Japanese production management and defines it idealistically as an inventory control system where work and materials are constantly on the move, 'a sort of hand to mouth mode of operation characterized by stockless production'. Oliver and Wilkinson (1992) expand upon this by describing JIT as a waste-minimizing system which seeks to match production exactly to market demand. They go on to denote three conditions necessary for its operation: swift machine set-up times; simple unidirectional material flow; and the implementation of TQM practices. On the basis of their quantitative analysis of recent developments in the UK, these authors argue that JIT is now becoming common practice in manufacturing firms.

To what extent is JIT established in the Japanese transplants of South Wales? The real picture is more complex than the above analyses would suggest. Only four out of the 15 firms surveyed claimed to use a JIT system, of which one operated in the autocomponents sector, two were in consumer electronics and one in plastics.

However, this does not mean that the remaining companies conformed to the opposing – and sometimes inaccurate – 'Fordist', 'just-in-case', high-buffer, ideal type. Many followed partial lean production strategies based on maintaining strict manning levels and constantly monitoring work in progress, stock levels and immediate product demand.

Both Sony and AIWA claimed to operate pure JIT systems, an unusual achievement for UK-based consumer electronics assemblers since a large proportion of the high value added electronic components are imported from the Far East. Over a period of twenty years, Sony developed its 'global localization' strategy resulting in a fully integrated TV production plant at Bridgend. Key assemblies such as cathode ray tubes were manufactured in-house whilst reportedly, 90 per cent of other components were supplied 'locally', that is, from the UK and other European Union countries. This complex network of suppliers delivered materials and components to the factory every two hours on average, some direct, some via local warehouses. The AIWA plant at Newport operated a more imperfect form of JIT since many of its electronics components were imported from the Far East. However, the company claimed to maintain close control over order schedules from its foreign suppliers – including detailed procedures for monitoring all supplier transport containers – to the extent that weekly shipments were possible, with daily supplies received just-in-time via port-based warehouses.

Calsonic's JIT system was designed to meet the multiple daily supply requirements of Rover–Honda, Nissan and other prominent vehicle assemblers. The management at this ex-Rover plant described their system as far more stressed and tightly controlled than previous practice. In earlier times, the plant would receive a weekly order for a supply of radiator assemblies which was rarely subsequently refined in terms of daily despatch requirements. Orders were received over the phone and casually adjusted over the phone if necessary. This loose form of control, along with large batch production and the prevalence of buffers on the shop-floor, created a relatively relaxed system of coordinating supply with customer demand.

Under the new regime, the systematic reduction of buffers and machine set-up times facilitated smaller batch sizes and a more precise JIT supply and delivery system. Calsonic's main customers provided fairly accurate monthly estimates of supply requirements and from these, bi-weekly and weekly forecasts were generated. Through interaction with the customer on Electronic Data Interchange, production planners were able to use these forecasts to issue daily shift production plans which incorporated any final day-to-day adjustments. From these, the planners established tightly controlled product despatch timetables, involving normally three des-patches per day to each customer at different fixed times.

These critical despatch schedules intensified the stress of mass production on the Calsonic shop-floor. The system exerted a continual disciplinary pressure on the teams and shifts responsible for meeting the customer's quality and quantity requirements on time. Any team of operators failing to meet these requirements was expected to work on until such problems were resolved. If the deadline was still missed then Calsonic was forced to deliver free of charge to the affected customer. Consistent failures placed contracts and jobs in jeopardy. And of course, we are not talking about one deadline but a whole series of routine deadlines for each customer, each day.

Although the majority of firms surveyed did not operate such closely controlled JIT systems, they did attempt to tighten their production schedules and reduce work in progress and stock levels. For those supplier transplants locked into long-term, 'cooperative' relationships with the JIT assemblers, these objectives could be undermined by the ability of the latter to pass their costs down the supply chain. A number of managers spoke bitterly of this. One said:

No, this company does not operate JIT. And exactly what is JIT may I ask? Who can define it, can you? I certainly can't. I believe the concept of JIT is an idea that has been blown up out of all proportion by the media and you academics. And it's all very well for the big final assemblers such as those in the auto industry to claim to work a JIT system, which they might well do, I don't know. But in fact, all they are doing is pushing their stock holdings down the supplier chain. And it's logistically impossible for all these suppliers to themselves run a JIT system. So at some early stage, one level of suppliers will have to pick up the bill by holding excessive levels of stocks.

And from a supplier to Sony:

I don't know what system Sony operate. All I know is that their order schedules are unplanned and chaotic. We can't do anything else other than keep good stock levels with which to supply them.

Notwithstanding these countervailing pressures, most of the Japanese transplants still attempted to regulate their production costs by maintaining leaner production control measures. Every firm operated a system for generating monthly, weekly, sometimes daily estimates of likely sales demand. And this was often accompanied by procedures which secured management accountability for work in progress and stock levels.

The ramifications of these control measures can be profound on the shop-floor. For the production operator, 'minimal human and material waste' in the form of low stock and low buffers, translates into no break or respite from the continuous grind of mass-production. Indeed, lean production control, whether in the form of JIT or more prosaic forms of reducing inventory costs, forms a critical component in management's repertoire of measures which aim to close up the pores of the working day. This is one of the more 'mundane' factors which characterize labour regulation within Japanese transplants.

Another is the simple practice of bell-to-bell working. One ex-British Steel shop steward remarked on this:

I must admit, coming from British Steel I was astounded by it at first. What it boils down to is that in a Japanese plant your life is controlled by a buzzer.

Few analyses of Japanese working practices dwell to any extent on the discipline of bell-to-bell working. Yet the manner in which this is imposed on transplant workforces makes it one of the more obvious manifestations of the Japanese obsession with reducing idle time and squeezing out 60 minutes of useful work from every worker in every hour.

Every one of the firms in the survey practised this down to the letter, using bells or sirens to announce the beginning and end of each break. Typically, workers were granted two ten-minute tea breaks and one half-hour lunch break each day. Observations at a number of plants during break periods highlighted exactly how precious these few minutes were. If the Japanese managements wanted their sixty minutes of work every hour, then similarly, operators were forced to scramble around to ensure that ten minutes eating, smoking and resting time could be extracted from every break. A number of times, at the moment when the break bell rang, affected groups of operators would immediately drop tools and race each other to the canteen, as if in a 100 metres Olympic final. This appeared to the observer as a kind of 'McDonaldized' break system (Ritzer, 1993) taken to extremes.

Operators who did not report back to their workstations at the end-of-break bell, or who did not seek permission to visit the toilet during work periods, would be immediately subject to the disciplinary procedure. But some managers were not even satisfied with this. At Matsushita Electric, for example, until 1990, two sirens would be sounded for starting work. The first came three minutes early as a warning. Workers were supposed to return to their workstations in preparation for the second siren. But more often than not, they would cram a final coffee or cigarette into the last three minutes and race to their workstations 30 seconds before the second siren. But Matsushita resented this. During the Cardiff plant's 1990 pay negotiations, management refused to offer its shop-floor a pay rise unless operators agreed to report to workstations, and be ready to commence work with tools in hand, immediately upon hearing the first siren. With bitterness, the workforce was forced to donate to the company three minutes break time, that is, nine minutes a day, 45 minutes a week, in order to receive a cost-of-living wage increase. It is this order of 'attention to detail' which tends to separate the Japanese from many British manufacturers.

Labour Utilization and the New Working Practices

The survey investigated the Japanese firms' use of those new working practices which seek a more efficient utilization of labour on the shop-

Table 2.2 *Use of new working practices (N = 15)*

Practice	Number of companies where used	Percentage of companies where used
Teamworking	6	40
Customer philosophy	11	73
Flexible working, in principle	12	80
Job rotation	7	46
Use of floats	10	66
Operator's involvement in job design	0	0
Operators responsible for SPC	1	6

floor: practices such as teamworking and other labour flexibility measures. The survey results are summarized in Table 2.2.

Teamworking and Labour Flexibility

The concept of Japanese-style teamworking suffers from a distinct lack of clarity in definition. One of its pioneers has described the practice as the cellular organization of labour and machinery in accordance with continuous-flow principles. Here, machines are grouped by product family rather than function, and each team member is required to operate the different machines in turn, moving items through a processing sequence, one piece at a time (Toyota Motor Corporation, 1992). Some writers have taken a more prosaic view, reducing this idealized craft-based version to one of mere multi-machine minding (Monden, 1983) whilst others have complicated things further by arguing that single process-based cells are also operable and may be used where large machines dedicated to particular functions are common, such as in a press shop (Alford, 1994).

If the precise format of the typical team organization is unclear, at least most managerialist writers agree on its purpose. That is, teamworking simplifies factory material flow and minimizes manning levels; and, on an ideological level, it mobilizes a sense of 'ownership', autonomy and business orientation amongst team members (Oliver and Wilkinson, 1992). Moreover, on the basis of primarily quantitative data analysis, many such writers also agree that teamworking has become a prevalent facet of work organization within both Japanese and British firms in the UK (for example, IRS, 1990; Oliver and Wilkinson, 1992).

Unfortunately, what is missing from this type of discussion is a sense of shop-floor politics. Teamworking is constructed as a mechanism of workplace efficiency or as a mode of work organization which may be of mere 'technical interest'. The idea that it could represent a significant managerial instrument of labour regulation which critically undermines traditional shop-floor controls over the labour process tends to get glossed over.

How have the Japanese exploited teamworking in their South Wales transplants? In fact, as Table 2.2 shows, less than half of the firms surveyed operated teamworking as a distinctive form of work organization. Furthermore, only Calsonic, in the auto sector, organized production into ideal typical cells.

At this factory, small teams consisting of between six and twelve operators were given the responsibility of producing families of car radiator assemblies for specific customers. Each team had its own leader, an elite operator who represented the 'totally flexible worker'. The team leader was responsible for such matters as the multi-task development of all team members, labour deployment and team performance. The latter was also monitored openly by the use of a combination of digital and manual display boards showing production targets; production performance; defect levels; individual operators' task proficiencies; and, under the heading of 'team morale', individual absenteeism records.

Case study analysis would be needed to establish the extent to which teamworking in this plant changed worker attitudes. But on the basis of the survey investigations there was little evidence of self-management or 'worker empowerment'. The company maintained strict lines of accountability from teamworker to teamleader to foreman to production manager; orders were received from supervision and expected to be strictly obeyed.

Nevertheless, it is ironical that this pre-war, multi-union site managed to organize a more fundamental restructuring of work organization than most of the greenfield Japanese plants in the survey. In fact, the crucial difference here is that much modular assembly work in the auto industry actually lends itself to a team-based organization rather than a conventional assembly line; and more importantly, competitive pressures within this sector are ensuring that established companies introduce the practice as a low-manning, labour-intensifying measure by purging the shop-floor of its traditional labour demarcations and controls.

In contrast, the greenfield transplants in the electronics sector had no legacies of shop-floor control to contend with. These companies continued to exploit rigidly fragmented labour processes organized along single, straight assembly lines in accordance with the traditions of this sector. Their teams merely comprised the total number of operators on the line, which could sometimes extend to above 50 workers. And again, their purpose was not to facilitate 'total flexibility' or 'self-management'. 'Teamworking' was a euphemism for the creation of organized units that could be held accountable for line output and defect performance. As a manager in one of the larger plants explained:

> We operate an informal team structure which might change even on a daily basis, but these teams are not organized for the purpose of team *working*, more for ease of communications and to provide a line of accountability to the team or line leader. The team might consist of around ten operatives and each will be coordinated by line leaders who really take up the role of the traditional charge hands.

A majority of the firms surveyed, whether using team organization or not, were attempting to enlist their employees into a 'customer ethos' to ensure that individual operators meet the needs of downstream 'customers' (Delbridge *et al.*, 1992). For example, a personnel manager at one company stated:

> Every one of our operatives is supposed to regard other operatives upstream or downstream of the line as customers. And his downstream customers are expected to, and will, create a fuss if the work they receive is not up to scratch. We've always supported this explicit customer philosophy promoting the 'individual as customer' idea. Not only will operatives complain to each other about any colleague's poor work but they also register complaints, sometimes bitter complaints, with the Company Advisory Board.

This, of course, was a new workplace individualism presented from management's standpoint. In fact, the needs of the external customer *were* consistently brought to the attention of shop-floor operators through continual quality campaigns, communications meetings and kaizen. It is likely that workers did have a greater sense of responsibility to the customer and the market. But this customer awareness did not necessarily extend to social relations between workmates. For example, when quizzed about the 'block assurance' customer/supplier system supposedly operating at their plant, two stewards at Matsushita Electric commented:

> No way! How can we check our own work let alone other people's work? We haven't got any time. And the idea that you could give your own people a telling-off for bad quality! You're joking! We're all on the same grade on the shop floor, we're all the same. If I were to turn round and give my mate a bollocking he'll just look at me and say 'Fuck off, who do you think you are?'

And on the idea of 'ownership'?:

> Ownership of work? You've got to challenge this terminology strongly. What's it supposed to mean? You only have the bloody unit in front of you for two seconds. So how are you supposed to own it?

There was no evidence, then, that the organization of workers into teams, in whatever form, acted to enrich the labour process. Even the practice of multi-tasking was confined to narrow limits. In line with many other inward investors in the UK, the Japanese transplants were more concerned to incorporate total labour flexibility into their employment contracts than to put this principle into practice (Peck and Stone, 1992; Morris *et al.*, 1994). Although over three-quarters of the firms had full flexibility agreements with their trade unions, less than half operated any form of job-rotation. For many operators, life on the line meant staying at the same position day in day out performing similar task routines. The only flexibility involved was in their ability to adjust these routines for different model changes on the same line. As a manager at Sony put it:

> Some of our women on the main CTV line might move around the line on occasions, but this is unusual. The idea of operator flexibility here lies in their ability to handle different models on a daily basis.

When quizzed about the enriching potential of job flexibility and rotation, many managers expressed a candid cynicism. One commented:

> I believe that this idea of continual movement between tasks to enrich the work process is frankly a lot of bullshit. Most workers prefer to stay in the same spot most of the time. They prefer one continuous boring routine to a number of continuous boring routines. And most of all they prefer working with the same people.

Indeed, a similar view was expressed by a GMB shop steward:

> The GMB agreement is that there's no demarcation whatsoever on the shop-floor. But in practice operatives do tend to stay on the spot doing the same

job. The most common reason for moving around is when you're covering for absenteeism. It's not done for flexibility's sake. If you've got people absent from a busy line then the supervision will throw other operatives on. Many of our people don't like it mind, especially the older ones. When people have been doing the same job all their lives they get used to it. They regard the job as their job, it sort of belongs to them. So they hate being moved off it.

For most of these transplants, full functional flexibility and productive efficiency did not go hand in hand. Although many of the firms did employ 'floats', elite operators who performed any task upon request in order to cover for sudden surges in demand for particular product lines, line-balancing problems and absenteeism, in most cases these made up less than 10 per cent of the shop-floor workforce. Maximizing output and minimizing waste formed the driving logic behind continuous, lean production. Concepts such as 'enrichment' and 'empowerment' just did not come into the equation. Production supervisors were held accountable for line performance, and they knew from experience that they could extract more output from groups of operators performing the same daily tasks than from others who were continually switching lines.

Placing full flexibility into labour contracts therefore served two purposes. Firstly, it provided management sufficient flexibility in labour deployment to allow for absenteeism and fluctuations in product demand. Secondly, it legitimized the imposition of managerial prerogatives; and it suppressed the emergence of rank-and-file controls over the labour process in the form of skill and job demarcations, regulation of effort rates, and so on. And these principles of management–controlled flexibility were not negotiable. One shop steward reflected on the activities of an unsuspecting young manager recently recruited at Matsushita Electric:

He's an unusual character for this place. He actually went around the lines talking to the girls about their work and discovered that they were all bored stiff. He even asked me my opinion. And I told him that there's a large number of youngsters here who get bored easily, and some of them might appreciate flexibility more than the older ones. But the supervisors are all completely anti-flexibility. They've got their efficient lines and they want to keep them.

So this manager drew up a plan. He'd discovered some of the operatives were pissed off with doing the same job day in day out, so he came up with these new job-rotation ideas. I don't disagree with him, actually. But the management aren't going to allow it to happen. Rotation will affect efficiency and rejects. This guy's new,so he's got a lot to learn. But the best of luck to him. He'll need it in this place.

Job Design

The Japanese work organizational paradigm is supposed to provide some space for direct production workers to participate in job design through such activities as statistical process control (SPC), kaizen and team briefings. Some writers build this aspect of 'worker democracy' into a post-Taylorist, flexible-specialization perspective which assumes that direct management control now has no place in factories characterized by the devolvement of decision-making to the shop-floor (Piore and Sabel, 1984). Braverman's (1974) dichotomy between the conception and execution of tasks effectively becomes redundant.

However, not much evidence of this could be detected amongst the Japanese transplants in South Wales. The limited worker involvement in kaizen is discussed in the next section, and the non-participative nature of team briefings in the next chapter. As far as monitoring and adjusting production line work through SPC is concerned, only two companies in the survey ever involved their operators in this. And one of these, Calsonic, was recently forced to cancel its SPC programmes due to worker apathy.

The role of the industrial engineer in these factories provides a more constructive indicator of worker involvement in job design. For, as Jurgens et al. have argued, 'no job is more characteristic for Taylorism-Fordism than that of the industrial engineer, whose job is to prescribe in detail the times and motions which the workers should use when performing their work' (1993, p. 19). To what extent had the work of these engineers altered or even become redundant in the supposedly 'democratic', post-Taylorist Japanese transplants?

The answer was very little at all. At all of the larger plants, teams of industrial engineers were employed to carry out routine work-measurement utilizing traditional time-and-motion studies. These were used in customary fashion for setting targets, for line balancing and for cost and benefit analysis. At AIWA for example, one industrial engineer was employed for every 30 operatives.

In fact, for most of these firms, it takes some imagination to envisage how matters could be any different once production tasks had become so fragmented and shaped by the exigencies of the continuous-flow production lines. However, the irony here was the extent to which some of these Japanese managements resolutely rejected *any* worker input into job design. For example, one personnel manager stated firmly that:

> Company procedures govern the way we organize work. Indeed, the company highly disapproves of the idea of allowing workers to change methods by themselves; this practice is just not accepted. All operatives must comply with the company procedures.

And another:

> The idea of workers designing their own jobs is frowned upon. Individual innovation with regard to work design is most certainly not the company philosophy here. It's our Japanese managers who are responsible for establishing all work procedures.

At Calsonic, teams of industrial engineers formed key personnel in the firm's 'management-led kaizens' in which managers and engineers, rather than operators, designed and implemented major adjustments to work organization. Conventional time-and-motion techniques were applied here. In a recent and typical exercise examined in some detail by the author, the engineers attacked production-line buffers in one area by reducing non-value-added process steps from 66 to 37 operations; manning levels decreased from 80 to 74 operatives; and 'drumbeat' production throughput increased from 2.35 units to 2.8 units per man hour.

Such productivity improvements were clearly a function of both improved capital and labour utilization and labour intensification. And as practical exercises in the systematic increase in the rate of extraction of surplus value, they will always run counter to the interests of shop-floor operators. However, the fundamental difference between this industrial engineering process and traditional British practice is that the former is not subject to trade union control or influence. Not one transplant sanctioned any trade union input over the setting of standards or work reorganization. One ex-British Steel shop steward, now employed at Matsushita Electric stated:

> They stand over the operative for half an hour, or an hour maybe, timing the job, and then they make a calculation for the whole eight hours. But it's a different ball game when you're knackering yourself trying to keep to these standards for eight hours a day.
>
> I just find it all extraordinary here. I mean, it's impractical. You go flat out for one hour, you can't help it when you're being watched, when there's

> someone looking at you, right over your shoulder all the time. And then they expect you to keep this up for eight hours a day. They're impossible targets, most of them.

And trade union influence?

> At British Steel, when we had the big time-and-motion studies, the shop stewards always participated to make sure the whole thing was fair and above board. And the management would always ask our permission first! But here the whole thing is indiscriminate. Ask our permission, my arse! The time-and-motion people just suddenly appear, and we're not even allowed to watch them. Okay, we might complain about a target here and there, but you never get anywhere. The company never allows us to see the records and measurements.

The targets established by these studies were rarely employed in conjunction with individual bonus systems. They were certainly used to establish line performance targets and to facilitate line balancing. But it was more than this. The untrammelled process of industrial engineering could sometimes be effectively exploited to assert management control in both a highly symbolic and an absolute fashion. The same steward again:

> But it's strange, weird really. They know full well we can't reach some of these targets. It's just stupid. They seem to take more satisfaction in the work study findings, in the actual work measuring, than they do in us reaching their impossible targets. They just like the watching. There's nothing worse than having someone standing over your shoulders all the time knowing they're watching your every move.

Total Quality Management Practices

Product and process quality concerns were integral to the manufacturing philosophies of the different transplants. Many managers stressed that whether or not specific quality assurance mechanisms and structures were in place, quality was seen as the hallmark and a central philosophy of the firm. They also believed that the concept of continuous improvement formed part of everyday thinking in the office and on the shop-floor.

In most factories, this philosophy was embodied in the vast array of quality campaign banners, slogans, charts and symbols that were encountered wherever one walked on the shop-floor. The AIWA plant at Newbridge provided a typical example. Shop-floor trade unionists had to endure the presence of a large embroidered banner, fashioned in trade union style, overhanging the main shop. It was decorated with symbols such as the Welsh leek and the Polaris star, which, as a personnel manager explained, signified that 'the plant is to be the guiding light for all of AIWA's global factories. We aim to meet these productivity and quality challenges and become AIWA's leading plant.' This corporate ideology supported the company's ACE 95 campaign – AIWA's Challenge for Excellence – which, as the workers were continually reminded through a plethora of posters, banners and briefings, demanded that they exceed all production targets by 150 per cent and reduce product defects to below 1 per cent.

Different Total Quality Management (TQM) practices give material expression to the concept of continuous improvement. The principles of TQM place considerable emphasis on enlarging employees' responsibilities, reorganizing work and increasing employees' involvement in problem-solving activities (Geary, 1994, p. 643). The management literature stresses that the central TQM objective here is meeting the customer's needs through the continuous improvement of both product and process quality.

The extent of the use of TQM practices in the transplants is summarized in Tables 2.3 and 2.4. This section will focus upon kaizens and quality circles.

The terms kaizen and quality circle were often used interchangeably by the different management interviewees despite the more precise, separate definitions in the literature. Kaizen is both a philosophy and a specific concrete practice for involving workers in quality improvement. As a philosophy, it stresses a new pro-enterprise attitude which is based on a management–labour consensus of general support for continuous

Table 2.3 *Use of different quality improvement practices (N = 15)*

Quality improvement practice	Number of firms where used	Percentage of firms where used
Kaizen	5	33
Quality circles	5	33
Kaizen/QC conferences	2	13
Suggestion schemes	3	20

Table 2.4 *Companies using kaizens and quality circles: organized times and participation rates*

Company	Kaizen/QCs held in company time	Kaizen/QCs held in workers' time	Participation rates
Calsonic	Yes	Yes	40%
AIWA	No	Yes	Majority
Matsushita Electric	Yes	No	Supervision only
Sony	No	Yes	Majority
Hitachi	Yes	No	Figs. unavailable
Electronic Harnesses	Yes	No	Supervision only
Matsushita EC	Yes	No	Supervision only
Sekisui	Yes	No	100%
Diaplastics	Yes	No	Figs. unavailable
Takiron	Yes	No	Majority

improvement at the workplace and, in particular, for the development of a consistent process-oriented way of thinking (Imai, 1986). In practical terms, this may mean involving the whole workforce in small-group activity which seeks gradual improvements to the efficient operation of different production processes. Quality circles also comprise small groups of employees, normally led by a teamleader or supervisor, who meet voluntarily to improve quality and productivity in their own area (Oliver and Wilkinson, 1992). Therefore, as far as the institutional mechanisms of continuous improvement are concerned, the kaizen group is little different from the quality circle.

Kaizens and quality circles are also mechanisms of labour exploitation. Under the cloak of a benign 'one team' ideology, workers become involved in securing for their employer higher levels of capital and labour utilization, reductions in idle time, an intensification of labour and a more sophisticated form of worker subordination. They do this by apparently offering to management knowledge of those facets of individual tacit skills and customary practice which provide workers with the means to exert some control over the labour process. Therefore, kaizen and quality circles act to convert rank-and-file control into management control: 'the company has an ambiguous, but inescapable, relation to worker know-how; it is at once a threat to the company, for it can lead to worker-control-in-work, but when rendered generalizable through the imperative that everything belongs to the company, it becomes a boost to the enterprise' (Garrahan and Stewart, 1992, p. 76).

Although the outcome of such a system might still reproduce a classic separation of conception and execution of tasks – since 'kaizened' production work remains highly fragmented and repetitive – the process of worker participation may, nevertheless, represent a marked shift from Taylorism, since workers themselves are acting as 'little industrial engineers'. To what extent, then, did the workers in the Japanese transplants in South Wales participate in their own exploitation in post-Taylorist fashion?

As Table 2.3 shows, two-thirds of the Japanese firms ran some form of continuous-improvement group, although only two of these operated the full structure of local groups reporting to factory-level conventions. Most just met at the shop level, regularly reporting their deliberations to lower management. However, Table 2.4 indicates a less impressive picture. Participation rates were variable to say the least, with three of the firms restricting kaizen activity to supervision only. Two firms, Matsushita Electric and Yuasa Batteries, originally organized plant-wide groups, but these were eventually disbanded due to a lack of interest on the shop-floor. A third, Electronic Harnesses, put a stop to full participation because of management fears that employees were straying beyond their remit. One manager stated:

> Our Japanese management felt that too much of the group discussion was directed towards wider issues such as production engineering and working practices, and wider corporate issues such as pay or management.
> Insufficient time was spent on quality issues, improving product quality, in other words real continuous improvement. The management felt that these groups should be discussing quality and nothing else.

Moreover, in some firms, particularly the smaller enterprises, the kaizen/QC groups tended to be informal affairs with little of the organization and accountability suggested by the literature. Nevertheless, full kaizen activity appeared to be operational in at least a number of the larger manufacturers. Calsonic, in the auto sector, was one of the more dynamic of these.

Calsonic operated kaizens at two levels. Management-led kaizens dominated by senior managers and engineers were responsible for all substantial work reorganization. An example of this activity was outlined in the 'job design' section above. At a lower level, the company organized 40 kaizen groups, each comprising between 4 to 8 members, to discuss small-scale continuous improvements. Significantly, management interviewees reported that this initiative came from a number of British managers and that the idea of using participative kaizen techniques in the plant was initially met with a lack of interest from the British-based Japanese managers.

These worker kaizens were controlled by management-appointed facilitators. They were responsible for monitoring and shaping the three key stages of the kaizen process: brainstorming, data analysis and adoption. Brainstorming is consultancy-speak for problem-identifying, which was described as the freewheeling of ideas, 'encouraging people to come up with ideas from the top of their heads whilst under a state of enlightenment'. But for some, this state of enlightenment too often drifted into disenchantment. As one manager stated:

> The operatives have taken to brainstorming of sorts, but most kaizens I've attended, and that's quite a few, have tended to generate into slanging matches which tend to put people under pressure.

Once ideas were 'thrown up into the air' and recorded, each group went through a 'democratic' voting process to prioritize the most practical suggestions. The groups met in company time, but once suggested improvements were prioritized members often worked in their own time to collect and analyse data and to formulate countermeasures to each problem. The maintenance of strict documentary procedures allowed management to monitor the process at all times. The end results of this kaizen activity would be presented to senior management and, if approved, implemented and proceduralized.

Does such worker behaviour amount to a break from Taylorism? None of the kaizen groups in any firm in the survey were involved in fundamental aspects of work design. At Calsonic, for example, kaizen produced incremental improvements in matters such as component rejects and small process hold-ups, but this did not constitute essential industrial engineering work. And although Graham (1994) describes a process by which American operators working in a Japanese auto transplant come to perform time-and-motion studies on their fellow workers after being trained in the techniques of industrial engineering, there was little evidence of such activity in South Wales. In one instance, where an enterprising worker attempted this at Calsonic, his colleagues reacted with a predictable sense of shop-floor solidarity. A quality manager:

Sometimes there's been more opposition from the shop-floor. It's still the case that only 40 per cent participate in the groups, but we've also had more specific problems. For example, during one kaizen exercise an operative got out a stop-watch and timed the activities of his colleagues. If an industrial engineer had done this there would not have been a problem, but because he was an operative it caused an outrage. He was sent to Coventry by the whole of the shop-floor, and as far as I'm aware he still is. However, he's a big lad. He can handle it.

Overall, then, the evidence from South Wales suggests that this 'partially autonomous form of worker participation' represents less the reversal of the Taylorist emphasis upon the specialist engineer (Wood, 1989) and more, as Wood himself also admits, strict management supervision of limited worker involvement in perfecting task routines, after which workers are 'returned to Taylorized jobs'. The Japanese manufacturers in the region sometimes differed in their approach to reaching this latter objective. The Calsonics, the AIWAs and the Sonys allowed their workforces a hint of autonomy in the process of proceduralizing work routines whilst other firms would sanction no worker input at all. But in all cases, the outcome was the same: fragmented tasks, tightly supervised work routines, minimum waste, and maximum levels of output from a minimum number of low-paid workers. Therefore, as Thompson (1989) observes, such mechanisms of employee participation hardly constitute meaningful forms of workplace democracy or job enrichment. Neither do they undermine the processes of direct management control: 'certainly, the delegation to workgroups of some immediate and localized production decisions, such as those on the monitoring of product quality, can happily coexist within managerial structures of directive control' (1989, p. 226).

To conclude this chapter, the survey data demonstrate that a distinctive, post-Taylorist Japanese work organizational paradigm has not been gradually installed along the South Wales valleys. Although a number of plants displayed some of the salient features commonly associated with Japanese management practice, not one conformed with the idealized 'Japanese model', which stresses multi-skilled labour processes, self-managing workteams, total flexibility, and opportunities for full worker participation in job design and process improvement.

The transplants did not display fundamentally different characteristics from their market competitors, because even if their managements were disposed to experiment with different work organizational forms in unfamiliar environmental conditions, intense global market pressures do not provide the necessary space for such innovation. Moreover, the presence of the Japanese in South Wales and elsewhere in the European Union is primarily a function of the rising value of the yen, EU market protectionism and advantageous local labour market conditions. The logic of their capital accumulation strategies in these circumstances will always be to efficiently exploit these markets to the full rather than venture into new 'empowering' labour processes and employment relations.

However, I am not arguing that the predominantly young workers in these Japanese transplants experience exactly the same employment conditions as previous generations of British manufacturing workers. Some things have changed. In the economic and political environment of footloose capital, de-industrialization, mass unemployment, weakened trade unions and a pusillanimous left politics, many Japanese inward investors have succeeded in exploiting their greenfield sites by suppressing the emergence of rank-and-file controls over the labour process. Indeed, as Tomaney (1990) has argued, such firms have merely extended and redeveloped existing forms of labour control and efficiency maximization. And although these changes might represent 'rather more mundane management priorities than is generally applied by references to Japanization' (Elger and Smith, 1994b, p. 48), as we shall discover when we come to the British case study, the workers on the receiving end of this less fundamental 'management of change' might nevertheless be forgiven for viewing such developments with some trepidation.

Moreover, it is when we consider Japanese manufacturing practice from the standpoint of labour rather than business, that a more obvious pattern emerges. Labouring under the different types of lean production control practised by their Japanese managements, the South-Wales-based transplant workers have become more completely subordinated to the supervisor, to the machine and to the intensified pace of production. Their time spent productively at workstations has been maximized by reducing production line buffers; by reducing stocks and work-in-progress; by more accurately synchronizing their output with customer demand; and by the strict policing of disciplined bell-to-bell working. Similarly, the strict managerial regulation of labour deployment ensures that shop-floor labour power is more efficiently consumed. The transplant labour processes most certainly varied in accordance with the diverse technical requirements of different production technologies, products and product markets, but management's exploitation of labour and skills was more homogeneous. That is, there was no variation in the prohibition of traditional union-controlled job demarcations; or in the maintenance of task fragmentation; or in the narrow enlargement of certain jobs by task accretion – whether through team organization or management-controlled flexibility on conventional assembly lines.

Furthermore, for most transplant workers meaningful personal involvement in the processes of job design and continuous improvement was at best highly restricted. The different transplant managements emphatically denied the possibility of trade union influence over work measurement whilst the limited kaizen-style activities were strictly management-controlled to ensure their focus on raising labour productivity and effort-intensification.

The next chapter considers the extent to which these highly disciplined production regimes are supported by both ideological measures seeking worker cooperation and systems of non-adversarial industrial relations.

Notes

1   Wales has the highest percentage of full-time workers earning below 68 per cent of average UK gross weekly earnings – the decency threshold set by the Council of Europe (Hetherington, 1994). Moreover, in 1990, one in three of all full-time workers in the region earned less than the Low Pay Unit's low-pay threshold of £157 a week. In the same year, there were 216,500 such low-paid workers in Wales: 92,500 men and 124,000 women (Labour Research, 1990).

2   This figure excludes the small number of Japanese firms employing less than 25 workers.

3   With the partial exception of Sony, these Japanese transplants were primarily manufacturing enterprises producing different consumer goods, components and materials for British and European markets. Perhaps the most striking aspect of their workforce composition was that although the firms employed few design staff – and some used subcontractors for plant maintenance – on average, the number of indirect staff still amounted to 30 per cent of the total workforce. Apart from management and administration, most of the latter comprised shop-floor supervision, industrial engineering and quality-control personnel. Thus, just as Lincoln and Kalleberg (1990) noted in their survey of employers' practices in Japan and the USA, despite dominant perceptions to the contrary, the 'flat hierarchy' and the principle of multi-skilled direct production workers taking on many of the tasks of redundant indirect employees are not characteristics of Japanese work organization.

The transplants also employed a relatively high proportion of women employees. Overall, women constitute nearly 50 per cent of all transplant workers in the region although this figure obscures disparities across sectors and occupations. In particular, women are concentrated in the electronics sector where most are employed as bottom-grade production operators.

4   Fourteen of the fifteen participating firms recognized trade unions (see Chapter 3). Calsonic maintained the multi-union tradition inherited from Rover (recognizing the TGWU; TGWU-ACTSS; AEEU; and MSF), although it had persuaded these different site unions to merge into a single bargaining unit.

5   Some management interviewees described how they compared shop-floor wage rates through participation in local wage surveys and more informal joint-consultation in local employers' associations.

6   The generally rudimentary, low-skill nature of these labour processes is further demonstrated by considering the extent and quality of training required for the operators to perform their work. In keeping with the view that Japanese firms devote far more resources to training than their British competitors (Pang and Oliver, 1988; Keep, 1991), and assuming that this should represent something more substantial than 'on the job' or brief induction training, each transplant management was asked whether formal NVQ skills training was offered to shop-floor operators. Five of the eleven firms did provide such training, but with the exception of a small minority of senior operators, this only extended to the most basic NVQ level 1. Moreover, the absence of NVQ certification from the remaining six plants was not the result of parsimonious attitudes towards employee training; it merely reflected a more candid appraisal of both requisite operators' skill levels and the dishonest nature of contemporary state-funded youth training. As a Sony manager commented: 'Let's be honest. I know, and so to be fair do the operatives, that it is ridiculous to think that their jobs could be "NVQable". I'm greatly concerned that so many companies are offering this sort of NVQ training and claiming NVQ skills for so many jobs that just don't warrant them. It's an abuse of the system and the Government knows it.'

3 JAPANESE HUMAN RESOURCE MANAGEMENT IN SOUTH WALES

Lean production places certain demands on the management of the employment relationship. The processes which enhance managerial control, increase effort rates and reduce the porosity of the working day require a supportive and durable human resource management framework for sustaining this intensification of labour exploitation. The term 'human resource management' (HRM) is preferred to traditional 'personnel policy' in this context because it denotes 'not just a capacity to think strategically but some distinctive view of the strategic direction that should be pursued' (Guest, 1991, p. 42).

Managerialist writers and organization theorists tend to present this strategic direction in terms of an explicit articulation between a Japanese JIT/TQM paradigm and a coherent HRM policy. For example, Oliver and Wilkinson argue that the fragility and high dependency relations characteristic of lean production systems 'demand a workforce that is dependable, hard working, flexible and unlikely to disrupt production' (1992, p. 331). And the point is often made that Japanese management cannot be understood without considering 'hard' systems of production control together with 'soft' systems of employee motivation and management leadership. As Trevor has put it, 'those who look only at either the "hard" or the "soft" are missing the point. "Hard" and "soft" are not opposites but the two sides of the same picture; and they both serve the same company ends' (1988, p. 143).

However, such analyses fail to consider how the necessary 'fit' between the demands of a production system and the management of labour may take on a more conventional form. That is, the assumption that 'soft' HRM (Storey, 1992) is not only the clever solution, but the only solution, to the labour problems thrown up by 'hard' production management overlooks the possibility that in an environment of mass unemployment, more assertive management and relatively weak trade unionism, 'hard' HRM can be both cheaper and more effective.

This chapter explores these questions further by providing a critical review of Japanese HRM policy in South Wales. It investigates the various management practices which seek to secure worker compliance with the dictates of lean production (practices governing recruitment, the employment contract, employee communications and trade unions) and the extent to which these provide a 'fit' with the transplants' labour control strategies. It also considers how these practices are mediated by such broader factors as local labour market and industrial relations traditions and how the firms endeavour to exploit the latter to further the accumulation of capital.

Employee Recruitment and Selection

The use of more rigorous employee recruitment and selection procedures appears to be a growing phenomenon in the UK, especially for certain sections of the workforce for whom this has not previously been the case, such as shop-floor workers (Townley, 1991). Although for some firms this development may well be a corollary of management's need to develop sophisticated monitoring procedures in the context of more flexible and autonomous work groups, for most employers changes in recruitment policy should be viewed in the context of the mass unemployment of the past two decades. In this economic environment of slack labour markets, factory managements are displaying a quite rational demand for prime candidates from mass applications, candidates of sufficient quality to withstand the pressures and disciplines of intensified lean production. It should also come as no surprise that Japanese firms in the UK have become adept at exploiting different types of recruitment and appraisal practices, each tailored to the needs of individual firms, but displaying uniformity in their aims of securing labour compliance and shop-floor discipline.

The Japanese transplants in South Wales were no different. Their practices stood in clear contrast to the more casual hire-and-fire systems characteristic of many British firms in Wales (Morgan and Sayer, 1988). The different Japanese managements carefully assessed worker attitudes and performance either during protracted selection interviews or by subsequent careful surveillance of probationary and temporary labour. Similarly, once recruited into the permanent workforce, many employees in these plants became subject to systematic supervisory evaluation of their shop-floor conduct using techniques that bore some similarities with the *satei* system in Japan (Endo, 1994). This chapter focuses upon employee assessment during the process of selection for employment.

Selection Practices

Calsonic's procedures exemplified one of the more thorough multi-stage screening processes investigated. Decent jobs are both scarce and precious in the area surrounding the plant's Llanelli location. Consequently, as one manager bluntly put it, 'any one vacancy receives mountains of application forms which are then vetted to filter out the rubbish'. Following this, selected interviewees had to overcome a daunting series of obstacles in their attempts to secure paid employment. Preliminary interviews assessed basic character and aptitude; a more demanding series of tests measured numerical, verbal, non-verbal and spatial abilities; extensive interviews with functional and line management judged character and conduct against key selection criteria; and surviving candidates often then endured yet another aptitude test. The management at this brownfield auto-components factory was leaving nothing to chance in its attempts to reshape and control shop-floor culture. Indeed, at the time of the survey, the company was on the verge of introducing a further hurdle in the form of a 16-point personality test.

The selection process for production line workers at Matsushita Electronic Magnetrons was equally measured and protracted. In addition to a similar series of interviews and both manual and aptitude tests, applicants were enticed into revealing their true selves during informal walkabouts around the factory. Here, supervisors engaged them in apparent 'friendly chat' whilst noting their attitudes to work, commitment, flexibility and so on. As one manager put it:

> What we are looking for here is the whole person, correct attitudes, people who will fit into our team ethos. And crucially they must be reliable people, reliable characters, the types you would expect to have a good absenteeism record.

Not all of the firms utilized these relatively sophisticated techniques, however. Many relied upon more rudimentary recruitment procedures. Nevertheless, by exploiting both probationary systems and temporary labour they were able to reach the same objective of securing recruits with acceptable work attitudes and adequate performance and attendance records. For example, applicants for TV and video production line jobs at Matsushita Electric in Cardiff underwent just a brief interview and two basic aptitude tests. But once employed as probationary labour – and more recently temporary labour – new recruits became subject to a more systematic and measured assessment of character and performance. One personnel manager said:

> To give you an idea of the selection process, we handled the last 100 applicants for the latest batch of temporary vacancies in one Friday afternoon. It's when we've got them as temps that we monitor their performance. That's basically, timekeeping, attitudes and work standards. Good performers are kept on, the rest are discharged.

The customarily intimate nature of the Welsh valley communities, and the ways in which this sometimes placed character development under overt scrutiny, allowed some managers to put more informal processes into play. At the Sekisui plant, for example, no formal recruitment procedures existed. Instead, these matters came under the sole control of the plant's paternalistic deputy managing director who made his selection decisions purely on the basis of his firsthand knowledge of local people:

> For most of the jobs we have on offer I only recruit individuals from the local community here and I only recruit people who I myself know [said with a wry smile]. I'm not embarrassed about this, it merely reflects the close-knit nature of our local Welsh communities. And what's more, I'll only recruit blokes with a good steady attitude. I will not take on militants and extremists. I'm only interested in good family men, men like carpenters and builders.

The specific selection criteria employed by these firms are shown in Table 3.1. These criteria do place as much emphasis upon behavioural characteristics as technical skills; but they were not used in the 'soft HRM' sense as part of a subtle monitoring process of autonomous work groups (Townley, 1991). Instead, attributes such as positive attitudes to flexibility, work commitment and, above all, timekeeping, were integral to the Japanese managements' demand for raw recruits who might more easily adapt to the stress and discipline of intensified lean production.

Despite their application of a variety of aptitude tests described above, few firms sought new recruits with particular manual skills. This was clearly a function of the low-skill nature of the labour process. Young women with experience of rapid light assembly work in the clothing

Table 3.1 *Selection criteria (N = 15)*

Selection criteria	Number of firms citing criterion	Percentage of firms
Youth	5	33
Dexterity/basic electrical mechanical skills	11	73
Attitudes to flexibility and team ethos	11	73
Prepared to work long hours	7	47
Absenteeism and timekeeping	14	93
General work attitude and commitment	10	66
Education	2	13
Domestic background	4	26

industry might be preferred for recruitment onto the electronic production lines whilst men employed as machine minders might be asked how they would go about changing the oil in their car or whether they possessed any DIY skills, but that was the limit to the technical proficiency required.

One-third of the firms surveyed cited youth as an important criterion.[1] This was particularly apparent in the larger firms operating in electronics and autocomponent production where, traditionally, trade unions have been well organized and have maintained their independence. For these firms, the recruitment of young workers constituted an important prerequisite of a workforce socialization process aimed at securing compliance and even the acceptance of managerial prerogatives. This was a prime objective at the brownfield Calsonic plant, for example, where the new Japanese management inherited an ageing workforce. The company's recruitment strategy sought to undermine the shop-floor's collectivist attitudes and accumulation of workers' gains by, as one manager said, seeking 'flexible, committed workers who are prepared to work long hours and accept new ideas'. As the first stage towards achieving this, Calsonic introduced an age bar restricting shop-floor recruitment to those aged under 25.

However, such ageist policies were not always congruent with these Japanese managements' requirement to maintain a highly disciplined and committed workforce. As both Morris *et al.* (1994) and Palmer (1996) discovered, some Japanese transplants in the UK have encountered significant labour retention and utilization problems arising from their mass recruitment of undisciplined young school-leavers. It is for this reason that many Japanese transplant managers in South Wales now prefer to recruit younger workers who also display some evidence of responsibility and discipline. Accordingly, a good number of these managers emphasized their preference for married men aged between 20 and 30 whilst stability in previous employment was a key criterion for young women.

Life on the shop-floor in these Japanese plants is harsh, regimented and stressful. Continuous, lean production means what it implies. But if it is not to be subject to frequent disruption this form of production also demands a good degree of labour retention. Therefore, questions of labour turnover and absenteeism became paramount concerns for production management and explained why the demand for workers with acceptable timekeeping, attendance and work attitudes featured so strongly in the selection criteria. Indeed, many of the management interviewees reported regular recourse to formal disciplinary procedures to ensure that these attributes are maintained. But in most companies, exploitation of temporary and probationary labour served as the most effective filtering mechanism. New recruits who found it difficult to accept the disciplines of attendance were abruptly shown the door if they had not already voted with their feet. As one personnel manager admitted:

> The company is willing to be patient and wait for certain improvements in operatives who may be lacking in skill, but we're a lot firmer with anyone who dislikes the company culture and the way we're used to doing things. I've got to admit, we do have some problems here. The Japanese managers run this factory as a highly disciplined regime. They frown upon operatives talking to each other too much, they greatly discourage people taking time off the section – operatives always have to seek permission to go to the toilet, for example. As a result, the shop-floor often get annoyed and irritated, they get fed up with being treated like children. A lot of the new women just can't handle it. Many of them leave during the probationary period.

Equal Opportunity Policies

As the principles of 'empowerment' and 'egalitarianism' are salient features of Japanese employment ideology, one might expect Japanese firms to take leading positions in supporting equal opportunity policies aimed at eliminating various forms of workplace discrimination. The reality in South Wales was somewhat different, however. Of the 15 firms which participated in the survey, only five maintained a simple equal opportunities statement. More pertinently, none of these firms developed working procedures aimed at implementing the principles of equity outlined in their statements.

The management interviewees did not regard equal opportunities as a particularly important issue, and few understood the term as one which addressed structural forms of discrimination. One manager typically remarked that, 'equal opportunities should be a natural practice rather than something which is formalized, not something run by procedures which you are forced to think about'.

As far as both horizontal and vertical gender segregation are concerned, Japanese employment policies in South Wales clearly replicate and reinforce existing patterns of labour market segmentation in the region's manufacturing industry. Male workers tended to concentrate in those engineering sectors where labour processes comprised primarily 'hard' mechanical work and process machinery operation. Women predominated in the electronics sector where traditional assumptions governing women's suitability for light and rapid assembly work prevailed. Similarly, as the previous chapter outlined, a clear intra-plant horizontal segregation between male 'machine operators' working on automated equipment and female manual assemblers obtained.

Vertical gender segregation was equally manifest. Most female operators found themselves trapped in the lowest shop-floor grades, earning around £140 per week. Few were able to break out into supervisory, let alone management positions. For example, at AIWA, where women constituted 66 per cent of the shop-floor workforce, just three women reached the supervisory grade. None had achieved management status. At most plants, managers attributed this to a 'lack of assertiveness' or 'lack of interest in career-making'. One typically commented:

> I don't believe that many women want to get on in manufacturing industry. We get little enthusiasm from the girls when we do our career tours at the local schools ... and the many women we do employ don't want to get above the level of supervision anyway. They don't want more than this because of their responsibilities at home with the housework.

By contrast, in her analysis of the experiences of women workers in

Japanese electronic plants in Wales and Ireland, Saso (1990) discovered that many women operators displayed a more positive attitude towards work than their male colleagues. She attributes the above gender inequalities to a combination of factors: the high turnover rate of young women due primarily to childbirth and the lack of crèche facilities; the sexist assumptions of Japanese transplant managers (she might have included the British as well); and the extra long hours of work expected of supervisory staff.

Such factors do present significant constraints against progress towards gender equality at work. Nevertheless, they are also mere symptoms of the discrimination which arises from the connections between gender relations and the dynamics of capitalist social relations. The capital accumulation strategies of these Japanese transplants sought to maximize the surplus pumped from labour power in an environment of advantageous local labour markets. Consequently, the electronics transplants restricted themselves to exploiting an endless supply of young, malleable female labour from the depressed valleys for repetitive production line work rather than experiment with practical equal opportunity programmes. Moreover, economic conditions in the region ensured that these large pools of labour remained particularly cheap. As one union official commented:

> The Japanese employers in this region will always set their pay rates in accordance with the general rate at that particular moment for that particular area and industry. The rate which is being paid will be the rate that the Japanese company has researched. And in truth, these companies, despite the low wages, are able to attract labour. I mean, the pay is pretty near the bone. It comes close to what we're arguing for a minimum wage. But employers are saying to us that if they increase the wage rate then we'll lose jobs. So in a sense, we're stuck in a square pegged hole. We're caged in by unemployment. We've got no opportunity for arguing and campaigning on pay. We can't say that there's a firm down the road that can pay more because there just isn't one. They're all paying low wages.

The logics of capital accumulation in many of these transplants, logics which incorporated exploitative gender relations, therefore sustained the extraction of surplus value from large pools of low-wage female labour power in those sectors and occupations that are conventionally designated as a 'woman's domain of employment'. As a result, most of the electronics transplants in South Wales were quite content to continue replacing departing mothers with younger girls from their captive labour markets. Indeed, even Matsushita Electric's Cardiff plant preferred to bus many of its female workers in from the valleys rather than recruit from immediately outside the factory gates in the city's more temperamental labour markets. That is, with the exception of one group. The company did venture into Cardiff's ethnic minority communities to exploit these similarly segmented inner-city labour markets. The plant was the only one in the survey to employ a number of black workers (68 operators, around 5 per cent of the shop-floor workforce). Not one of these occupied any supervisory or management positions.

Finally, few, if any, of these Japanese firms paid any attention to the employment rights of the disabled. When questions of continuous production, line discipline, bell-to-bell working and absenteeism are paramount, disability rights just do not come into managerial reckoning. And as with so much equal opportunity policy elsewhere, companies were more concerned with promoting corporate image than creating egalitarian substance. For example, one manager at Gooding Sanken was particularly keen to show off the plant's facilities for the disabled such as special toilets and ramp entrances to all buildings. Only one thing spoiled the presentation – the plant employed not one disabled worker!

Job Security Policies

Japanese firms are often praised by Western observers for their ability to offer lifetime employment to their workforces. However, as a number of analyses of Japanese employment practice have demonstrated, the segmented hierarchy of the Japanese labour force, built upon a mass of subcontractors and temporary workers at its base, has ensured that job security and welfare for a minority employed in large corporations are secured at the expense of low wages, poor conditions and job insecurity for the majority (Littler, 1982; Mitsui, 1987; Kumazawa and Yamada, 1988).

Studies of Japanese employment practices in the UK have found little evidence of any attempts to transfer these structural arrangements into this country. Nevertheless, many Japanese firms do attempt to offer a measure of long-term commitment to their workforces even though job security is rarely drafted explicitly into the labour contract (Pang and Oliver, 1988; Oliver and Wilkinson, 1992). How is this commitment to job security achieved in the context of British labour markets and employment

Table 3.2 *Employment flexibility practices*

Company	Employment flexibility measures
Calsonic	Temporary workers (14% of directs); contractual overtime; labour redeployment.
AIWA	Temporary workers and extended probation (30% of directs); contractual overtime.
Matsushita Electric	Temporary workers (16% of directs); contractual overtime; annualized hours.
Sony	Temporary workers ('substantial numbers in the autumn period').
Gooding Sanken	Extended probation; contractual overtime; unpaid lay-off periods.
Electronic Harnesses	Temporary workers (23% of directs); contractual overtime.
Yuasa Batteries	Contractual overtime; labour redeployment.
Matsushita E.C.	Temporary workers (8% of directs); contractual overtime.
Matsushita E.M.	Temporary workers (21% of directs); annualized hours scheme.
Sekisui	Labour redeployment.
Dynic	Temporary workers (20% of directs); reduced working week arrangements.

traditions? Can any comparisons be made between the employment policies followed by UK-based Japanese transplants and their parent companies in Japan?

In South Wales, eleven of the surveyed transplants claimed to support a long-term job-security philosophy. To further this they exploited different types of employment flexibility practice. Table 3.2 summarizes these. Apart from routine labour redeployment, the three principal measures adopted were the systematic use of temporary labour; contractual overtime; and annualized hours.

The employment of temporary labour featured strongly. As previously observed, the careful monitoring of production line temporary workers serves as an effective employee selection mechanism. In addition, this type of employment contract allows companies to swiftly lay off or top up sections of the workforce, as and when demanded by product market fluctuations.

In some firms, this employment flexibility was achieved under the cloak of the ostensibly inoffensive fixed-term probationary system, which, conventionally, is supposed to allow firms to filter out incompetent new recruits. However, in practice probation could become more elastic in its implementation. At AIWA, for example, many of the plant's 300 temporary workers were classed as probationers. The least that can be said of the fixed-term labour contract is that its length has a measure of certainty attached to it. In contrast, the tenure of employment for probationers can be cut or extended at the whim of management and the market. As one manager admitted:

> It can be increased to 6 months, 9 months, 12 months, sometimes 18 months. It will partially depend on the state of the market. Temporary status may lengthen if the market is uncertain but it may also lengthen if we're not quite satisfied with the quality of the individual that we've taken on ... and eventually if we're just not satisfied then I'm afraid we get rid of them.

In Japan, manufacturing companies habitually extend working hours in order to enhance flexibility in production, effectively substituting human buffers for the material reductions introduced by just-in-time production (Endo, 1991). In similar fashion, nearly half of the Japanese firms in South Wales reported the use of contractual overtime as an explicit component of their lean-manning policies. At Electronic Harnesses, for example, overtime working clearly facilitated management attempts to negotiate fluctuating product demand with a relatively small core workforce. As one manager stated:

> The size of the workforce is such that we work to the bone, there is never any surplus. The downside to this is that when the company gets busy then overtime has to come into operation and the company does have high overtime expectations. We insist that all operatives work a reasonable amount of overtime as part of their labour contract.

A key question here concerns the definition of a 'reasonable amount'. At many companies, a 'reasonable amount' actually meant a considerable amount. At Yuasa Batteries for instance, overtime accounted for 15 per cent of payroll costs. Similarly, at Calsonic, a demand that operators work at least two hours extra mid-week and five or six hours on a Saturday was made a key recruitment selection criterion. And these were minimum amounts. The Calsonic management admitted that some operators in the plant's labour intensive manufacturing areas consistently work a 70-hour week.

This picture suggests that 'policy overtime' under lean production regimes has taken on a new dimension. Nichols (1986) observes that many analyses of the decline of British manufacturing industry have placed the blame fairly and squarely at the door of trade unions and 'restrictive practices' such as both union regulation of working hours and shop stewards' attempts to ensure an equitable distribution of paid overtime amongst their members. However, whilst the Japanese in South Wales are quite happy to exploit the tendency of British workers to clock up longer hours than their counterparts elsewhere in the European Union (Hughes, 1994; Labour Research Department, 1994),[2] they have refused to countenance any measure of union regulation of this, whether in the form of shorter working week agreements or overtime distribution practices such as 'one in, all in' and the use of rotas. Therefore, what is distinctive here is not so much the explicit use of overtime to secure consistently low manning levels against fluctuating product demand but the ease with which this is now achieved within a non-regulatory framework. Put another way, the relatively untrammelled extraction of absolute surplus value from overworked though 'secure' core workforces has become the salient feature of Japanese 'policy overtime'.

Ostensibly, flexible working arrangements in the form of annualized hours systems seem a more innocuous form of the management of working time. They are currently applied to around 9 per cent of the UK workforce (Taylor, 1994). Reshuffling the distribution of total working hours over a one-year period provides employers with greater flexibility in matching workers' hours to market demands; in addition, it cuts labour costs by eliminating payments for overtime and reducing absenteeism. Accordingly, four of the Japanese firms exploited some form of flexible hours arrangement, and of these, two used standard annualized hours schemes. Whilst the flexibility which accrues to employers may also be sold to workers in terms of 'personal control over time management', those on the receiving end of these policies may not necessarily perceive them in such a positive fashion. When, in 1992, Matsushita Electric in Cardiff attempted to introduce annualized hours, its workforce embarked upon a campaign of resistance focusing on both the uncertainty in working hours involved and the principle of working unpaid overtime. Eventually, in the depths of a recession, the company secured compliance by intimidation: it threatened to sack any employee who failed to sign the new labour contract.

Although by no means exact emulation, these examples do demonstrate certain similarities with employment policy in Japan. 'Job security' for those who labour under different Japanese regimes in South Wales comes at a hefty price. The downsizing of lean production depends on a core workforce which is subject to both long working hours and the continual stress of intensive work methods. And it may also depend on the employment of temporary and probationary workers who enjoy no job security or employment rights but who still suffer the same intensified exploitation at the point of production.

Employee Communications and Single Status

Different management techniques aimed at consolidating the new balance of power at the workplace have accompanied the recent decline of trade union influence in the UK. New methods of direct communications, which seek to bypass trade unions as the principal channel of information to workers, represent one example of these. Another is the development of single status and harmonization measures designed to obscure fundamental class divisions and interests. Both techniques are commonly associated with Japanese management practice.

Small group-based communications, in the form of team briefings, constitute one of the more common mechanisms of direct communications between managers and workers. A number of recent surveys clearly indicate that team briefings are now routine practice in British manufacturing industry (IDS, 1992a; Marchington *et al.*, 1992; and Millward, 1994). Moreover, one author, on the basis of the latest Workplace Industrial Relations Survey findings, has gone on to assert that whilst worker involvement via trade unions has declined, the team briefing can be viewed as 'the channel that increased in extent to the greatest degree [and] was the one with the greatest potential for employees to play an active part [in their companies]' (Millward, 1994, p. 86).

Surveys of Japanese firms in the UK have demonstrated that communications techniques such as team briefings are both common and well established. The Japanese firms operating in South Wales proved to be no exception here, with all but one reporting the use of team briefings, the majority on a daily basis. A much smaller proportion of these firms also organized factory conventions for the whole workforce.

According to management theory, the function of a team briefing is to promote employee involvement and team building by encouraging two-way communications as well as to impart management-approved information to subordinates (IDS, 1992a). However, the picture to emerge from the survey is that rather than exhibit potential for Millward's (1994) notion of worker involvement, Japanese team briefings bear a clear democratic deficit. Direct communications tended to be strictly top–down processes, focusing purely on narrow productionist issues rather than wider factory politics. Management interviewees in firm after firm stressed that the real purpose of the Japanese team briefing system is merely to provide succinct briefs to production teams in order to explain the day's production targets; to establish labour deployment to meet those targets; and to address production and quality defects and any individual operator performance problems. The following summary from an AIWA manager was typical:

> Our line briefings are held at the start of each shift; they're led by the line supervisors and last about five minutes. They will discuss the day's targets, and of course questions of quality and defects will also be dealt with, including who on the line has been responsible for any quality problems. And if people need a telling-off it's at these meetings that they'll get it.

A number of managers expressed concern at the lack of employee feedback during these sessions, although this reticence was hardly surprising considering the limitations of the briefing agendas. A GMB union official reflected on this:

> Yes, I've seen these team briefings in operation. But I've never felt that they've been of real value. The Japanese managers might think they are, but really, as they themselves will admit, they're only used to help the workforce make sure that their 50 units of production go out the door each day. Team briefings are used as a pep talk to make sure that production targets are met. I certainly don't see them harming us. If that were true, then surely it should indicate that the whole aspect of company policy and company news rather than these narrow production specifics were on the team briefing agendas. But they're not. So I'm not worried about it cutting across the information coming from the GMB because team briefings were never designed to do that.

As we shall see in Chapter 8, this understanding of a neutral impact of team briefings on trade union communications maybe somewhat optimistic, but it does highlight the real link between Japanese 'employee involvement' and the needs of production. Stressed lean production

Table 3.3 *Single-status conditions (N = 15)*

Single-status condition	Percentage of firms where condition obtains
Harmonized pay system	33
Hours	66
Equal sick pay	26
Equal pension scheme★	62
Clocking	80
Single grading scheme	26
Single-status canteen	80
Single-status car park	66
Company uniform	86

★ Two firms reported no pension scheme provision for any employees.

systems have no requirement for experiments in worker self-management and participation. They demand highly disciplined workers with minds focused solely on the day's production targets. Thus, as Morris *et al.* have argued, Japanese direct communication methods provide a further means of maintaining firm discipline on the line, constituting another sense in which 'Japanese transplant management might be considered "strict" or "autocratic"' (1994, p. 92).

Many Japanese firms incorporate single-status conditions into their employment contracts with the purpose of diminishing 'them and us' attitudes and class antagonisms. This is not done for its own sake. Worker acceptance of single status and the associated notion of membership of 'one big, happy and equal family' offers employers clear advantages in terms of management surveillance of the shop-floor and reducing resistance to work intensification. For these reasons, nearly all of the firms in South Wales supported some form of harmonization, although, as Table 3.3 suggests, for many firms the principle had less impact upon those more fundamental conditions of work which attract major personnel costs or which impact upon management control.

The more cosmetic manifestations of equality, such as single canteens or the wearing of uniforms, were indeed common; but unequal sick pay provision and other more traditional distinctions between shop-floor workers and staff/management remained intact. When these impacted directly on those concerns which are central to the management of lean production, such as absenteeism, then the distinctions could be extreme.

For example, many of the companies paid full sick pay to their management and salaried staff whilst their hourly paid suffered the hardship of Statutory Sick Pay (SSP). And ironically, this was excused by resort to the very status-based arguments that the Japanese are supposed to be abandoning. As one manager put it:

> You have to remember that managers have a higher standard of living, they couldn't survive, they couldn't pay their mortgages if they had to rely solely on the SSP scheme. Okay, we apply it to everyone else, but SSP is just totally inappropriate for managers.

Equality of status between managers, staff and workers, therefore, had little real material basis in these firms. However, this did not inhibit their mobilization of egalitarian corporate ideologies. Many managers were keen to stress the importance which their Japanese employers placed on the idea of regarding the company as 'one team', comprising managers and employees willingly working together with unity of purpose. A director at one company provided a typical example of this:

> Our Japanese managers talk constantly of teams and team philosophy and all in terms of the family, regarding the company as a family. There is a continual stress on the idea that all employees should be pulling together as one team. Our idea of teamworking is that everybody in the firm is a member of the same family and that there should be no distinctions between individuals within this family.

The Japanese managing director of this company produced a list of the key management philosophies and slogans to be instilled into the British managers at his Welsh transplant. These were printed in all management handbooks. He spelt out his 'corporate team philosophy' in the following idiosyncratic way:

OBJECTIVE 8

Two Families
Working place is another family.
Create sharing happiness and bitterness in family (workplace).
Have an attraction to be able to motivate and improve moral of family (work).

This was a company where members of the same 'family' could be disciplined for talking to each other on the line and where most production operators earned just £140 per week. 'Happiness' and 'sharing' were therefore in short supply. The same ideologies could also be enlisted to support the needs of production at particular times of the year. At AIWA, for example, habitual last-minute management requests for overtime during busy production periods often caused anger and resentment amongst the predominantly female workforce. Apart from problems of fatigue, many women with children encountered difficulties in arranging childcare at short notice. In order to reduce this opposition, the AIWA senior management frequently instructed managers and staff to themselves man the line and 'dirty their hands' in a symbolic gesture of 'solidarity' with the women. Similarly, other staff workers were forced to work on in their offices, unpaid, until the production line targets were achieved.

In different ways, therefore, single status and direct communications often served on the one hand to obscure real class inequalities and power imbalances at the workplace, whilst on the other, they served to maintain management's leverage over worker effort.

Industrial Relations

The 'new realism' in contemporary industrial relations, characterized by the emergence of harmonious working relationships between compliant trade unions and company managements (Bassett, 1987), is often regarded as an essential support for the highly stressed, low-waste JIT/TQM production system. This is because a more adversarial form of industrial relations will inevitably cause periodic and severe disruption to factory output (Oliver and Wilkinson, 1992; Milsome, 1993; Morris et al., 1994). This section considers the extent to which the Japanese transplants have succeeded in fashioning a new consensual relationship with their recognized trade unions. Or, what Millward (1994) has defined as the construction of the Japanese pattern of a 'new industrial relations'.

In a region notable for its union traditions, where, 'belonging to a union is as natural as breathing' (Morgan and Sayer, 1988, p. 180), and given the tendency of some UK-based Japanese inward investors to tolerate some form of union organization, it is not surprising that 14 out of the 15 firms surveyed recognized trade unions.[3] Moreover, in line with other surveys of Japanese HRM policies, nearly all of these firms operated single union agreements. The brownfield Calsonic plant provided the one exception, though even here the management persuaded the four site unions to merge into a single bargaining unit.

The practice of recognizing single unions has a long history in the UK (Millward 1994), but until the 1970s and 1980s it was less common in manufacturing industry. And, in the context of declining membership nationwide, it was the introduction of single-unionism into these Japanese manufacturing plants that caused the greatest political fallout within the Welsh trade union movement (Munday, 1990; Morris *et al.*, 1994). Although single-union deals facilitate the introduction of full labour flexibility into labour contracts through their implicit negation of traditional job demarcations, this was not the only factor to shape the different transplants' industrial relations policies. Of equal importance was a determination to fashion a hybrid company unionism with an underlying objective of building company loyalty and worker commitment at the expense of wider worker solidarity. According to the General Secretary of the Welsh TUC (one of the leading figures involved in attracting the early Japanese investors to Wales):

> They [the Japanese] just couldn't understand the British practice of multi-plant unionism. They just could not accept the idea of recognizing trade unions which also had members working in companies that were in competition with them. They saw this as a question of conflicting loyalties. They stressed that their employees, if trade union members, had to display just one form of loyalty, a loyalty to their own employer.
>
> So what developed was a compromise between the UK multi-union tradition and Japanese 'yellow unions'. This was that as long as the Japanese did not join the different employer federations in the UK, then the recognized union would not involve itself with disputes outside of the company. What emerged was a sort of red circling of industrial relations in the Japanese firms which met their real concerns about the problems of extraneous factors and actions common in British industrial relations.[4]

The old EETPU – now the electrical section of the AEEU – is the union most commonly associated with Japanese single-union agreements in the UK. However, prior to the mid-1980s, these membership agreements were distributed fairly evenly between the major engineering unions in South Wales. It was only after this period that hostilities between the TUC unions in Wales erupted, ostensibly over the controversial issue of no-strike deals, though propelled by an obsession with signing up new recruits within the context of a membership haemorrhage in the Welsh coal and steel industries (Morris *et al.*, 1994). And it was then that the EETPU started to monopolize the signing of recognition agreements with the Japanese. The General Secretary of the Welsh TUC again:

> In 1984, the EETPU in Wales came out with a new, revolutionary view of themselves which was about removing the image of the EETPU electrician. Instead, they saw themselves as general workers. One newspaper described the new EETPU member as anybody who worked under a light bulb. It was quite accurate and it became a major issue because they began poaching members. What's more, between 1984 and 1986, which was the big period of Japanese investment in Wales, the EETPU virtually got a full house. They had their own intelligence units, they had a full-time office in Japan, they developed sophisticated presentational packages, they invested in new training facilities to upskill their members, and they had their no-strike sales pitch. Other unions hated it. They weren't getting their own goodies any more, and they regarded the EETPU approach as short-selling trade unionism and as pushing the unions into the gutter. For most of them no strikes meant no rights.

In fact, although many firms in the survey did have their own no-strike agreements, the management interviewees placed more emphasis upon the general decline in overt labour militancy in South Wales. The actual agreements are not legally enforceable. Consequently, they were regarded in a more limited sense as symbolizing company harmony and cooperation rather than enforcing it. Indeed, the union officers interviewed stressed that the dispute record within the Japanese plants in South Wales was no different to the suppression of strike activity elsewhere in British–owned firms in the region. Sporadic walkouts have occurred at Hitachi, Sekisui and Matsushita Electric; during the national engineering dispute over the shorter working week in 1989, the Sony workforce walked out on strike only to be rapidly recalled by embarrassed AEEU union officers who regarded their action as a 'mistake and a misinterpretation of national directives'; and more recently in 1994, the Matsushita Electric workforce maintained a solid two-month overtime ban during a pay dispute.

Moreover, as with any unionized workplace, the propensity of the workers in these Japanese plants to enforce their collective workplace rights, including the right to take industrial action, was also a function of both national union policy and plant-level union leadership. At the relatively trouble-free Sony plant for example, one union officer claimed that the performance of the 'new realist' AEEU local stewards was such that 'the company regarded the AEEU as their own union, they put their arms around them, totally embrace them, and they couldn't be happier with their industrial relations record'. And it is no coincidence that the majority of the seven transplants which placed their negotiating machinery within the confines of company councils, or advisory boards,[5] based on the consensus model pioneered at Toshiba in Plymouth (Trevor, 1988), were those which recognized the AEEU. In these firms, management control over both council membership and bargaining agendas – along with the exploitation of procedures which ensure that any disagreements can be 'talked out' until management objectives are secured – all act to assure the attainment of a decidedly one-sided form of 'consensus'. Consequently, as both Broad's (1994) and Grant's (1996) different case studies of Japanese transplant Company Councils demonstrate, shop stewards and workers can rapidly become disillusioned at the realization that those questions which are central to shop-floor interests are defined as management prerogatives.

That is not to say that those firms which negotiated with the more traditional union-controlled negotiating committees[6] did not seek incorporation and acquiescence. Indeed, in some of these firms, the same management objectives were secured by use of more explicit forms of coercion. For instance, as the GMB convenor at Matsushita Electric stated:

> One of the methods the Japanese use in their industrial relations here is when there is a 'final, final offer', and the Japanese put a lot of stress on the 'final, final', then the offer must be recommended by the JSSC [Joint Shop Stewards Committee] even though you may have your own personal misgivings. If the package is not recommended then they withdraw the whole package. You all lose your pay rise. It's industrial blackmail frankly. The number of times I've had to tell the stewards not to be obstreperous. You're forced into a position where you have to accept, even if it runs against your principles.

Nevertheless, sometimes distinctive national union policies and local steward activism supportive of independent trade unionism can make a difference here. As Lucio and Weston (1992) argue, trade unions are manifold and complex organizations and they react to different managerial strategies in a variety of ways. Just because the AEEU choose the concessionary approach to Japanese management does not mean to say that all other unions must follow suit. Thus, 'there can be no uniformity of inevitable outcome of human resource management' (p. 216). For example, union membership densities within the surveyed firms varied from 35 per cent to 95 per cent and although the higher densities tended to obtain in the longer-established plants, independent union activity also impacted on this. A GMB regional officer argued that:

> The GMB densities tend to be higher than the AEEU because we've always been more aggressive, we've always worked harder on the basic union issues ... and I have to admit that the Japanese don't exactly welcome us with open arms. In fact they keep us at arm's length most of the time, even at Panasonics [Matsushita Electric] where we're one of the oldest established unions in any Japanese plant over here. Over the years we've had to take an aggressive approach. We've had to continually try to prove to the management that the members actually want us. And this was much easier in the 1970s when the Panasonics and the AIWAs first came because we were operating under different political conditions then. But these days it's a lot more difficult. We really have to be on our toes.

Thus, in some of these Japanese transplants, labour organization is maintained by conscientious and committed union activists just as it is in many British-owned factories. The GMB tended to bombard its members with leaflets and newsletters to keep the union message alive. Union campaigns on such bread-and-butter issues as wages, employment conditions and health and safety were all regular events. Sometimes these were reinforced by strike ballots, even though they were rarely won. A good number of the management interviewees reported likewise that although strikes were a rarity, negotiations with their unions were conducted in a traditional, combative atmosphere within an industrial relations that was certainly not as harmonious as the literature often suggests. As a Sekisui manager admitted, life on the shop-floor is subject to continual local arguments and conflicts between supervision and 'traditional union men, traditional union thinkers'.

The case of one such 'traditional union thinker', an ex-British Steel shop steward now employed at one of the larger and longer-established transplants, is instructive here. It exemplifies how personal courage, perseverance and deeply-held convictions can engender both a widespread trade union consciousness and effective resistance to Japanese managerial prerogatives:

> When I first came here about ten years ago I thought I'd walked right into a concentration camp. The workers were treated terribly, they had no rights at all. They were just being walked over by the bully boys. But we've come a

long way since then. I don't want to blow my own trumpet but we've changed things quite a bit here now. The members stand up to the management and we've won new rights, we've got a sick pay scheme now, bereavement leave, and these things are important.

Needless to say, the application of traditional union principles coupled with strong leadership incurred a number of personal costs:

Soon after I started work I was always bumping into some of the men from the Llanwern steelworks who'd also managed to get a job here, and they used to continually get on at me, urging me to stand, because to tell you the truth the union at this plant was next to useless in those days. At this time I was a clerk in the personnel office of all places. It was my wife [a shopfloor supervisor], who got me a job here as a sort of odd job man … anyway, after a lot of thought I decided to stand for the union, and I got elected.

Two days later I got called up by senior management and one of the directors said to me, 'we know you, we know who you are, you're a Llanwern man, a union agitator. We've got our eyes on you. One false move and you're out, so's your wife.' It was real blackmail. I got chucked out of the department and they put me on cleaning duties, picking up litter from the boundary fences, that sort of thing. I'm back in the factory now but I've been moved from shit job to shit job ever since. But I'm careful, mind. I won't let them get me. I always keep to procedure, never break the rules. It's the only way to stay safe in this place.

This is not the language of pro-business 'new realism'. In fact, industrial relations in these Japanese firms were more complex and differentiated than the functionalist HRM paradigm suggests. Many of the plants were unionized because such is the tradition in South Wales. And although the region's right-wing union officialdom has acted to compromise the tradition of a free, independent trade unionism, the harsh reality of life on the shop-floor under these highly disciplined, intensive production regimes provides a countervailing force here. As one union officer admitted, 'they really are stressed systems. And the work is exactly the same day in, day out. It must get boring and frustrating. So people do get comfortable with the idea that they have a union to call on, something to fall back upon.'

In reaction to attendant problems of labour discipline and control, some of the more recent Japanese arrivals have expended time and money on the construction of more 'harmonious' industrial relations systems based on

management-driven advisory boards. These aim to suppress the independent, collective articulation of rank and file interests. In contrast, a number
of the older – and larger – plants in this depressed region are content to
exploit, in a traditional manner, labour's structural dependence on the
employer for its livelihood. That is, by gaining broad acceptance of the
capitalist notion of managerial prerogative whilst seeking to manage local
conflicts over questions of reward distribution, labour discipline, and so
on. And as I will demonstrate in Chapter 7, just as with British employers,
the success of these different strategies is itself dependent upon coherent
management, the relative strength of plant labour organization and wider
political and economic conditions which impact upon the balance of
power between capital and labour.

To conclude this chapter, although some facets of the different transplants'
HRM policies differed in detail, their objectives were markedly similar.
That is, these Japanese managements were quite consistent in their careful
attempts to recruit and regulate teams of workers with the attributes
necessary to sustain the highly intensive and disciplined nature of their
lean production regimes. Few policies were detected that could be
characterized as 'soft' in the sense of offering real opportunities for
employee involvement and significant two-way dialogue with management. The more distinctive HRM practices, such as new recruitment
techniques, direct communications (and teamworking), were notable for
the ways in which they consistently attempted to secure individual and
team accountability for productive performance rather than open up any
potential for meaningful worker participation.

   The process of reaching these straightforward labour management
objectives was facilitated by the ways in which some features of Japanese
HRM policy replicate, indeed take advantage of, existing structural
conditions in the South Wales labour markets. For example, the abundant
pools of cheap, malleable, low-skilled labour, unsocialized in the ways and
traditions of labour organization, and segmented in terms of gender and to
a much lesser extent race, served these companies well. And in the 'hot
house conditions' of high unemployment and intensified market
competition (Morgan and Sayer, 1988), to which might be added the
debilitating constraints imposed by the Government's anti-trade-union
legislation, organized labour resistance to management control can be
critically restricted, though as the survey demonstrated, not completely
suppressed.

In many respects, therefore, a 'fit' between Japanese transplant work organization and the management of the employment relationship in South Wales did obtain. This was not one of fashioning new, enterprising work attitudes in a context of 'enriched' and 'empowering' labour processes. Instead, the imposition of managerial prerogatives, the suppression of rank-and-file worker controls, the extant fragmentation of production line tasks and the consequent intensification of labour under lean production demanded a more prosaic, though still strategic, HRM policy. That is, in the distinctive contemporary political and economic climate, such measures as careful recruitment techniques, the disciplining exploitation of temporary workers, the diligent control of company communications and the different attempts to restrict independent trade union activity all significantly contributed to management attempts to secure worker 'cooperation' and compliance on the shop-floor.

Notes

1   On the basis of pure observation, this youth criterion appeared to be under-reported. Many of the factories visited employed large numbers of young workers, most in their late teens and early 20s, which suggests informal if not formal age discrimination practices.

2   Although between 1983 and 1992 average hours worked each week in European Union countries declined by 4 per cent, in the UK the fall was the lowest at 1 per cent. Moreover, nearly half of the 7 million male workers in the EU countries who work a 48-hour week are employed in the UK (LRD, Fact Service, September 1994). Hughes (1994) has shown how the tendency to work excessive hours has risen strongly in the deregulated labour market. Focusing on employees who work more than 30 hours per week, he calculates that over 20 per cent of these worked more than 48 hours per week in 1991 (compared to 15.6 per cent in 1984); and for male employees the increase in the incidence of such excessive hours amounted to 35 per cent over the same period.

3   Of the 14 transplants which recognized trade unions, 13 had single-union agreements (seven with the AEEU, four with the GMB, and two with the TGWU) whilst the remaining one had a long-standing multi-union recognition agreement with the TGWU, AEEU, MSF and TGWU-ACTSS.

It should be noted that this propensity to recognize trade unions extended primarily to manual workers. Only two of these 14 firms included white collar workers in their union agreements, and one of these was the multi-union brownfield plant.

4   Interview field notes, 28.9.94.

5   The seven transplants which organized company councils were Matsushita Electric, Hitachi, Electronic Harnesses, Yuasa Batteries, Matsushita Electronic Components, Matsushita Electronic Magnetrons and Diaplastics. Three of these transplants (Matsushita Electric, Hitachi and Diaplastics) also recognized conventional union negotiating committees for bargaining purposes.

      Seven more transplants only used negotiating committees for bargaining and consultation purposes: Calsonic, AIWA, Sony, Gooding Sanken, Sekisui, Takiron and Star Micronics.

6   See note 5.

4

LOCAL AND GLOBAL CONTEXTS TO THE RESTRUCTURING OF WORK AT A BRITISH FACTORY

The survey of Japanese transplants established that whilst prevailing notions of a 'post-Taylorist', 'post-industrial' Japanese management paradigm are in fact groundless, this does not mean that there is nothing sufficiently distinctive about Japanese management practices in the UK to warrant investigation of their diffusion into indigenous firms. For, as the last two chapters have made clear, despite their work organizational differences, Japanese firms in South Wales do share certain similarities in their meticulous approach to the control and 'management by detail' of capital and labour power resources. In all cases, this is aimed at securing greater leverage over worker effort and worker compliance to boot.

Two key empirical questions arise from this. Firstly, if the sum total of Japanese transplant operations in the UK is to assume a significance greater than that of constituting merely a novel branch of MNC transplant activity employing only a relatively small number of workers nationwide, then we need to demonstrate clear connections between the distinguishing features of these Japanese firms and changes in management practices in similar British firms. Secondly, even if such a relation can be outlined, a more comprehensive analysis requires an understanding of the process of workplace change by explicating political developments at the point of production. That means seeking the views of managers, and above all, affected workers, whose opinions should take centre stage in any critique of contemporary changes in capitalist production methods. This requires switching methodologies by moving from the survey to the in-depth case study approach.

The book's remaining chapters effect this by providing an analysis of both quantitative and qualitative research data accumulated over nearly two years during a restructuring of work and workplace relations at a long-established autocomponents factory located in South-west Wales. The author makes no apology here for this focus on just one company. Apart from the general point that such an in-depth approach often provides unrivalled opportunities for exhaustive study of the processes of change, this particular factory offered two additional benefits which could not easily be disregarded. Firstly, the plant management was prepared to provide unhindered access to its shop-floor and white collar workforce in terms of workplace observations, formal and informal interviews and questionnaire distribution. Secondly, and this was crucial for the research, these facilities were offered at the very same time that the factory was embarking on a major exercise of transforming its working practices, a process which the plant management explicitly attributed to Japanese competition and influence.

What follows is an investigation of the similarities between local Japanese management practice and specific innovations introduced at the British plant. And more importantly, the accumulation of data during a period of significant change for shop-floor workers provides evidence of the ways in which capitalist social relations of production ensure that the processes of the management of change at work are not unproblematic. In so doing, the following chapters provide an in-depth exploration of the contradictions, conflicts and class struggles which remain inherent to the contemporary capitalist labour process.

The Case Study

The case study firm has been given the pseudonym 'CarPress'. It occupies a 30-acre site on the outskirts of an old coastal town located in South Wales, hereafter referred to as 'Oldport'. Oldport is a traditional working class community with a proud industrial history built upon coal and steel. Although it has undergone a metamorphosis since the end of the last world war, involving the complete demise of the latter industries, the town remains an important centre for employment in an area that contains the largest concentration of manufacturing industry in Wales (Moreton, 1990).

The substantial diversification of the local industrial base should not obscure the fact that Oldport and the surrounding area remain dependent on an economic demand for hard metal in one form or another. Despite a series of rationalizations, the giant British Steel works at nearby Port

Talbot still dwarfs other local enterprises. And a plethora of autocomponent, general engineering and steel fabrication companies means that, if they are lucky, the workers in these male-dominated industries will spend most of their working lives using different skills and technologies in the process of shaping and fabricating steels and other metals into a variety of forms for further capitalist production.

I use the term 'lucky' in the context of the mass unemployment which continues to overshadow and oppress many of the old industrial towns of South Wales – and Oldport is no exception here. As a number of comments from the workers at CarPress will testify, the fear of losing one's job is a threat that remains at the back of everyone's mind, it is something that undermines both the stability and aspirations of every household in the community.

Its official unemployment rate fluctuated between 10 and 20 per cent throughout much of the 1980s and early 1990s; and in 1991, 43 per cent of Oldport's 16–64-year-olds were either unemployed or economically inactive. However, bad as they are, these statistics disguise a more serious position for the younger inhabitants of the town. At the time of the last Government Census in 1991, 36 per cent of Oldport's 16–20-year-olds were either unemployed or registered on government schemes; the rate for young males stood at 40 per cent. These figures reflect the fact that, recent inward investment notwithstanding, much of the restructuring of job opportunities in Wales has not been helpful to the cause of youth employment. The local diversification in the Oldport area failed to generate sufficient new manufacturing jobs to offset the decline in coal and steel; only the service sector enjoyed a significant expansion (Harris, 1987). Moreover, although manufacturing industry in Wales fared better than elsewhere in the UK during the two major recessions at the beginning and end of the 1980s, this relative resilience failed to translate into the creation of new manufacturing jobs for the youngsters coming onto the labour market. The more fortunate of Oldport's young job seekers, many of them women, have managed to secure low-paid, often casual employment in the area's expanding service and tourism industries. But many others are either unemployed, or forced into worthless government training schemes.

The problems of unemployment in general, and youth unemployment in particular, are important here. This is because, as we shall see, they contribute to an environment of fear which the management at CarPress was able to adroitly exploit in its efforts to introduce a number of new floor working practices which undermined the collective interests of its shop-floor workforce.

CarPress is a body-in-white presswork and fabrications company. It operates autonomously within the CarPress Engineering Group of autocomponent manufacturers which is itself owned by a major German steel multinational conglomerate. Despite this foreign ownership – which is a recent development – the case study remains 'British' in almost every other respect. That is, in terms of management style, industrial relations traditions, union organization, and so on.

CarPress's Oldport factory started life in 1961 as part of BMC's Fisher and Ludlow Division. It was set up as a satellite plant with the purpose of feeding pressed parts and assemblies to the main BMC auto factories at Longbridge and Cowley. During this period, large amounts of new manufacturing capital were invested well away from the well-organized, high-cost labour areas in the Midlands and the South. As with most investments on greenfield sites today, many employers were seeking to take advantage of the vulnerability of labour in regions such as the North-west and South Wales where the decline of traditional industries and consequent unemployment placed labour in a difficult bargaining position (Beynon, 1984).

In those days, in contrast to the carefully planned and phased production at recent Nissan and Toyota investments in the UK, greenfield site organization could be chaotic. One manager and ex-apprentice reminisced:

I remember all of the schools in Oldport were invited to send kids in for mass interviews for apprenticeships. You won't see that sort of thing these days! Luckily, I was accepted for one of these. It was a classic greenfield site. There was little local experience of the auto industry apart from a nearby car radiator factory. And people were interviewed by the hundreds because the area was undergoing quite rapid industrial change with a lot of the older industries dying out, coal and tinplate especially. When I started in May 1961, there was hardly anything in the factory running at all. The administration was housed off-site in an old guest house, the press shop was built but it was empty of presses and I had to spend my first year in a rented bakery which was used as a training shop.

By the end of 1962, initial production had commenced in the two main manufacturing areas – the press and assembly shops. Press lines and multi-weld sections began the fabrication of complete door sets for Alex Issigonis's new BMC Mini. Over the next two years, line capacity was increased for the production of Mini sub-frames, Austin/Morris 1100 door sets, Austin Maxi and Austin/Morris 1800 floors and a variety of other pressed assemblies such as engine compartment valances and wheel arches.

In 1965, BMC merged with another body pressings company, Pressed Steel, to form British Motor Holdings. Three years later BMH merged with the Leyland Group to create British Leyland. By this time the Oldport factory employed nearly 2,000 workers, a figure that was maintained throughout most of the 1970s.

However, bad times were approaching. During the 1980s, a combination of recession, increased market competition and maladroit corporate management caused a disastrous drop in the newly named Austin Rover's domestic and foreign market share. As a result, a process of wholesale sacking took hold throughout the decade (Williams *et al.*, 1994a). The Oldport workforce took its fair share of the redundancies and between 1981 and 1988 suffered a reduction from 1,723 to 928.

Even in these circumstances, nothing could prepare the workforce for the helter-skelter of events that started in July 1988 when Margaret Thatcher's Conservative government completed its sale of Rover to British Aerospace. Despite Rover's earlier public reassurances to the contrary, British Aerospace announced the closure of the Oldport factory just four days after the privatization (Lovering and Hayter, 1993). Subsequent union and community campaigns made little impression on the new BAe management. Then, in January 1989, just two months before the Oldport shut-down was due to come into effect, a new player arrived on the scene. A Stevenage-based autocomponents supplier, CarPress Engineering, announced that it was holding talks with BAe-Rover with a view to taking over the factory. Coincidentally, this company also started life in the early 1960s and through a process of acquisition rapidly expanded its operations to ten factories located in the South and South-east of England. This expansion was partially driven by an explicit anti-union policy. As one CarPress director admitted, 'the principle concern here was the need to respond to the union militancy which damaged the industry in the 1960s. It was essentially a multi-plant strategy for strike breaking.'

After two months of inter-firm negotiations, which were complicated by a series of strikes and walkouts over questions of employment conditions and union recognition rights, the sale was completed. The local media jubilantly reported that the factory's remaining 750 jobs were safe. But within 12 months these were again under threat.

In May 1990, the CarPress Engineering Group succumbed to a hostile takeover bid by a firm of property speculators owned by a major Australian industrial conglomerate. A number of CarPress directors resigned, convinced that their company would become subject to a classic asset-stripping operation. In the event, financial problems within the parent Australian firm forced the sale of CarPress, more or less intact, to a German steel and engineering company which was in turn acquired by another German steel conglomerate in December 1991.

Up to this point, the changing fortunes of the Oldport factory were of marginal interest to the main actors involved. However, once the plant was integrated into the German MNC's automotive division, contemporary global changes in the autocomponents industry started to move in its favour. The major car assemblers began shifting towards single sourcing of supplies to control component price and quality. At the same time, the benefits of economies of scale, along with the assemblers' encouragement of suppliers to develop a presence in each of their global markets, combined to bring into effect industrial concentration and the emergence of an international oligopoly of component suppliers (Amin and Smith, 1991). CarPress had become a member of one of these oligopolies.

As a result, the factory remained a major supplier to the Rover car assembly operation. But it also succeeded in building up a European and Japanese customer base on a long-term, single-supplier basis. In 1992, as much as 90 per cent of the factory's output was destined for Rover. Management aimed to reduce this to 40 per cent over five years. By 1995, the Oldport plant had become a principal first-tier supplier to Toyota and GM Opel. It also secured important long-term contracts for body-in-white parts with Honda and Mercedes Benz.

Work Organization and the Labour Process

When the research started, CarPress employed 718 men and 45 women,[1] 763 managers and workers in all. Since the factory was principally a manufacturing unit, over 600 of these employees were hourly paid, mainly semi-skilled operators and skilled production support workers. The white collar workforce approached nearly 150 in number, comprising managers and staff employed in the finance, sales and marketing, quality assurance, engineering, manufacturing and human resource functions.

The shop-floor was 100 per cent unionized: the TGWU represented semi–skilled production operators whilst the AEEU covered all skilled groups. Upon acquiring the Oldport factory the CarPress management immediately derecognized MSF in all office areas. Despite this, 95 per cent of MSF members retained their membership, so that management was forced to accept a more informal process of white collar union representation and negotiation.

When the factory was built in 1961 it was regarded as one of the most advanced press and assembly shops in Europe. The long, rectangular main production building divided exactly in half between the press and assembly shops and contained production, maintenance and toolroom areas. Bottlenecks and buffers notwithstanding, it was designed to receive steel coil and strip in the goods inwards bay at one end of the building and then, in the course of the production process, material would flow through the two main shops eventually arriving as completed assemblies on the despatch deck at the opposite end of the building. All superfluous scrap metal was channelled into a novel underground recycling system where metal would be compressed into large cube blocks.

The labour processes in the main shop-floor and engineering areas will now be described in turn.

The Press Shop

The main press shop contained over 100 presses ranging from 30- to 1100-ton capacity. Most were located along three bays and arranged in groups of four or five machines along 17 straight production lines.

The process of manufacturing a complex pressed part, such as a car door, requires a line of presses each set up with a different pair of dies designed to press the blanked steel into a particular shape. As Williams *et al.* (1994b) have observed, this process has hardly changed over the past 50 years. Each part travels once through the line of presses receiving successive 'blows' from the hydraulic rams so that the required shape materializes at the final press on the line. The CarPress shop also housed one line of automatic transfer presses which can carry out these successive operations within the same press. But most of the shop was organized along traditional lines with each group of presses working in tandem and linked by portable conveyors moving the steel parts from machine to machine.

The press shop operators worked an alternating day and night shift system. Each shift comprised 85 operators supported by supervision.

There are, of course, many additional tasks to be performed in the steel pressing process by toolmakers and toolsetters, maintenance workers, crane drivers, fork lift truck drivers and so on, all of which are considered later. But the principal labour process belongs to the press operators. Their machines dominated the whole factory. Standing as towers of hard metal and oil-based grime, they generated a continual rhythmic din of muffled thuds and metallic strikes as their rams cycled every four or five seconds of the working day.

The shop typically achieved 1 million 'blows' on a weekly throughput of 800 tons of steel. To accomplish this, operators worked with speed, consistency and efficiency. Many of them performed in pairs. At the first press along a typical line of five, operators standing each side of a conveyor would pick up a blanked steel sheet, place this into the bed of the press so that it sat correctly on the lower die (or 'tool') and then activate the ram with a single push–button electrical switch. Immediately, a metal safety bar would be released and come flying upwards to hit out of the way any unlucky operator who might have absent-mindedly remained by the bed. Once the ram cycled the operators pushed the pressed part out onto the next conveyor belt at the opposite end of the press bed and repeated the whole operation by loading the next blanked sheet. The same task routines were performed at each press down the line.

Williams *et al.* (1994b) argue that although the efficiency of press shops may differ on an international basis because of variable machine setup and downtime performance, the actual speed of the press operation tends to be a universal, as it is technically determined by press design, and in particular, cycle time. However, although this may hold for some automated presses, the argument fails to take into account the impact of capitalist social relations and the accompanying capital–labour conflict over the speed of work, as the next chapter will demonstrate. In fact, the speed of the production operation in the CarPress press shop was a function of both the targets or 'scores' set by management and the variability of labour power, as well as cycle times. But it was always rapid. Press throughput could vary between 100 and as much as 1,000 parts per hour, according to the complexity of part design. A typical rate was about 350. That is, six parts, or six of the above task routines every minute. Therefore, it would be misleading to describe the physical labour process of the press operator purely in terms of the simple coordination of a few basic tasks. It is a process that is characterized by a rapid tempo and consistent body movement; as the operators handle heavy steel parts their bodies rhythmically sway in and out of the presses between conveyor and press bed, at all times avoiding the bruising knock of the safety bar.

The work was degrading and dehumanizing. It was the strength of organized labour rather than any objective task assessment which enabled the workers to defend their semi-skilled status. The production operators themselves sardonically dismissed any alternative interpretation of their work. The following view was typical:

> So you people talk about job enrichment! What's that supposed to mean? You should come down and work on our line for a few days and then maybe you'd see some sense. I mean, all you're doing is feeding fucking parts into a machine and pressing buttons all day long. How can you ever get any satisfaction out of that?

Marx (1976) wrote that, 'in the factory we have a lifeless mechanism [the machine] which is independent of the workers, who are incorporated into it as its living appendages' (p. 548). This observation still applies in contemporary workplaces. Many CarPress workers spoke of the physical fatigue caused by 'being on your feet all the time' and a mental fatigue resulting from the boredom of 'being married to your machine'. For example, another press shop operator felt that:

> You see, as an operator you're just an extension of the actual machine, you're not a person. As soon as you clock in each morning you switch off, you just leave your brain at the clocking station.

The operators continually complained of being treated as numbers and not always in the sense of 'numbers on cards' or numbered units of labour. Most presses were fitted with clocks which registered the hourly quantity of parts produced. These facilitated calculation of operator and plant performance, and therefore served as precise little instruments of management control. Some CarPress managers were so obsessed with production, output and productivity that their attitudes to the shop-floor workforce really were conditioned solely by the numbers on these clocks. As another operator put it:

> I'll tell you what I think of this company. This company treats people as numbers and it's numbers we will always be. It doesn't care about me as a human being. The only thing that this company and it's management are really concerned about is the number that's on my clock at the end of the day. Nothing else.

The Assembly Shop

The organization of production and technology in the assembly shop was more complex. The basic manufacturing process consisted of welding together the different pressed parts and components required for the manufacture of car body assemblies. For body-in-white plants, three production stages are needed for this. Firstly, pressed parts are welded together to form sub-assemblies; then these sub-assemblies are welded together along with additional components to form major parts like doors or sub-frames; and finally, these parts undergo different labour intensive metal finishing processes, such as de-burring, smoothing and small dent removal, all performed with the use of a variety of heavy hand tools.

Jurgens *et al.* (1993) have identified three levels of welding mechanization currently used in the industry to complete this manufacturing process: manual welding guns; robots; and multispot welding processes. The CarPress assembly shop used all three of these: manual equipment such as pedestal welders, hanging gun spot welders and conventional CO_2 welding gear; different clusters of multi-welders (which accomplish more than one weld simultaneously); and both a robotic automated transfer line for high volume production and clusters of smaller robots for smaller volumes.

In their analysis of the restructuring of working practices in the industry, Jurgens *et al.* also highlight, *inter alia*, the interrelationship between specific national and local corporate technological strategies. In particular, they identify a tripartite division between a German – and to a lesser extent American – reliance on investment in modern automated transfer lines; a Japanese preference for the modernized organization of existing technologies; and a less coherent British position, which, lacking sufficient resources to follow the German path, is therefore attempting to imitate the Japanese, albeit in piecemeal fashion. In a curious way, the CarPress assembly shop provided a microcosm of this.

The most advanced technology in the plant was used exclusively for a multi-million-pound contract to manufacture dashboards for Opel in Germany. It consisted of a dedicated robotic transfer line employing discrete groups of teamworkers welding together different sub-assemblies and feeding these into the automated final assembly system.

Two groups of teams responsible for producing different body-in-white parts for Toyota and Honda provided the 'Japanese' representation. Although the Honda team relied on advanced, more flexible robot systems, emphasis in both sections was placed on the rational organization of discrete welding units in cellular formation rather than automation.

Finally, the largest areas were 'British' and dedicated mainly to Rover production. These comprised row upon row of the older welding machines, often manned by the same operators day in, day out. Apart from the press shop, it was in these areas that the CarPress managers were particularly keen to introduce teamworking and other new working practices.

This segmented work organization had little impact on the essential physical labour processes in the assembly shop. Although the Opel and Japanese teamworkers took on a number of additional tasks which will be considered in Chapter 6, the basic task routines nevertheless remained constant across the different assembly sections.

Once again, the work had a low skill content. Operators would simply pick up the necessary pressed parts and metal fasteners from line side pallets, place these into their machine jigs and then activate the weld either by hand gun, pedestal arm, or push button switch. Management-set targets aimed to ensure that operators maintained this cycle, typically, every 12 seconds of the working day. And although to the observer the work appeared less arduous than press shop work, most operators experienced it as pure drudgery. As in the press shop, it was economic compulsion and the crack of the foreman's whip that kept many on their toes, as the following comments demonstrate:

> No, there's no job satisfaction here. How can there be? We're not involved in the job at all. I tell you, the management here are all fucking pigs. I mean, they say to you 'right you go over here and you over there and *work*'. They don't care about you at all. All they want is the score out, you do the score and that's it. Basically, they treat you like a machine, like a robot. I'm afraid the style of work is totally monotonous, and if unemployment was lower I'd be out of here like a shot. And I'd work for less money.

And another:

> I come in every morning and I'm usually on a dreamer. It often takes me two hours to get going properly. It's the same job, week in week out, there's never any change. And it's a low skill factor job. You know how to do it inside ten minutes; all you need is speed and synchronization. So the satisfaction is in the pay and the knowledge that you've got a good paying job. There's nothing else.

Sometimes, in order to balance production lines, the foremen would lend and borrow labour across the press-shop/assembly-shop divide. However, the press shop workers were not keen on this; they tended to look down on their assembly shop colleagues because for some men, heavy manual work carries a certain prestige. As one said, 'we're handling ten tons of steel per shift and that's heavy work I can tell you ... next door they're doing women's work playing with their little nuts and little bits of metal'. The lack of any dignity in mass-production labour, the boredom and relentless grind of the work, often gives rise to such irrational internal working-class divisions. In fact, the work in the assembly shop, like the press shop, was neither men's work nor women's work. It was just hard work.

Plant Maintenance and the Toolroom

CarPress employed 189 skilled workers, all men, in its maintenance and toolroom departments. Some of these tradesmen were specialist electricians, electronic technicians and mechanics; others, over a number of years, were forced to bridge the traditional electrical-mechanical divide by learning new technical skills outside of their particular specialisms. During the 1970s and 80s, such workers fought hard against this 'multi-skilling' in order to maintain some control over their specialist skills and through this to retain a certain dignity of labour that is absent from the production line (Beynon, 1984; Willman and Winch, 1985; Roberts, 1993). But at CarPress, as we shall see in Chapter 6, explicit de-skilling and multi-tasking are now a greater threat than multi-skilling.

For many of these workers – and some of their sympathetic managers – the contemporary changes in skilled work were seen as a function of the growing domination of mass-production over the supportive craft roles. As the maintenance manager complained, 'unfortunately, in this place, production is the god that drives the whole thing. We seldom have any windows during the day that enable us to get onto the machinery to do the essential preventative maintenance work.' Because of this, most CarPress maintenance workers harboured increasing resentment at the resulting stress, work intensification and irrational marginalization of their essential work. One fitter put it like this:

> The work was more relaxed here years ago, and there's a simple reason for that. There were just more people working here. Now it's got a lot tighter.

> The company has cut down on the workforce drastically. So the whole workplace has become stressed up due to a sheer drop in numbers while at the same time our workload hasn't dropped at all. They're still running all of the same machines flat out. If anything they're running them without breaks more than they ever used to.
>
> And it's a different firm now. It's more stressful being a maintenance worker because there's no real preventative maintenance being done. We can't do it because we don't have the materials or the men. So what we're doing is fire fighting rather than fire preventing. They just expect us to come running when things begin breaking down.

In most auto plants, toolrooms are responsible for manufacturing and maintaining press dies and welding jigs. The work demands a range of predominantly mechanical skills in fitting and machining. At CarPress, the toolroom's main function was restricted to the maintenance and installation of the plant's 1,200 press dies and 600 assembly jig fixtures, rather than new die manufacture. For, in the interests of capitalist efficiency and profit-making, the factory, like many others, was now subcontracting die manufacture to engineering specialists. By depressing wages and conditions, these firms were able to capitalize on their low prices. Not surprisingly, many of the toolmakers resented the dilution of skills that accompanied these changes. One commented:

> We used to be real toolmakers. That was our job, our craft. But these days there's no money or investment going into the shop at all. The company's no longer prepared to invest in new machinery because most of our toolmaking work is now subcontracted. Don't get me wrong, refurbishing has always been part of the job here, but we've also had real toolmaking to do as well. Now all it's about is regrinding and first aid and this has resulted in a definite loss of skills. I just think that nowadays we seem to be doing everything *but* toolmaking.

And another:

> I think there's one sort of teamworking that's okay. When we were under Austin Rover we were always doing everything for ourselves. We'd make new heads and other parts, we would all chip in doing different jobs. But now all this work's being sent out, we've lost it. The management are always telling us that it's only chicken shit but we know it's not, it's the quality work that's going.

Many of these tradesmen felt that their jobs and skills were coming under threat from internal sources as well. Since the Rover sell-off, the organization of technical work in the engineering and quality functions had undergone some significant changes involving a weakening of the demarcation between shop-floor and office. For example, one of the more satisfying elements of the toolmaker's job is the testing of die prototypes for new part designs, or 'tryout' as it is called in the trade. The careful adjustment and modification of dies, jigs and machines involves a wide range of practical and reflexive skills. However, despite all the fashionable talk of a post-Taylorist synthesis of the conception and execution of tasks, many CarPress toolroom workers were discovering that the restructuring of the relationship between shop-floor and technical workers was, if anything, acting to reinforce the de-skilling process. CarPress's white collar engineers were colonizing 'tryout' work for themselves. A toolmaker:

> It seems to me that the toolroom is just full of white coats and white collars these days. They all seem totally unaffected by the cuts. Maybe it's because the managers are empire building, I don't know. But it's also because the engineers are taking over the best of our work. They are. They're taking the work that needs all the ideas and real skills, the tryout work. It's the sort of work that needs a bit of creativity. But now we're losing that as well.

Engineering

These changes in the toolroom, and the accompanying restructuring of work in CarPress's office areas, did not necessarily confer enhanced skills and opportunities on all 137 staff employees. Most of these were managers, supervisors and engineers employed in production, engineering and quality functions with a small number of supporting administrative staff. Despite the above shop-floor resentment, many of these workers were also experiencing their own particular forms of loss of job control and skill. The case of the engineering department was typical here.

Under the previous Rover management, the department was involved solely with part design. In those days the drawing office was fairly large, housing mainly component designers and jig and tool draughtsmen responsible for designing press dies and welding machine fixtures. Associated questions of sales and project management generated abstract problems safely located elsewhere in a West-Midlands-based administrative centre. The CarPress takeover changed all of that. The engineering director put it like this:

> After the takeover we suddenly changed from being a large satellite
> manufacturer to being a supplier to a range of customers. So we had to
> change our philosophy from one of volume supplier to one of quality
> supplier. We had to suddenly start thinking about the customer's needs. And
> this involved a major cultural change in relation to both product and financial
> questions. We had to become a commercial enterprise virtually overnight.
> Basically, it's now about customer engineering.

For the engineering department, this meant assuming overall responsibility for the management of the whole contract from initial conceptualizing all the way through to production and sales. What the business schools like to call 'simultaneous engineering'. CarPress's design engineers became 'customer engineers', learning the disciplines of contract, customer liaison and product management as well as the prototype development and 'tryout' work described above. However, this did not necessarily have a positive impact on skill and job content. Although the company introduced CAD technology and other advanced information systems, the quantity and quality of design work diminished. On occasions, the department would 'get the envelope' from the customer, designer-speak for receiving the basic conceptual parameters from which draughtsmen and women generate their drawings and specifications. But increasingly, any design work of substance was being transferred to external contractors.

Contemporary analysis of these types of changes tends to be driven by an assumption that the demise of old craft skills, whether in the drawing office or on the shop-floor, is a sign of the inevitable progress of advanced capitalism. This is not in the negative sense of the 'progress' of capitalist accumulation and control outlined by Braverman (1974); indeed, for some writers, it is not something to be regretted at all. Instead, we are often asked to accept the restructuring of the work of core employees as an accumulation of new responsibilities and new knowledge-based skills which more than compensate for the loss of traditional craft expertise. For example, Lash and Urry (1994) have argued that in Japanese companies such changes bring workers into an increasingly skilful interaction with different information-intensive systems. Through these reflexive processes, Japanese workers and their employers are held to benefit from an 'accumulation of cultural capital' in the form of new training, new skills and so on.

Although the work of the CarPress engineers underwent a similar transformation, many did not see these changes in such a positive light.

The following view of a tooling engineer typified the general bitterness caused by the loss of draughting skills:

> It's definitely changed over the years. We used to be far more involved in design. Previously a lot of the design work would be done in-house, or it would come straight from the customer and we'd do some modifications. But now we're only working on the management of new projects. These days, the tooling's designed by whoever, it's made by whoever and handed straight over to production. As I see it, the whole thing's just turned into cheque book engineering.

And:

> I suppose it had to happen. A lot of firms seem to be getting rid of design these days. It's being subcontracted out all the time. Personally, I prefer it as it was. I was brought up in a real drawing office environment. I've got nothing against the system, I suppose it works, but there's much less job satisfaction now and a lot less skill. Our job used to be about starting the job off on the board. We used to put ideas onto paper with drawing pencils and then you'd gradually develop the job yourself and see the thing materialize. But not any more.

This is not to say that CarPress's engineers dismissed out of hand the new ways of working and the responsibilities that went with them. Like many engineers, they enjoyed rising to the challenge of solving new sets of problems. It was just that they felt the process had limits of acceptability. And whilst human interaction with new computer information systems could be appealing, many nevertheless resented the de-skilling which accompanied the loss of the primary interaction between engineer and machine. They could not understand how anyone could be classed as a skilled engineer without having a practical appreciation of machinery and tooling and a knowledge of the technical parameters associated with the different production processes. But as part of its internal restructuring, the engineering department began to recruit such individuals, young 'customer engineers', well versed in the procedures of contract management but lacking a basic understanding of practical engineering principles. The experienced engineers were clearly disgruntled at the divestment of 'cultural capital' which this approach signified. As a project teamleader put it:

> Most of these youngsters might have good qualifications, the HNCs and degrees, but none have the formal engineering training and the skills that go

with it. The skills involved in actually understanding a process, understanding how a machine tool works, how a press works, getting close to it and understanding the technical problems that you get with these types of machines ... I suppose it's a reflection of the way the job is changing. I've got to admit, many of the youngsters may be sharper than us at costing and estimating. But they're not engineers.

The Impact of Japanese Management

The foregoing preliminary account of the organization of work at CarPress sets the local context for our analysis of the implementation of 'Japanese-style' new working practices which unfolds over the next four chapters. It also demonstrates that irrespective of the impact of new management techniques, the plant's work organization has not remained static since its inception in 1961. The advent of new technologies, new product markets and new customer relationships along with competitive pressures for demanning and a 'commercialization of the labour contract' (O'Connell Davidson, 1993) through external subcontracting, have all made their impact on the labour process. So has internal job restructuring. But we also need to consider the wider environmental context of the change process and how external contingencies at the global and national level, particularly the growth of Japanese inward investment, have affected the local factory and local attitudes.

The British autocomponent industry has for some time been caught between a pincer movement. This consists of a general decline in the fortunes of the hand that feeds it, the British auto assembly sector, and the simultaneous propensity of the latter to both reduce local content and squeeze the prices of the remaining UK suppliers. As Amin and Smith (1991) have outlined, since the early 1970s, the UK has gone from being 'a sizeable manufacturer of cars which once dominated the domestic markets and exported over a third of its output, to a significantly smaller actor in both the domestic and export markets' (p. 174). At the same time, the auto sector multinationals have rationalized capacity and restructured their operations to generate plant-based economies of scale through either task or car model specialization. Amin and Smith point out that this process of vertical integration put many British autocomponent suppliers out of business during the 1980s. But it also had a significant impact on remaining suppliers of the likes of CarPress. The major car assemblers reduced their supplier volume by awarding larger and longer term contracts to an upper tier of prime suppliers. In so doing, they were able to exert substantial control over these suppliers by overseeing price reductions and insisting on better quality, innovative capability and delivery. This is not a process of corporate intervention that is peculiar to the Japanese, although they are particular experts at it. For example, Opel, one of CarPress's largest customers, recently embarked upon a major internal efficiency drive along these lines. It resulted in significant cost reductions of bought-in parts (Parkes, 1993).

Japan's phenomenal success in global car exports coincided with these changes. Between 1973 and 1985 the Japanese auto industry expanded to such an extent that it eventually controlled 29 per cent of global output and totally dominated world intercontinental trade movements (Bloomfield, 1991; Jurgens et al., 1993). This presented a real threat to Western manufacturers. It contributed to the emergence of an ideology of 'factory survival' in the West, where managements increasingly raised the nightmare of superior Japanese productivity in their attempts to expedite job rationalization and the introduction of new working practices. Of course, the history of low wages, work intensification and exploitation of small subcontractors that underpinned this Japanese 'miracle' was conveniently overlooked here (Garrahan and Stewart, 1992).

Managerial apprehension of Japanese industrial expansionism also had a more direct material impact. For instance, in 1993, the European Union commissioned the influential Boston Report into the competitive gap between European and Japanese autocomponent suppliers. The report's conclusions, right or wrong, that a massive productivity gap in favour of the Japanese required halving by 1999 if the European industry was to survive (Done, 1993), started to provoke corporate action. One CarPress director commented on this and related influences:

> Yes, our parent company in Germany is very heavy on the Boston Report at the moment. The company was one of the driving forces behind it in the EC, and it's certainly having an impact here. And there are similar influences elsewhere. For example, Rover with their RG2000 quality audits and Ford are the same with A1. They're always trying to drive down our costs. They can be a bloody nuisance as well. Particularly when times are bad in the industry you tend to get the representatives from some of these customers coming in and crawling all over you, looking at your quality procedures and working practices.

Perceptions of superior Japanese management performance, therefore, contribute to the diffusion of new management techniques. Also of importance to suppliers is the sheer presence of the Japanese auto assemblers in the UK and the potential of new business. It has been estimated that by the late 1990s, something like £2 billion worth of EC-sourced components will be flowing into the three Japanese assemblers in the UK – Nissan, Honda and Toyota (Griffiths, 1992). But those indigenous companies which are successful in gaining prime supplier contracts are also paying a price. With the balance of power between these different capitals clearly in favour of the Japanese assemblers, suppliers can no longer fix, or even negotiate, component prices in the traditional manner. Instead, they are forced to open up their books to the Japanese, allowing the latter to determine how costs and prices are calculated, and through this to set in motion a price-lowering process. They are also forced to accept the intrusion of the Japanese customer into the area of monitoring quite intimate aspects of their quality and performance (Done, 1990; Griffiths, 1992).[2]

Too much of the contemporary debate on the 'Japanization of British industry' has dwelt solely on the extent of Japanese management innovation without attending to the pertinent practical question of how the *process of diffusion* between Japanese-owned or 'Japanized' firms and British firms might take effect. At CarPress, diffusion from the likes of Toyota, Honda, Rover and Opel was accomplished primarily through the development of the type of close customer relationships outlined above. These relationships were realized through determined sales strategies, persistent customer liaison and the additional highly proactive role of such external agencies as the Welsh Development Agency.[3]

Rover was the chief protagonist in this change process. The introduction of new working practices at CarPress, like many other British companies, has been slow, incremental and subject to both management incoherence and periodic trade union resistance. But certain defining moments in the Oldport factory's recent history did represent significant catalysts of change.

One of these was Rover's decision to sell the plant. This was not done in response to any overcapacity of capital in relation to product demand. Apart from securing immediate financial gain, the sale acted to commercialize the Oldport labour contract, squeeze unit labour costs and, thereby, both reduce Rover's overall production costs and increase its profits.

A post-privatization, long-term customer–supplier relationship was forged. Although Rover remained CarPress's largest customer, the nature of the commercial relationship changed. CarPress's production manager summed this up in the following way:

> When we were a Rover plant we produced no budget accounts to speak of. We were dealing purely in wooden dollars, supplying parts to Oxford, Longbridge and Swindon. Now things have changed. Everything has got to be justified. We're accountable for all our budgets and costs and we're all far more commercially aware than we used to be. Now the site is a profit centre, and each section within it is a cost centre, so we've had to become more open with our figures. It also means that we've been forced to keep to tighter profit margins, which Rover and the rest of our customers enforce on virtually every contract. The result of all this is that we now have to get smarter in the way we manufacture.

Rover took a keen interest in the methods used to achieve these cost reductions. As the firm at the forefront of the 'Japanization of work organization' in the British car industry (Oliver and Wilkinson, 1992), it followed the Japanese practice of demanding surveillance of CarPress's attempts to introduce changes on the shop-floor. Various mechanisms were used to accomplish this.

For example, the increasing use of a new style of factory audit, extending far beyond matters of product quality, constituted a significant supplier-control device. Rover applies its RG2000 audit to every one of its prime suppliers. The company's audit personnel regularly visit firms like CarPress every year, armed like industrial bureaucrats with their packs of assessment forms, audit criteria and interview notes and making critical judgements on working practices, personnel policy and business performance.[4]

Day-to-day customer–supplier interactions were equally important for shaping the process of change. CarPress managers and engineers attended many routine meetings with Rover liaison staff to discuss product and process quality including such 'technical' matters as 'cost-down', the managerialist euphemism for reducing part prices by intensifying work effort. And as we shall see in Chapter 7, Rover's interventions even extended to direct interference in shop-floor disputes.

CarPress's Japanese and German customers applied similar instruments of surveillance and control over the factory's product quality, process and business organization. As a result, the density of interaction between these major customers and CarPress managers and technical staff reached relatively high levels. This enabled many senior staff to formulate their own subjective assessments of Japanese management style and innovation. Apart from regular meetings at different Rover plants, most managers and technical staff visited Toyota and Honda's British factories at some time; many did this on a routine basis to address both substantial problems and some of the minutiae of contractual, engineering and quality matters. A relatively high number of engineers and managers also visited parent factories in Japan itself.

The diffusion of ideas and ideology followed further parallel routes. Some managers were well-read in the latest business school offerings on the 'Japanese miracle'; many had the seminal works of Dr Deming and the more quixotic Tom Peters on their bookshelves. In addition, the majority of managers and senior staff, and even some shop stewards, had at various times attended local seminars on Japanese management practice organized by the WDA and other business agencies. More recently, as we note in Chapter 6, CarPress established a series of courses on teamworking and other new working practices for managers and shop-floor workers. These were organized by a local brand of the ubiquitous British management consultant with additional input from Honda and Toyota.

Although many managers and engineers expressed admiration for certain aspects of Japanese management performance, and most accepted the drive for a restructuring of work and employment relations on the CarPress shop-floor, one could nevertheless discern an irritation with the notion that British companies should blindly follow the Japanese path. On the general level this was often expressed in crude nationalistic terms. For example, one production supervisor complained:

> Okay, maybe some Japanese companies have got some good ideas, though I suspect as many of them are American as Japanese. But I would have thought that this country, as pioneers in the industrial revolution, should have some ideas of its own rather than follow the lead of some old third-rate country. Where have our ideas gone?

And a project engineer:

> No, I wouldn't want to see a 'Japanization of industry' as you put it. No, we're a different race, we're different people. We couldn't accept all the regimentation that you get over there. They're all 'yes men'. They like taking their orders. And they don't complain or offer any resistance. They don't seem to be the type of

people who can take decisions as individuals. Everything's done in groups and all their decision-making takes a hell of a long time.

There was also a resentment of any implication that British managers were inefficient and weak 'labour-pushers' by comparison. Different managers consistently criticized the generally held view that Japanese plants are more productive than their British counterparts in terms of profit performance and both capital and labour utilization. Moreover, with almost universal conviction, these managers and engineers rejected as pure myth the idea that Japanese firms are structured around flat hierarchies. They argued that Japanese managers benefited from a superior number of staff supporting the function of control over the production process.[5] In contrast, it was the understaffed British managements, rather than their Japanese counterparts, who suffered stress and overwork. The CarPress production manager expressed it this way:

In any case, not all the Japanese firms are lean producers. As far as I'm concerned many of them are mob-handed. Take Toyota for example. The management seem to have three or four levels of staff to back them up. Far more than we have here. And they're certainly not as efficient as they make out. Personally, I don't believe from what I've seen at Toyota and from what I've learned elsewhere that the Japs work their men as fast as the equivalent CarPress worker.

And a similar view from a robotics engineer:

Well, I've visited a number of plants in Japan and they all tend to give me the same impression. You talk about lean production but there's always plenty of people doing the same job. They never move out of the company and they never seem to change jobs. In some respects I don't suppose you can blame them. Their kids go to the company school, they went to the company school and they all live in their company houses. So they start with a company and never leave it. But many of them seem overmanned to me. When I was there for meetings with the customer I'd be covering six or seven disciplines. Electrical work, electronics, welding and so forth. But they couldn't understand this approach. They always had the same men strictly covering the same narrow range of disciplines.

Despite these caveats, the management seemed convinced that shop-floor working practices and employment relations required restructuring if CarPress was to rise to the challenge of Japanese greenfield, hi-tech investment. Throughout much of its history, capital investment in the

British car industry has suffered at the expense of corporate demands for immediate profits and dividend payments (Greenhalgh and Kilminster 1993); and despite recent waves of international modernization, many British plants have retained their low investment records (Jurgens *et al.*, 1993). In keeping with this tradition, the CarPress board of directors consistently refused to consider long-term capital investment on a coherent, strategic basis, preferring the cheaper option of organizational change and specific technological investments when demanded by the customer. Needless to say, the company's shop-floor managers resented this. Many wistfully reflected on the Japanese propensity to carefully plan and financially support the introduction of sophisticated dedicated capital equipment. As one quality manager said, 'in this place, things are antiquated in comparison ... what we need is an injection of modern technology and Japanese philosophy'.

In truth, however, the management was more envious of the Japanese capacity to exploit young, malleable labour on its greenfield sites. Although, on the basis of their regular visits to different Toyota and Honda plants, Japanese transplant workers were variously described as, 'brainwashed, vacant and empty', 'fully indoctrinated' and 'behaving as robots', this does not mean that things would be any different if these workers were placed under the control of the CarPress management. Far from it. In reality, any expressions of 'pity' merely translated into regret that the CarPress workforce could not be equally subordinated. Indeed, one objective of the change process was to undermine the defensive, collectivist culture on the CarPress shop-floor. As the operations director expressed it:

> We need to change our shop-floor culture by getting the workers out of this plant, by taking them to some of these Japanese factories. They've never left it in their lives, they've never seen anything else. And the problem we have is that our younger recruits are always gradually contaminated by the older workforce, they rapidly get 'queered' so to speak. In the past, any evidence of individual initiative has always been swamped by an attitude of 'protect your brother'.

What were the attitudes of the shop-floor workers to notions of 'Japanization' and change at the workplace? Were they as uniformly unyielding as the above comment suggests? In fact, as we shall see, although they revealed a clear sense of collective interests, in terms of the demand for fair treatment and greater control over their working lives, in the initial stages of the research there existed no consensus on whether the introduction of a new 'Japanese style' of management might support or hinder this. Why was this?

Beynon's description of the 'factory consciousness' displayed by shop stewards at Ford highlights how a trade unionist's class politics and ideology can become essentially factory-based. That is, a factory consciousness with an ideology whose cutting edge is confined to the arena of production, shaping a class politics which is often isolated within the confines of the plant (1984, pp. 117, 374). A similar analysis can be applied to the CarPress rank and file. Indeed, it has a particular bearing in the context of the UK in the 1990s, where the temporary demise of radical left-wing politics and extra-parliamentary working-class activity leaves little for factory workers, or their stewards, to cut themselves off from. Since the Rover sell-off, the CarPress shop stewards enjoyed few opportunities for joint plant campaigns or even political discussions with fellow car workers from other plants. And unlike the management and technical staff, their members had virtually no contact with the workers employed by the different customers who were intent on changing CarPress's working practices and shop-floor culture. Apart from those employees who had friends or relatives working for a Japanese company in the area, the only information on the nature of Japanese practices came from the media and the internal tendentious source of formal company communications. Therefore, although the introduction of Japanese management innovations had potentially damaging implications for working-class interests on the CarPress shop-floor, the recipients of these changes accumulated little of the required knowledge for developing a coherent and united political response. An extant 'factory consciousness' was starting to work against them.[6]

Despite this, a good number of the workers interviewed did display an antipathy towards the idea that their working lives should somehow become 'Japanized'. It reflected a resentment of any imposition of an 'alien Japanese work ethic' which might merely compound the existing levels of stress on the shop-floor. Like some of their bosses, this fear would sometimes be dressed explicitly in racist terms. As one operator cynically remarked, 'you talk about hard work, loyalty, discipline, but the Japanese are like that aren't they? They all like to get on a daily sweat for a bowl of rice. But that sort of life is not for me, this is Wales not Japan!' Others held equally unambiguous views on the nature of Japanese work intensification and discipline. An assembly shop operator felt that:

> We're told that the Japanese way is the only way to work, that people are happier working for Japanese companies. But I'm not so sure that's the case. They've got this teamworking and they work just as hard, if not harder, than we do. The Japanese are the worst taskmasters of all, they're worse than here. As I see it, in these Japanese firms everything has to be done their way or else. If you don't like it then you either shut up or they show you the door.

And a crane driver:

> I don't know what the Japanese working practices are about. What I do know is that they're continually cutting manning. I know about lean production, it's bad news, it's what they're trying on here. It's all threat, threat, threat. As far as I'm concerned the Japanese way is about screwing the maximum amount of work from the minimum amount of men.

However, prior to the introduction of the new working practices, a surprising number of other workers were less critical on these questions. This ambivalence could be partially attributed to a lack of awareness of the likely impact of new management techniques on the labour process and management–labour relations. But it also reflected a blind hope that anything might be better than the existing production regime. Such attitudes are not unusual amongst those whose working lives have become grotesquely disfigured by the dehumanizing hard work, drudgery and monotony of traditional Taylorist forms of mass-production;[7] and they become entirely logical in the context of the coercive forms of management that accompany this.

The relationship between the CarPress management and the shop-floor was indeed characterized by intimidation, fear and antagonism. When given the chance to express themselves, time and again these workers referred to being treated as 'animals', as 'cattle', as 'slaves' and as 'Jews in a concentration camp'. Like the following two assembly shop operators, many spoke of management in brusque, contemptuous terms:

> Yeah, I'm talking about fear. A fear of management and a fear of losing your job. I mean the management here are a bunch of fucking liars. You can't trust 'em any further than you could toss 'em. They tell us one thing and you get the opposite.

And another:

> These managers are pigs. They'll screw you into the ground. All they're interested in is getting blood out of you.

These were not the comments of a small group of marginalized dissidents. They were particularly embittered articulations of the opinions of the majority. One foreman expressed the fear that continually aggressive and arrogant management attempts to exert greater control over the shop-floor were creating 'an evil simmering of hatred'. And so, as we shall discover, they were, to the extent that the most hardened outsider might occasionally be shocked by its intensity. But this hatred had meaning and purpose; it did not hit out at everything in its path. It was certainly not 'anarchistic' as some managers liked to refer to it. One toolmaker commented that, 'I suppose if I was a manager I'd probably be the same as them, I'd try and make as much money in the shortest time possible. That's just the system, isn't it?' Similarly, another said, 'I know that at the end of the day we have to rely on the man upstairs, I understand that, I accept that. It's just that the man upstairs is a clown.'

These people were not rejecting capitalist managerial prerogative. But they did reject the explicit coercion and exploitation that accompanies direct management control whilst simultaneously recognizing that factory production has a social basis in which management has a coordinating role. As Beynon (1984) puts it, workers' views on management can have both structural and moral dimensions, 'the one structural, which places the action of management within the structure of the large capitalist corporation; the other moral, which involves a criticism of the action management takes in the plant and a moral judgement of the managers as men' (p. 112). At CarPress, the workers understood that complex production processes require professional management. They did not believe that this was forthcoming from their own managers. Neither did they believe that these managers aspired to any sense of collective morality and decency, as the following cry of despair makes clear:

> You just wouldn't believe the attitudes of the management here. They're so defensive. Sometimes, you know, we would like to discuss our work problems with them, we're open to that. But they can't do it, they're not capable of it. They retreat into a sort of defensive shell and not only refuse to talk to you but they end up treating you like shit.
>
> You'd be appalled at some of the things they say to us. You might be working away, sweating like hell probably, and the boss [a director] will walk past you down the gangway and shout out, 'I know you're only putting on a show because I'm here you Welsh wogs!' They say dreadful things like that, dreadful language. Outsiders just wouldn't believe it.

> So how can you have teamworking here? You know if this were a rugby football team it'd be like your team captain giving you a right dressing-down or a kick in the teeth minutes before you're due to run on the pitch. It's not the workforce, it's the management who's got the wrong attitude for teamworking.

In these circumstances it was not surprising that some workers clearly supported the notion of introducing a new style of 'Japanese management' at CarPress. A typical reaction from this group was, 'I like the Japanese way, I like the way the Japanese management and workers are all at one.' Two women in the assembly shop similarly believed that, 'they all work together don't they? They do seem to have a good way of working, I think it will come here one day, I do hope so,' and, 'I honestly feel that the Japanese would look after you better because they treat you all the same.' But these were vague egalitarian aspirations based on hope rather than substance. They were also tempered by a cynical realism, itself conditioned by weary experience of membership of a subordinated producer class in the Western system of consumer capitalism. As a shop-floor inspector put it:

> But the Japanese are a different breed to us, they're brought up in a different way. We're not like that and never will be. Everybody's talking about the Japanese. What's that place called over there? Toyota Town? Where all the workers get their houses, their schools and the rest of it. And all we get is a lousy wage packet and redundancy. And when we get made redundant our managers always get promoted, they never lose their jobs. So as I say, we'll never be like the Japanese, we'll always be different.

In the context of the supposedly 'classless' 1990s, some people might be forgiven for thinking that factories like CarPress represent curious anachronisms, abandoned by the new 'soft management' and the 'consensual' industrial relations environment that goes with it. But, as will become clear, this is too simple a view. The remaining chapters will demonstrate that the politics of production in this factory are not outdated. The company's attempts to restore the 'right to manage' and exert greater leverage over worker effort through the introduction of new management techniques bridge a continuum of coercion and control; a continuum spanning the crude macho management of the likes of Michael Edwardes in the 1980s to the more refined contemporary Japanese techniques. It is a contemporary politics of production still characterized by class conflict over the undisguised managerial objective of maximizing surplus value by means of maintaining control over the capitalist labour process.

Notes

1   The low number of women employees exemplifies a gender bias which is typical for the auto industry in the UK. Chapter 8 explores this in more detail.

2   This approach to the control of suppliers bears many similarities to current practice in Japan, where suppliers are forced to relinquish their freedom and independence once a contract with any of the giant Japanese corporations is signed. As Sakai puts it, suppliers are 'told what to make, when to put it on the line, and how much it will get for delivery. If the company that placed an order feels a profit squeeze, it can easily order the subcontractor to reduce its final price. If hard times continue, the larger company can demand yet another cut. If it gets to the point that the subcontractor is losing money on each unit it's producing and has cut expenses and streamlined production to the utmost, the "parent" company could demand that it buy some new piece of equipment to increase productivity' (1990, p. 40).

3   Significantly, just as the British state has taken up a proactive role in enticing Japanese firms into the UK in order to weaken organized labour, its Welsh arm, in the form of the Welsh Development Agency, is equally active in securing the adoption of Japanese-approved new working practices in British owned suppliers in Wales. The WDA has now established a 'Source Wales' programme aimed at persuading major manufacturers to source their components locally through the promotion of 'best practice' within Welsh suppliers.

   To achieve this, Source Wales has set itself up both as a broker for customers and suppliers and as a management consultant. Its officials move on to the premises of an enlisted manufacturer and act as a temporary procurement arm of that customer. Simultaneously, Source Wales acts as management consultant to potential suppliers, advising on the restructuring of management practices and providing the necessary resources, such as TEC management training. It then attempts to bring together approved suppliers with enlisted customers on a long-term contractual basis. Its officials stress that Japanese companies tend to be as much interested in potential suppliers' quality of management as their quality of production. That is, they take a particular interest in the ability of managements *to push through* some of the changes in working practices necessary for achieving longer-term quality production standards. (Field notes, interviews with the director of Source Wales, Welsh Development Agency, 2.3.94.)

4   The audit criteria encompass a variety of different indicators of the

restructuring of work and employment relations, each of which are marked on to a 0 to 3 score. For example, there are sections covering: procedures for minimizing the risk of discontinuity of production (a euphemism for strike-breaking); personnel policy matters which include health and safety, the behaviour and appearance of employees, single status, the physical integration of management with the workforce locations, company communications and employee involvement; and work changes which include wider questions of the development of coherent strategies for organizational change as well as particular work practices such as teamworking.

5   This view is congruent with the evidence provided in Chapter 2 (note 3).

6   An important example of this political constraint is discussed in Chapter 7.

7   Parker and Slaughter (1988) discovered similar attitudes amongst workers confronted with new management techniques at the GM-Toyota NUMMI plant in California and at different USA Chrysler plants; the literature suggests that they are also common in Japan itself (Milkman, 1991).

5 LEAN PRODUCTION CONTROL AND LABOUR INTENSIFICATION

The seductive maxim 'working smarter rather than harder' has become a mantra of the various apologists for the new management techniques of the 1990s. In fact, workers in manufacturing industry – subject to an increased exercise of managerial prerogative in the distinctive political and economic conditions of the past 15 years – are now working harder as much as smarter. Over this period, British manufacturing industry has displayed a clear tendency towards a reduction in the porosity of the working day which is not always overtly strategic but which instead may occur slowly and steadily, often in an uneven and piecemeal fashion (Elger, 1990a; 1990b; Nichols, 1991).

Elger's overviews of a number of British case studies suggest that rather than aim for a fundamental workplace restructuring through either technological innovation or work reorganization, many employers are attempting to improve productivity through demanning and task flexibility. These types of changes exhibit a bias towards 'the horizontal enlargement rather than multi-skilling of jobs and towards an intensification of labour, especially via the reduced porosity of work routines' (1990b, p. 38). Similarly, in their analysis of contemporary changes to working practices in the auto industry, Marsden et al. (1985) argue that different reports of people working harder are neither here nor there; what is more pertinent is the evidence of additional time people are working, that is, the additional time they actually spend on their feet performing labour, which thus closes up the porosity of the working day. Although such an approach runs the risk of discounting individual subjective assessments of effort, it does highlight an essential point. That is, what is central to the intensification of labour and therefore more important than the exact nature of the different management attempts to improve productivity and their impact on worker perceptions is, as Nichols puts it, 'that more labour is squeezed out in a given time, or – the same idea looked at the other way around – that the porosity of the working day is closed up as more labour gets squeezed into it' (1991, p. 573).

Nichols goes on to suggest that the more mundane, piecemeal changes to manufacturing working practices impact upon general work rates to, if anything, a greater extent than the crude increase of effort brought about by a fear of macho management. That is, as well as raising output per worker by 'speed-up' and multi-machine minding, these new practices act to close up the porosity of the working day by reducing break times; by reducing any idle time in production periods; and by introducing task accretion.

At CarPress, both the macho and the incremental approach to management served to induce a progressive increase in work rates. Some changes were effected by a slow process of chipping away at custom and practice; some were subject to negotiated agreement; and others were enforced by managerial threat and coercion.

During the 1980s, demanning and the compensatory development of labour flexibility practices constituted principle features of this process as they did in many other British factories. But following the change in status of the plant from a satellite pressed part manufacturing operation to an independent first-tier supplier feeding a number of JIT final assemblers, the CarPress management faced new pressures to exert greater control over labour utilization and work rates. In particular, the new demands of the customer, shifts in the nature of the plant's production control system, the inadequacies of ageing machinery and persistent internal and external pressures to drive down unit labour costs all warranted an explicit attack on the production operators' ability to partially control their own working time. This chapter provides an analysis of the impact of these changes at the point of production whilst Chapter 6 extends the enquiry to the implementation of labour flexibility and such new practices as teamworking and kaizen. Rather than treat these processes as unproblematic, the analysis draws out the contradictions and conflicts that accompany labour intensification in the contemporary workplace.

The Production Control System

CarPress's production control arrangements contained elements of just-in-time organization. Outwardly, the system did appear to conform to Ohno's (1988) well-known supermarket analogy, where the exact quantity of the necessary materials arrive at the factory gates just in time for consumption in the process of production, and the required type and exact quantity of finished parts are despatched to the customer just in time for further productive consumption. To effect this, the plant developed close, long-term contractual relationships with its main steel suppliers and customers. Consequently, tightly coordinated order/supply arrangements ensured that the necessary sizes and specifications of steel coil and strip arrived at the factory just four hours before they were needed for production. At the opposite end of the operation, exact quantities of the required pressed assemblies were despatched to the customer typically four times a day, five days a week.

Viewed from the factory's goods inwards and despatch bays, the production system had the likeness of a smooth, flow line, JIT control in classic textbook fashion. However, the process of investigating the inner workings of this black box exposed certain technological, organizational and labour relations constraints which created something more complex, imperfect and troublesome than external appearances suggested.

In Japan, JIT systems function to provide low-cost, low-stock production control which is essential for the financial viability of the Japanese multi-model marketing tradition. This in turn relies on small-batch production, whose efficiency, as Williams *et al.* point out, 'rests not on a mastery of production but on a mastery of unproductive time. More exactly, the Japanese do not seek reduced unproductive time for its own sake; instead they try to minimize the wasted breakdown time while what we may call the "contributing downtime" of set-up is used constructively to secure the downstream objective [of process efficiency]' (1994b, p. 64). In their study of different Japanese press shops, Williams *et al.* found that although machine utilization time varied between 68 per cent and 85 per cent, what united the different plants was their effective use of residual unproductive time, principally to ensure rapid die changes over single shifts. As a result, the Japan-based manufacturers are able to secure small batch production through technological means.

In the auto industry, Toyota pioneered these flexible manufacturing techniques by implementing Single Minute Exchange of Dies (SMED). Evoking Taylorian principles of rationality and efficiency, Shingo, the founder of the SMED system, argued that it is 'a scientific approach to set-up time reduction that can be applied in any factory to any machine' (1985, p. 26). By rationalizing the process through a combination of incremental improvements to manual die changing, the introduction of new working practices and the more recent employment of automated die side-loaders, Toyota and eventually many other Japanese manufacturers were able to reduce the set-up time frame from one of hours to minutes (Cusumano, 1985; Shingo, 1985).

At CarPress, a lack of both the necessary capital investment and coherent planning ensured that the factory's machine set-up process was a relatively backward affair. For most presses, die changing was a matter of transporting dies from toolroom to machine by a combination of slinging devices, overhead cranes and fork lift trucks; the same equipment was then used to load the dies onto the machine bolsters; finally, teams of toolsetters would carefully assemble and secure the die in a slow process of trial and error, ensuring that it was exactly centred in the bolster and that its shut height was sufficient to yield acceptable pressed parts.

Consequently, typical machine utilization rates measured just 49 per cent in 1994. Moreover, although long-established continuous improvement SMED meetings eventually contributed to a reduction in the proportion of total working time expended on die changes, such a potential gain was neutralized by an ineffectual management of tooling investment, machine allocation and labour deployment. The time lost due to faulty machines and tools, machines awaiting new jobs and labour shortages together amounted to 27 per cent of total working hours in 1993 and 34 per cent in 1994; they accounted for 52 per cent of downtime in 1993 and 74 per cent in 1994.[1] And the outcome of this was a negation of JIT in many areas of the shop-floor: most lines were forced to operate on the basis of three- to four-week cycles. That is, producing batches of typically 10,000 parts, sufficient to cover three or four weeks of supply.

However, although these different factors made authentic JIT inoperable they did not prevent the implementation of a less perfect lean production control system. Both the general impact of global competitive pressures and the particular interventions of the plant's major customers described in the previous chapter forced the management to effect simple labour and material cost reductions aimed at improving plant efficiency. In the four-year period leading up to the research, between 1989 and 1993, plant employment declined by 20 per cent whilst output per worker almost doubled. At the same time, stock and in-production buffers were being considerably squeezed. CarPress managed to double its stock/turnover ratios from 10.0 to 20.6 over this period; work in progress reduced from £1.1 million to £642,000; and WIP/turnover ratios almost trebled. In the context of lean production, stock/turnover ratios constitute significant indicators of productive efficiency and buffer levels

(Cusumano, 1985; Williams *et al.*, 1992). As Williams *et al.* have argued, this is because, 'low stocks are an important indicator of the physical integration of manufacturing operations and measures the manufacturer's ability to realise smooth continuous flow in multi-process manufacturing; flow is an important influence on productivity and costs because smooth flow takes out indirect handling labour and allows direct labour to work continuously and efficiently' (1992, p. 22).

In a number of ways, these changes in production control were congruent with arrangements in the Japanese transplants in South Wales. Compared to a customary 'Fordist' mass-production operation, the systematic reductions in manning levels, stocks and line-side buffers amounted to the implementation of a leaner and more work-intensive system which, as we shall see in the next section, was gradually refined during the period of the research.

Of course, the practical manufacturing constraints generated by the plant's poor record in the management of machinery sit rather oddly with these statistical indicators of productive efficiency. This contradiction will be addressed in due course. For the moment, what should be recognized is that, despite these constraints, the CarPress management succeeded in raising labour productivity and factory throughput to a significant degree. This was not operationalized in an overtly corporate-strategic sense; production control managers introduced their stock control measures and other cost reductions at the behest of external customers rather than CarPress's most senior manufacturing managers who concerned themselves more with maintaining output quantity. But the significant point to appreciate is that although the production control system was developing in a piecemeal way and could not be described as 'textbook' just-in-time, the process of stock and buffer reduction had clear implications for the intensification of labour, for the worker's capacity to take an unofficial breather. That is, just as Nichols has argued, neither the debates about what exactly should count as JIT (see for example, Wood, 1991; Jenkins, 1994) nor certain representations of these changes in British manufacturing as improvements in the technical efficiency of management should be allowed to 'distract from their significance for the closing up of the pores of the working day/labour intensification' (1991, p. 589). The material impact of these changes upon the shop-floor will now be considered.

Labour Intensification at the Point of Production

During the course of the research, two questionnaire-based attitude surveys were carried out at the plant. The first of these asked respondents whether they believed they were working harder compared to ten years ago. Of the 236 respondents with more than ten years' service, 69 per cent replied 'yes', 27 per cent 'no' and only 4 per cent were undecided. This result is consistent with what might be expected from the changes summarized in the previous section and it also verifies the qualitative data collected by means of employee interviews.

Most shop-floor operators perceived management's attempts to exert greater leverage over work effort as a multifaceted threat which materialized in a number of different ways. Many complained of a gradual but inexorable tightening of production targets and the unchallenged use of traditional work study methods to re-time jobs and remove 'excess' operators from the line. One press shop operator summed this up:

> The effect is that they give you more to do in target hours. And on top of this they give you extra tasks to fit in where you can. For example, during the old days under Rover you'd have quality men walking around doing regular quality checks on your work. And you'd have other admin staff coming around to write up the buy-off ticket to sign your job off. But now we have to do all that sort of extra work ourselves and they still expect you to get your pieces of work out per hour. In fact, you have to get more pieces out per hour. So when the management start to talk about 'back to basics' what they really mean is 'more work, more pain, less gain'.

Others spoke of management's attempts to mobilize the disciplinary pressure of competition from harder-working colleagues to extract greater work effort; and for many workers, perpetual management surveillance could sometimes effect a compulsion to relinquish informal breaks and to persevere on the line, as the following comment from one operator exemplifies:

> I've been working here for 17 years and for the last few years I just haven't enjoyed life at all. It all boils down to the attitude of management. These days I come to work and I feel like I'm in a concentration camp. I tell you, I dread coming in on nights, you're on your feet all the time and you get knackered, there's a real need for regular breaks. But we don't get them anymore. The management just treat you like kids, they keep looking at you, checking up on you all the time.

These perceptions accord with the results of investigations into changing effort rates elsewhere in British industry (Edwards and Whitston, 1991; Nichols and O'Connell Davidson, 1993). And they become quite predictable when placed within the context of the dynamics of capitalist social relations and the inherent pressures of capitalist production. As Marx (1976) commented on the connection between social controls over the length of the working week and the extraction of relative surplus value: 'capital's tendency, as soon as a prolongation of the hours of labour is once and for all forbidden, is to compensate for this by systematically raising the intensity of labour, and converting every improvement in machinery into a more perfect means of soaking up labour power' (p. 542).

Moreover, the contradiction referred to above, between the constraints of CarPress's inefficient technological organization of production and the pressures generated by the piecemeal development of lean production, resulted in the employment of additional labour-intensifying methods which corresponded to the tightly supervised, highly disciplined bell-to-bell practices used by the Japanese transplants in the region. If the CarPress management was either incapable or unwilling to modernize the plant's capital assets then it insisted that labour should take up the slack instead.

This was not necessarily a question of vindictiveness. At least not for some managers. Under circumstances which were partly of its own making, management exhausted all other options; it had no alternative but to squeeze labour. Many middle managers complained of an absence of modern production planning instruments and indeed, a lack of corporate commitment to long-term planning for the site. For example, at the time of the research, the company was investing over £1 million on a new computer-integrated information system, but this could only be used for financial control purposes rather than production planning. And these financial controls inevitably militated against the emergence of coherent production policies. One assembly shop superintendent remarked bitterly on this:

> My main problem is the financial restrictions on the budgets needed to keep the equipment running. It's like a noose continually tightening around your neck.
>
> The responsibility lies with senior management. They're obsessed with the idea that if you meet your budgets then you'll satisfy your customer. But this is crap. Because whatever we do here we seem to get ourselves into bad situations, log-jams, all sorts. And we don't seem to understand how to get

out of them. That's because there's insufficient production planning. There's never any detailed production planning from the top and there's never any long-term production planning either.

Faced with the pressures of reducing material buffers and machine downtime problems, many UK managers would be expected to rely on the safety valve of human buffers, usually in the form of overtime. But at CarPress, the rule of the customer had reduced this option.[2] As the chief production manager expressed it:

Our new concerns about productivity are now about complying with customer schedules and meeting strict budgets. The main rule now is that we must produce 'x' units of parts for the customer in 'x' period of time. Therefore, the pressure is on continually to perform to budget levels. Because of this, overtime has become the last option for us. It's a major cost. So all alternative avenues must be explored before we resort to it. We have to continually look at the question of more efficient labour utilization, labour redeployment and more flexibility.

So the situation on the shop-floor was this. Most materials were delivered to the plant just in time for production; in-production buffers were subject to systematic reduction; and corporate parsimony on capital investment in combination with ineffective production planning were producing unfavourable capital utilization rates. Accordingly, in the light of the customer's multi-requirement for a more flexible supply system, increased output and reduced costs, the only remaining option was to run the serviceable machines flat out and to squeeze 60 minutes of productive work from every worker in every hour. As one manager said, 'we had nowhere else to go. With no stores and not enough machines up and running we could not switch to alternatives. All we could do was put pressure on the supervision to crack the whip on the men, crack the whip on idle time.'

This principal objective of closing up the porosity of the working day was embodied in different sections of a new working-practices agreement introduced, despite rank-and-file union opposition (which is explored in some depth in Chapter 7), in the summer of 1994. The agreement ensured the introduction of such practices as bell-to-bell working; labour flexibility; teamworking; continuous improvement (or kaizen); single status; and the dismantling of seniority rights. Their impact on the labour process and employment relations is analysed throughout the remainder of the book. This chapter will now investigate one significant component of management's strategy. That is, the dismantling of a payment-by-results scheme which management had insisted on introducing at the time of the acquisition of the plant from Rover but which eventually came to bestow significant levels of individual operator control over working time; and the introduction of a more disciplined continuous production system through tightly supervised, measured day, bell-to-bell working.

Payment By Results

Generally speaking, the primary difference between piece-rate bonus systems and flat-rate systems such as measured day work is that, 'in a piece-rate factory the workers are disciplined by the rate. In a time-rate factory, where men are paid by the hour or week at the same rate, no matter how much work is produced, work discipline has to be established through organization' (Nichols and Beynon, 1977, p. 133). However, this description does overlook important qualitative differences in the degree of discipline, the degree of control, that can be exerted over the labour process. For example, although Burawoy's (1979) analysis of workers 'making out' in a piece-rate engineering factory in the USA makes the central point that such activities can be useful to capital in that they contribute to a process of simultaneously obscuring the creation of surplus value and securing worker consent, it also highlights the different ways in which workers exploit their tacit skills to maintain a degree of individual control over their work. As a result:

> Workers control their own machines instead of being controlled by them, and this enhances their autonomy. They put their machine into motion single handedly, and this creates the appearance that they can, as individuals, transform nature into useful commodities. The system of reward is based on individual rather than collective effort. (Burawoy, 1979, p. 81)

In fact, pure piece-rate systems are now a rarity in manufacturing industry. Instead, those factories operating individual incentive schemes on the shop-floor have tended to use payment by results (PBR) systems where, typically, basic wages are topped up by individual payments made on the basis of time allowed/time taken to produce a job (Conboy, 1976; Beaston, 1993). Measured day work (MDW) systems differ from this in that output and productivity are determined wholly by management organization rather than worker incentives. With MDW, it is the prerogative of management to specify the level of daily plant performance and to supervise both the measurement and execution of work to ensure that the required performance is achieved. Such systems are indispensable to highly disciplined, low-buffer, continuous production regimes; they demand controlled worker flexibility rather than autonomy, and strict management supervision rather than collusion with workers over practices such as 'making out'.

In the early years of the British auto industry, piece-work functioned as a system of control exactly as Nichols and Beynon describe it. Workers were rated for each individual operation performed, and if they produced their parts they were paid; if cars could not be sold and the production track was stopped then they were laid off. It was a form of casual labour that served management's interests well (Thornett, 1987). However, during the 1960s and 1970s, a period when organized labour in the industry steadily grew in confidence and militancy, piece-work systems increasingly became subject to both individual and union negotiation. As Brown (1973) observed, rate-fixers were forced to haggle over piece-rates rather than impose them, whilst the piecemeal growth of custom and practice, such as the periodic re-observation of work whenever the operator found the going tough, acted to mitigate the degree of management control exerted. Thus, with the balance of forces between capital and labour in this period sometimes favouring the latter, the tendency of piece-work was to drift in the direction of 'managerial indulgence' as managers became obsessed with getting work out the door and avoiding strikes.

Inevitably, the employers launched a counter-offensive in due course. Their attempts to effect a transition from piece-work to MDW became one of the major causes of strikes in the vehicle assembly industry during the 1970s, particularly at British Leyland and Chrysler (Friedman, 1977). The BL management embarked on a long-drawn-out campaign to implement MDW at the end of the 1960s. By 1971, after many sessions of troubled negotiations interrupted by periodic walkouts and strikes, agreements were signed for its introduction at all of BL's pressed-steel plants, including what was to become the CarPress factory in South Wales. However, the strength of the BL unions at this time ensured that even though piece-work was lost, the work rates governed by the new MDW systems were still subject to union negotiation and varying degrees of mutuality (Thornett, 1987; 1993).

This is an important point to note in the context of the CarPress acquisition of the ex-BL/Rover plant. At the company's other UK factories, unions were at best suffered rather than treated as equal negotiating partners; the principal personnel policy objective was to marginalize effective trade union organization. The management's more unitary style of industrial relations ensured that the weakly organized CarPress workforces in the South-east were unable to take full advantage of incentive bonus systems in the ways described above; indeed, at these plants, the company's perseverance with payment by results maintained significant levels of management control over work rates. The inherited MDW system at Oldport was perceived as a conspicuous threat to this control. With Rover, workers were expected to reach individual production targets commensurate with the required daily plant performance but strong trade union organization ensured that management only rarely took disciplinary action against individuals who failed to perform satisfactorily. Moreover, although writers such as Marsden *et al.* (1985) point out that the more macho Rover management of the 1980s partially succeeded in untying the hands of the company's industrial engineers, in fact the process of setting production targets was still subject to significant trade union influence. One CarPress industrial engineer recalled:

> Under the Rover management the rule was that the steward could always be present to stand with his member, to safeguard the union member against the possibility of the time study setting too high a standard. And of course the emotive thing was always the performance assessment. We used to get some really serious arguments over this. Mark, my mate on the next desk, used to get dreadful problems, he literally couldn't move around the factory without a steward tailing him all the time. It used to frighten him to walk into the assembly shop. He virtually needed a day pass to get into the place!

Mark, a staff union representative himself, had no hesitation in endorsing CarPress's drive to restore managerial prerogative on the shop-floor:

> It didn't matter what I was doing, setting up equipment, setting a standard, doing a study, it made no difference. They would always stand behind me, watching me. But when the CarPress management came they knocked all of that on the head. The management saw shop stewards standing around, not producing, and watching me sweat, watching me do all of the work. So now the union influence has declined, they certainly don't exert any control over me any more. As far as I'm concerned their days are over, and good riddance.

To eliminate such union activity, in 1990 the new CarPress management decided, against the grain, to jettison MDW and introduce its own trusted payment by results scheme based on targets set solely by management. Rather than countenance the endurance of Rover's system of partial mutuality, the company was prepared to concede to its South Wales workforce the limited degree of control that accompanies any individual PBR system but without allowing shop stewards any influence over the work measurement and target-setting process. In this way the hands of the industrial engineers really were untied, and an explicit process of work intensification ensued as the production standards established under the outgoing Rover management were systematically discarded in favour of more challenging targets.

The engineers under both Rover and CarPress managements assessed effort expenditure at 100 per cent BSI.[3] However, departing from British Standard work measurement practice, the CarPress management refused to include in their new standards what is known as 'outside work'; that is, time taken for tasks such as material handling operations, loading steel coils and so on; or even components of relaxation allowances, such as going to the toilet.[4] They were only interested in paying out bonus for pure productive labour time. Therefore, once the management secured agreement for its new bonus system, the CarPress industrial engineers set about using classic time-and-motion work study techniques in the process of establishing new, tougher standards for new jobs. The lack of an effective shop steward challenge enabled the engineers to mobilize their quasi-scientific methods of effort assessment to translate human motion into machine motion in a 'professional' quest for maximum labour utilization. But the management was also faced with literally hundreds of existing standards which required uprating. Lacking sufficient engineers to re-time these jobs, prevailing cycle times were adjusted by a standard factor to remove unproductive labour time. On this basis, new cycle times, issue times and production standards were generated. Of course, 'outside work' was not mysteriously removed from the real labour process; material handling, the removal of scrap and pallet changes remained routine tasks. The effect was to ratchet up the effort required to reach target scores.

However, although the management succeeded in securing greater leverage over the effort exerted during productive labour time, it simultaneously forfeited a degree of control over idle time. Like many individual incentive schemes, the CarPress bonus system was designed to intensify the extraction of relative surplus value from the shop-floor workforce. If a typical job received a 'standard performance' rating of 300 parts/hour then by hitting the 133 per cent target of 400/hour the scheme paid a premium of £1.50 per hour; hitting the 150 per cent target of 450/ hour paid £1.75 per hour; and operators reaching the 200 per cent level of 600 parts/hour enjoyed a bonus of £2 per hour. One industrial engineer commented:

> Some of the operators would regularly go for the 200 per cent target which was brilliant because, okay, you'd be paying out an extra £2 for every hour achieved at this rate but at the same time you'd be getting twice as much work out of them for the price of one man!

The problem for management was that although this was certainly true for one or two shop-floor mavericks, the vast majority of production operators maintained their own informal collective discipline over target attainment. A characteristic of the bonus system was that if a job received a 'standard performance' rating of, say, 300 parts/hour, then over an eight-hour working day an operator working at the 133 per cent incentive performance level of 400 parts/hour would complete the day's quota two hours early. The operator would then have the choice of accumulating bonus, taking a long break at the end of the shift (or periodic breaks during the shift), or a combination of the two. Despite the constraints imposed by the tightening of standards, the operators found that they still retained sufficient discretion and control – a simple control of speed of movement – to vary their work rates to achieve these various ends. And a collective shop-floor discipline ensured that most operators did not earn excessive bonus or finish their jobs too early, thereby exposing this control to the watchful eyes of the industrial engineers. One press shop superintendent expressed this as follows:

> Although there was never a ceiling, most of the operators created their own ceiling of 133. They'd go like the clappers to achieve it and then sit on their arses in the Wendy house [tea-room] playing cards or reading papers. I'd say, maybe about 10 to 15 per cent would go for above 133, a few might even go for 150 but you'd get a shop-floor reaction. For example, we used to have a policy of taking on a lot of temporary workers who had a tendency to go for gold. But the culture on the shop-floor was that you didn't go flat out or you'd do yourself out of a job. So the permanent operators used to lean on the temporary workers and threaten them if they didn't change their ways. And it worked of course.

Antagonism over work effort, between workers on the one hand endeavouring to create their own portions of time and supervision and industrial engineers on the other, insisting on the maximization of working time, has been described as a customary 'game' in capitalist mass-production, involving elements of both conflict and collusion (Burawoy, 1979; Jones, 1994). But in an environment of lean production, this 'game' rapidly becomes dysfunctional; it transforms into a more explicit class struggle. For example, the panoply of government and employer restrictions on the ability to strike induced the CarPress shop stewards and their members to implement alternative sanctions against management. Almost as a matter of routine, the bonus system would be turned against the company during a 'work to rule' when the whole of the shop-floor steadfastly refused to work above the minimum 100 per cent standard performance level. Constraints on output caused by machine downtime presented further possibilities for shop-floor resistance to managerial control. In the face of union opposition to the removal of unproductive labour from the new production standards, the management was forced to concede the payment of average bonus for any periods of inactivity that were beyond an operator's control, that is downtime. Of course, management assumed that whenever a machine became disabled the operators concerned would be immediately switched to alternative lines. In fact, the mediocre machine utilization rates outlined above often hindered this. And the shop-floor knew this. The general resentment at the implementation of tougher targets and reduced manning was sometimes channelled towards certain disabling actions. Despite management warnings, operators would often throw teabags and other rubbish into machine oil sumps or toss coke cans into press beds. They also possessed a portfolio of other more clandestine tricks which had an immediate effect on production. One ex-shop steward explained:

> It's the easiest thing in the world to fuck up the company if you know how. I'm not saying what, but we could make certain adjustments to our machines, you know? Then the foreman might come up to you and ask, 'Dai, how's your score, why's your machine not running?' And I'll tell him 'Well, I'm on downtime, boss; my machine's broken down and I've tried but I can't find a spare fitter.' In fact, they've cut down in the tool room that much that sometimes you might not get a fitter for weeks! So you'd end up getting your Nett up [target] and your bonus money while the Company's losing production!

In the context of the politico-economic conditions of the 1990s, which favoured capital in so many ways, a further management counter-attack was inevitable. The withdrawal of MDW in favour of PBR might have intensified the labour process to a degree, but it failed to compensate for low machine utilization rates by increasing labour utilization to the extent required by the evolving lean production regime. Production operators continued to forge their own versions of 'enrichment' and 'control'. As Beynon observed during his research at Ford, when given the chance workers will 'work slower; they work back the line; they share out jobs; they mess around – all to create that bit more space, that bit of room to lead "a normal life". Yet it is precisely this space, (call it autonomy or independence; call it control or humanity) which the march of capitalist expansion seeks to regulate and ultimately deny' (1984, p. 389). The CarPress management became obsessed with denying their own shop-floor workforce this private space. The personnel manager later commented:

> The working system we had then [1990–1994] was like the old flat earth syndrome in that people demanded that it must never be challenged. The underlying principle was that people would not work unless they had a target, an hourly target in terms of parts, money and breaks. But my argument was that our shop-floor workers are defined as hourly paid employees which means they're paid by the hour for their labour time. And when we pay an hourly rate our expectation should be for the full 100 per cent effort in every hour and not 45 minutes in every hour which was the attitude of most of them.

To secure this objective, the management ensured that the 1994 new working practices agreement re-imposed measured day work along with the gradual implementation of strict bell-to-bell working, Japanese style.[5]

The Restoration of Measured Day Work

Effective MDW systems require effective management. At CarPress, the demands of the customer were synchronized with available capital by traditional production planning methods; these demands were synchronized with available labour by crude coercion. The incentive bonus scheme was discarded in favour of a plant performance scheme which paid just £7.50 per week provided plant efficiency exceeded the agreed minimum of 133 per cent. However, the management was well aware that this would not compensate for the loss of individual incentive. Consequently, the new agreement stipulated that individual target performance must still be measured and any operator falling below their previous average performance would be subject to formal discipline. Effectively, in a move reminiscent of Marx's description of nineteenth-century factory despotism,[6] the rhythm of the machine was supposed to overshadow the self-control of the worker; and the self-policing of work effort surrendered to the superintendence of production.

Although some foremen voiced their satisfaction at this apparent return to 'the old days' when, as one reflected, 'you used to be an overseer as opposed to a supervisor, those were the days when the bully boy was king, the bigger the mouth you had the better', many, in truth, cast themselves as reluctant despots. Most were ex-shop-floor operators themselves. The new disciplinary arrangements offended their political sensibilities and resulted in an intensification of their own labour. One younger foreman, who admitted to being completely exhausted after just three years in the job, commented:

> You see, it's all about making me fully accountable for the whole performance. And to put it simply, that's to get a minimum of 133 out of every operator every day. The pressure can be unbearable. Most nights I go home, have a shower, have some tea and then just fall asleep because I'm totally knackered. The wife's always complaining that whenever I'm home I'm asleep. But even when you're awake you take work home in your head, your head's buzzing, you're writing mental notes all the time. It's just crazy! That's how I feel. When I was an operator at least I used to be able to go home and switch off. But not any more.

Another commented on the policing of work effort:

> My instructions are to push them to the limit. Just this morning my manager marched up to me and said he'd seen one of my men talking to a mate down at the other end of the plant. And he wanted to know what I'm going to do about it: why aren't I disciplining him? That's the key change in my job. It's gone from one of using the skill of talking and coaxing people to the use of pure discipline all the time.
>
> I reckon this has all been caused by the downfall of the trade unions. They've got no power any more. It's all about Maggie Thatcher. Believe me, our management used to say to us 'Well, now we've got Maggie, she's doing her stuff for us, let's take advantage of it, let's kick 'em in the balls.' And that's exactly what they're doing, and I'm afraid I'm stuck in the middle.

Not long after the disposal of payment by results, bell-to-bell working was introduced. This was not bell-to-bell in the sense of a gradual erosion of such shop-floor traditions as washing-up time or the relaxation of work at the end of each shift. Instead, the explicit aim was to secure the highly disciplined working time arrangements established at the various Japanese transplants in the region. But rather than precipitate a major dispute over this, the management decided to take a more careful incremental approach to its introduction; bell-to-bell by stealth, so to speak.

Normal day-workers clocked an eight-hour working day punctuated by a half-hour lunch break and two ten-minute tea breaks. Under the bonus system, operators were also allowed a four-and-a-half-minute rest each hour in addition to the longer time-buffers accumulated if individual targets were exceeded. The opening objective of the company's bell-to-bell system was to remove these longer discretionary breaks and, consequently, all supervisors were instructed to confine their operators to the line whether or not they were working.

Then, two months after this initial system commenced in the early autumn of 1994, the management announced that all informal tea breaks must cease forthwith. Although operators could still stop work each hour for an 'unofficial' rest, they were banned from taking cups of tea or from chatting together in groups. The official four-and-a-half-minute hourly relaxation time was effectively discarded. The intention here was to squeeze these little portions of time by forcing the operators into a state of ennui for which more production work was the only remedy. As the plant operations director put it:

> At the moment, with bell-to-bell continuous working we're not actually getting more parts out the door, the operators are taking longer to churn the stuff out. But we're hoping that will change. We're hoping that if they know they were capable of getting eight hours worth of output in five hours with a three-hour break, then with continuous working they can now go for nine hours output in eight hours by going a bit faster, going like they used to do. Okay, this will be without the breaks, but we're hoping this will come about due to the boredom. It is boring work. I'm convinced that gradually under the new continuous working system they'll start to go faster.

At this stage, the attitudes of CarPress's production operators were mixed. The withdrawal of PBR gave rise to predictable shop-floor divisions since such systems are characterized by clear inequities in effort and pay between individuals. They also contribute to uncertainties amongst shop stewards whose principal aim is to secure collective objectives for their members, such as general pay rises (Brown, 1973; Conboy, 1976; Tolliday and Zeitlin, 1986). The CarPress management sought to build on these divisions and pre-empt an open dispute by carefully introducing the system in stages. But this did not entirely succeed. As one ex–steward explained:

> I'm just totally against bell-to-bell. The old system worked. You had decent incentives there to make the bits the company wanted. You also had the incentive to earn your break. With the sort of work we are doing you need a break and you need it regular. And in any case we've been brainwashed for 30 years into accepting the idea that you have to get the job done and if things are getting behind to pull back that downtime, to speed up if need be. But what the company has done with introducing bell-to-bell, they've just imposed it on us, they've totally aggravated the workforce into slowing production down. We've been coerced into accepting a deal and it's been done by intimidation at the highest level.

During this period of implementation, plant efficiency fell from the agreed minimum of 133 to 128 per cent. In the press shop it fell to 125 per cent.[7] The new system was producing unintended outcomes; a resentful shop-floor was managing to maintain both a measure of discreet control and space for resistance. Under these circumstances, some workers displayed a degree of preference for the system's steady, consistent tempo of work over the spasmodic cycles they had become accustomed to. As one older worker admitted:

> Sometimes I actually prefer bell-to-bell because, in the assembly shop at least, it can be easier on the body, though I've got to admit it depends on the job. For some jobs it's much harder standing up all day under bell-to-bell. But the old system could be just as bad. It was giving some people heart attacks – stop go, stop go, going flat out half the time. If you pace the work that way some people are bound to have health problems. So I suppose you can't win either way, can you?

However, a clear majority of operators interviewed resented the disciplines that accompanied the new system. Younger workers were more firmly opposed than their older colleagues. Many expressed bitterness at their loss of the right to make money or time; the loss of individual choice and control. Some had not been long out of school and were hoping to experience a more adult and equal supervisor–subordinate relationship at the workplace. They were of course disappointed. Although these younger operators were generally more likely to acquiesce to changes in working practices than older workers, they still resented the constant surveillance that comes with bell-to-bell working, the 24-hour vigil of production management. Some youngsters in one group of interviewees were recently disciplined for having the temerity of going to the toilet without permission. One of these remarked:

> I was already on 150. I'd already made up the time, the ten minutes needed to allow me to go to the toilet, so I wasn't going to lose the company any production was I? So I nipped off to the toilet at 7.50 and came back at 7.52 and as a result I got a final warning. So did 20 of my mates that day. We were all totally cheesed off ... they treat us like school kids all the time. They're just bastards.

For different reasons, many women workers opposed the changes. As we shall see in Chapter 8, the relatively few women employed on the CarPress shop-floor were offered little in the way of assistance from management to compensate for their relative lack of height and strength that are prerequisites for some press and assembly operations. Consequently, the regime of steady, continuous working merely exacerbated the levels of toil and drudgery experienced. One woman in the press shop complained:

> I've got to admit that on the big presses I really hate it. I mean, it's hard work and you do have a need for regular breaks, you need to sit down and take a rest. But with bell-to-bell you're on your feet all the time. And on nights it's worse. We all dread nights. You're on your feet for even longer, for eight and a half hours a shift.

And another:

> I just don't like it at all. Before bell-to-bell individual operators had some control at least. We could do the job at our own pace, within reason. We could do the scores, take breaks when we needed them and wind down at the end of the day when you do need a rest.
>
> You really need that period to unwind. The work in this place will always be hard and monotonous, but at least when you worked at some speed you felt better. It might sound strange but you just felt better in mind and body. Your body felt better and your mind felt happier because by working fast you could give yourself something to aim for. You knew if you kept it up and

> completed your score you'd earn your break. But now with bell-to-bell it's slower but also harder and even more monotonous.

When the management consultants and business writers enthuse over the ideas of Japanese management pioneers Ohno, Shingo and the like, we must remember that they are articulating a management ideology, a particular class interest, rather than an objective appraisal of the implications of technical efficiency in capitalist production. Ohno wrote that, 'manpower reduction means raising the ratio of value-added work. The ideal is to have 100 percent value-added work. This has been my greatest concern while developing the Toyota production system' (1988, p. 58). It has also been the concern of the workers of CarPress. But they have different class interests. For most, the reduction of 'human waste' and 'idle time' amounted to growing fatigue; working without breaks; working under constant surveillance; seeking permission from the boss to go to the toilet; 'being treated like school kids all the time'; and 'being married to your machine'. And they were trying to fight back because they knew the intensifying pressures could only increase. One assembly shop operator said:

> We all know it's not going to be like it is now forever because the company is not going to be interested in the steady pace of the Japanese. They'll be wanting us to go flat out all the time. That's the bottom line. They want you to work at the rate that you used to do when you were chasing your target but instead of doing it from 7.00 until 1.00 and then taking a breather you'll be doing it all day, going flat out from 7.00 to 3.30. That's the management's bottom line.

In November 1994, a month after this particular interview, the company again turned the screw. It announced that *all* informal breaks and unofficial rests on the line must stop. Operators not working at their machines any time between official breaks would be subject to the disciplinary procedure. Operators not reaching the individual performance levels achieved under the old incentive system would also be disciplined. An authentic Japanese bell-to-bell system had been constructed, piece by piece.

This chapter has focused upon one significant feature of the trend towards labour intensification in British manufacturing industry today. That is, management's drive to eliminate idle time, to maximize labour utilization, and to reduce individual worker control over the pace and rhythm of work by the introduction of more disciplined production control systems.

Elger (1990a) notes that the distinctive political economy of the 1980s and 1990s has provided a definite impetus to the exercise of managerial prerogative, one result of which has led to intensifying pressures on the shop-floor. However, as this chapter shows, despite this supportive environment, the process of change is not unidirectional or trouble-free. Although, as we shall see in Chapter 7, some CarPress managers were clearly keen to take full advantage of the anti-union conditions established by successive Conservative governments, most senior manufacturing personnel were reluctant to take the initiative for this reason alone; they found themselves forced into the position of confronting labour over idle time by the general pressures of intense global competition in the auto industry and the particular cost-cutting interventions of the major vehicle assemblers.

For the workers at the receiving end of these changes, increased effort in the harsher, more disciplined manufacturing environment of the 1990s is not just about speed-up, or meeting tougher targets, or de-manning, or labour flexibility, important as these pressures still are. The attack on idle time is an attack on workers' own time; an attempt to undermine the ways in which workers' tacit skills are put to use to create a breathing space, a few moments to take your mind off the job, an opportunity to become temporarily divorced from the machine. It is a distinctly working-class form of 'empowerment' that does not sit happily with the fashionable sermons of the industrialists and management consultants. As such, it is a capacity that workers will seek to defend. For this reason more than any other, contemporary managerial attempts to exert greater leverage over work effort in the interests of 'efficiency' and 'enrichment' will remain subject to inner contradictions, tensions and frequent shop-floor resistance.

Notes

1 Press Shop Downtime Analysis Sheets, Materials Dept., CarPress Ltd.
2 The problems of machine reliability and poor set-up times ensured that budgetary cost constraints against overtime working did not extend to CarPress's craft workers and white collar engineers, both of whom worked considerable amounts of extra hours. See Chapter 8.
3 The BSI 0–100 rating scale based upon the notion that a typical worker

should produce x standard units of work per hour for his/her time-work rate of pay and $x + y$ units of work per hour at the expected incentive performance level. Translated into a ratings scale, it is assumed that the normal performance of time-workers is 75 standard units per hour and 100 standard units per hour at the expected incentive performance level. In other works, leaving aside inconvenient factors such as macho management, worker obstinacy and particular class conflicts on the shop-floor, Britain's work study engineers, working under the auspices of the British Standards Institute, decided that normal performance of time-workers was three-quarters of that of workers operating under incentive. (Source: BS3138: 1979.)

The BSI 100 scale is now the standard for the engineering industry. However, other scales which equate to, and operate under the same principles as the BSI 100 scale are also in use. CarPress used the 100/133 scale which corresponds to the BSI 75/100 scale.

4   Basic work cycle times (used for the purposes of both incentive payment calculation and production line balancing) normally comprise three components. 'Outside work' consists of work elements which must necessarily be performed by a worker outside the machine controlled time, such as material handling; 'inside work' consists of elements which can be performed by a worker within the machine controlled time (that is, machine operation); and a relaxation allowance which includes a fatigue allowance and attention to such personal needs as going to the toilet. Machine controlled time is defined as the time taken to complete that part of the work cycle which is determined only by factors peculiar to the machine. (Source: BS3138: 1979; BS3375: 1985).

5   The withdrawal of PBR in favour of MDW should not be construed merely as a process of the CarPress management catching up with its competitors. PBR systems are not anachronisms in British manufacturing industry. As Beaston (1993) has established, around 30 per cent of workers in British industry are still covered by individual PBR arrangements; and 51 per cent of firms in metal goods, engineering and vehicles use variations of individual incentive pay. However, Beaston also shows how the number of workers covered by both collective and PBR agreements has gone into decline since the 1970s whilst the use of performance related pay, merit pay and financial participation schemes has increased. This concerted management attack on workers' control over pay determination and associated work effort is now a general trend in British industry; it is also a particular requirement of the management of lean production.

6   K. Marx (1976), *Capital*, vol. I, pp. 548–50.

7   Management's counter-attack against individual workers who were blamed for this deteriorating shop-floor performance is described in Chapter 7.

6

Teamwork and Kaizen: Disempowering Shop-Floor Labour

Lean production regimes do not incorporate labour flexibility innovations in order to surrender control of the labour process to autonomous teams of multi-skilled, 'responsible' workers. Low waste mass-production requires, if anything, more meticulous forms of control than that utilized by conventional 'Fordist' management systems. As the survey of Japanese manufacturing transplants in South Wales indicated, in contrast to the empowering rhetoric contained in the ideological lexicon of labour flexibility and employee involvement, for reasons of efficiency, lean production operates on the basis of narrow, tightly controlled task flexibility coupled with only limited worker participation in continuous improvement of the production process.

Although such practices as teamworking and kaizen – or continuous improvement – can represent additional, sometimes more subtle mechanisms for securing managerial leverage over labour power than the coercive methods described in the previous chapter, they may still constitute forms of direct control. Indeed, as Lichtenstein (1988) and Geary (1995) have argued, these latest innovations bear remarkable similarities to past attempts by capital to undermine workers' collectivistic visions of a fair and decent shop-floor order. By attacking workers' lines of defence such as job demarcations, job classifications and seniority rights, contemporary labour flexibility strategies seek to return workers to the days of full managerial prerogative, when labour utilization was unhindered by union organization and when foremen enjoyed an unimpeded right to allocate labour to the different shop-floor tasks.

This chapter investigates how the introduction of teamworking and kaizen effected such a shift in the frontier of control at CarPress. It describes management's attempts to secure both improvements in labour utilization and a more efficient extraction of surplus value by expanding the process of functional flexibility in production. Moreover, in emphasizing social action on the shop-floor as the epicentre of the process of change, the analysis also gives some prominence to the attitudes and reactions of white collar engineers and supervisors and how the defence of their sectional interests contributed to an increase in management's direct control over work effort.

Labour Flexibility and 'Ownership'

The new working practices agreement came into effect during the autumn of 1994. It was signed in the aftermath of management's defeat of sustained shop-floor opposition, which, as we shall see in Chapter 7, involved the frustration of a series of rank-and-file actions and the eventual sacking of a number of scapegoated workers. Although multifaceted in approach, the agreement embodied the company's foremost objective of securing the workforce's commitment to the principle of 'total customer satisfaction' by ensuring that 'outdated industrial relations practices that restrict or threaten the interruption of customer supplies will be eliminated'.[1] Teamworking was considered the primary institutional means of achieving this.

As I explain in the next section, a minority of the shop-floor operators had been working in teams since 1992. The new agreement stipulated an immediate plant-wide introduction of both teamworking and kaizen together with the simplification of job classifications and the gradual implementation of various harmonization and single-status conditions. All employees were expected to perform any job or function for which they possessed the relevant skills whilst traditions such as seniority-based labour deployment were prohibited.

Although the organizational principles enshrined in the agreement formed a radical departure from existing practice for most areas of the shop-floor, the theory, if not the application, of these Japanese-style flexibility techniques was not completely new to the CarPress workforce. As Marsden et al. (1985) document, during the 1980s many senior managements in the British automobile industry attempted, often unsuccessfully, to attack union protected job demarcations by seeking the introduction of teamworking and other new labour utilization techniques. The Rover Group placed itself at the forefront of these management initiatives. However, despite winning agreement for the introduction of teamworking on its main production lines and cross-trade skill flexibility in plant maintenance areas, rank-and-file trade union opposition combined with middle management cynicism to ensure a distinctly limited degree of labour flexibility in practice (Marsden et al., 1985; Willman and Winch, 1985).

Biding its time, Rover eventually took advantage of a malleable labour organization demoralized by mass sackings in the industry when it introduced authentic teamworking and controlled labour flexibility on a systematic multi-plant basis towards the end of 1992 ('A Cowley Worker', 1993). Following this, Rover's actively interventionist stance towards its first-tier suppliers provided an important impetus to the introduction of the new working practices agreement at CarPress. However, the close assembler–supplier relationship was not the only influencing factor here. As the previous chapter demonstrated, lean production measures such as minimal material stores and low in-production buffers combined with poor capital utilization rates to compel the new CarPress management to maximize labour utilization rates. The way in which continuous bell-to-bell production subordinated workers both to their machines and their supervisors represented one major aspect of this. But it was not the sole one. CarPress also sought a more flexible and efficient consumption of labour power; not only did it require complete control over the time workers spent on the job, it also demanded full managerial prerogative over the allocation of workers to their different machines and tasks.

The management confronted two major obstacles here. Firstly, semi-skilled job demarcations on the basis of seniority. Secondly, skilled job demarcations on the basis of craft. Both of these will now be briefly considered.

Seniority – the Ownership of Jobs

Workers' seniority rights are more commonly associated with post-war labour deployment practices in American manufacturing industry. During the 1950s and 1960s, unions in such sectors as steel, automobiles and electricals succeeded in securing complex plant seniority systems based on the principle of offering first choice to longer-serving workers on questions of selection for lay-off, promotion and both intra-departmental and intra-plant mobility (Stone, 1974; Tolliday and Zeitlin, 1986; Lichtenstein, 1988). Ironically, before the war, some of the major

American corporations sowed the seeds for this by creating their own job classification and seniority procedures with the intention of building a sense of company loyalty and commitment amongst their workforces. But these early systems did not infringe upon managerial prerogatives to any great extent. They operated within the context of close supervision and strict discipline. Foremen still had the final say when it came to selection for lay-off and redeployment; 'troublemakers' and 'militants' were always excluded from the benefits of this form of company paternalism (Tolliday and Zeitlin, 1986; Lichtenstein, 1988).

This management control was gradually limited during the 1950s and 1960s as trade union organization started to flex its muscles. In the American auto industry, a series of union campaigns and labour disputes succeeded in enshrining seniority-based labour deployment in mutually agreed constitutional arrangements. These placed significant constraints on the foreman's ability to frustrate workers' job choices through arbitrary discharge in relation to either selection for redundancy or job allocation (Tolliday and Zeitlin, 1986, pp. 110–13). And by the 1980s, seniority presented a major obstacle in the path of management's quest for labour flexibility and more extensive shop-floor discipline.

In the UK, although jointly managed seniority-based labour deployment and promotion systems have operated in a small number of industries[2] the seniority principle has more commonly been protected by custom and practice and the strength of shop steward organization rather than bureaucratic regulation. In the British auto industry this resulted in a more informal regulatory system which was thin on specific shop-floor rules and procedures but which instead relied upon the defence of a set of rights residing in the 'collective memory' of different groups of car workers and their elected stewards (Jurgens et al., 1993). However, the effect was similar to the American experience in the sense that British car workers were led to expect an equitable and morally acceptable shop-floor order. For example, at CarPress the normative principles of seniority and ownership of preferred jobs and machines formed a central part of the 'collective memory' of the more experienced shop-floor workers. An assembly shop steward reflected on this:

> This seniority was always a sacred cow especially for the older operators here, and it was one of the main reasons that we fought hard against signing the new agreement. You've got to understand that it's wrong that an older man aged, say, between 55 and 60 could be asked to move from the

assembly shop to the press shop where the work is heavier and more stressful. You could have someone suffering from angina and those presses would just kill him. Over the years the scores have become harder, and anyone with any common sense could see that the press shop scores are just too hard for the older men.

I'm not saying that we never allowed some form of labour mobility, mind. We used our common sense. We would often agree to labour redeployment, but not always the way management wanted it. You see, before the new agreement was signed you might be a senior operator working on a decent job and churning out the parts, earning your bonus and at the same time helping the company meet its production targets. That's fair. You'd have earned that position. Then along would come someone like Les Williams [production manager] who'd try and do a double shuffle. He'd say we've got a new job that's needed urgently and so he might try and move the senior operator onto the new job and get him to sort out all the problems and lose his bonus into the bargain while the younger operator would end up with the easier job. Well, we used to be able to stop that sort of practice. We used to be able to stand up to management and say, 'Hey, fuck off! That's not mobility of labour that's just an abuse of labour!'

As this comment suggests, from the older worker's standpoint the claim to seniority at CarPress amounted to the avoidance of disadvantage rather than an assertion of positive rights. This principle influenced three areas of labour allocation: plant seniority governed selection for redundancy, in effect, 'last in first out'; departmental seniority governed the movement of labour between the assembly and press shops; and the more serious restraint on flexibility considered here, line seniority, governed the movement of workers between different production lines and machines.

Line seniority in the assembly shop presented a particular problem for management. Here especially, some jobs and target quotas were manifestly more arduous and demanding than others; the 'science' of time-and-motion work study rarely took full account of every machine idiosyncrasy or every manual difficulty associated with the more complex assembly operations. Consequently, the assembly shop stewards would invariably invoke seniority rights where the need arose to protect their members against the perceived whim and prejudice of production management. This tradition bred a sense of 'ownership' amongst the older operators which stood in stark contrast to the euphemistic form emphasized by the new management ideologies in which 'ownership', in reality, translates into individual accountability for performance. These operators defended an alternative and more benign ownership, a means of securing a degree of personal control over the quality and pace of work on the factory floor. It formed a serious handicap for the management's demand for more efficient and flexible labour utilization practices. As the chief production manager remarked:

> In the assembly shop you've got rows of fixed machines but you've also got the men fixed to the same machines. The challenge here is to overcome the rigid mentalities in this area where the men tend to regard the machines as their own, they really think they own the machine as it were. Now, thank heavens, the new agreement counters all this rigidity. Now, if you've been trained to do a job and you're capable of doing it, then no matter who you are, you will do it, no argument.

Prior to the new agreement, therefore, the foreman's options for labour deployment, particularly in the assembly shop, were shaped primarily by the operator's length of service. As a result, in similar ways to Burawoy's (1979) description of the seniority-based 'bumping' system in the USA, the more experienced CarPress workers enjoyed enhanced job security and control over their work. According to one manager, 'the logic here used to be that the older men always tended to gravitate towards the easiest jobs whilst younger operators were shunted towards the jobs with the harder targets'. It was a system of shop-floor control that was far from perfect; and in the context of the contemporary relaxation of collectivistic convictions, seniority will always be subject to a degree of internal working-class discord. For example, the second questionnaire survey (November 1995) indicated that only 15 per cent of assembly shop operators with less than five years' service supported it compared to 64 per cent of the largest group, operators with over ten years' service. Yet compared to the despotism of an unchallenged foreman's prerogative, this system of ownership was at least transparent and equitable in the long term.

Craft Demarcation – the Ownership of Skill

During the 1980s, Rover took a leading position in the car industry's attempts to undermine traditional craft demarcations in the maintenance and tooling functions. The company sought to improve machine breakdown response times by rationalizing the maintenance trades and establishing two new broad groups, mechanical and electrical, members of which would then form on-line maintenance crews (Marsden *et al.*, 1985). Following trends elsewhere in the engineering industry, this did not result in the creation of teams of new multi-skilled craftsmen; the intention was to secure cost savings by reducing the size of the skilled workforce and ensuring that assignments were expedited by way of low-skill task accretion (IDS, 1994b).

The skilled workers at the Oldport plant feared these developments, not so much because their bargaining position within external labour markets might be weakened (Hyman, 1988) but, more fundamentally, because the local market for their skills had all but disappeared. In such circumstances, the ownership and collective defence of tangible skills, which historically protected engineering tradesmen against the iniquities of Taylorized mass-production work, came under real threat. Many skilled men foresaw a looming encounter with Hobson's choice: accept de-skilling and the degradation of work that goes with it, or face the dole. These fears were exacerbated upon the arrival of the new CarPress management.

CarPress was not satisfied with the limited degree of cross-trade flexibility secured by Rover. In 1991, the company introduced a new group working agreement which deepened the process of task accretion. Traditionally, teams of slingers, crane operators and truck drivers performed the difficult task of transporting and manoeuvring 25-ton dies around the factory floor. Although the work was not classed as skilled, it contained many potential safety risks and entailed the employment of a number of tacit skills which could only be mastered over time. The new agreement sought a reduction in downtime and a further intensification of the craft labour process by expecting the various skilled groups to take on much of this work themselves. The affected workers were forced to accept the agreement or suffer the consequence of job loss.

In fact, the changes contributed to further job insecurity. As one crane driver complained:

> Our people didn't vote for the flexibility agreement, they voted for their jobs. But as a result you can be doing any job now ... just two years ago they gave the toolmakers a ten-point test. The management said that if they completed it then their jobs would be guaranteed. It was all about trying to get them to work flexibly. They asked them to do just about anything, from toolsetting to slinging, to driving, to cleaning toilets, to cleaning the boss's arse. The management said it was all done to save jobs. And has it? Has it hell! Since

then half the men have lost their jobs. Flexibility is a con. It's all a con, man! You just can't believe management.

The same worker expressed heartfelt bitterness at the company's hazardous devaluation of his own tacit skills:

And now they're putting people to work with you who've got no idea of safety at all. I needed a six-week training course to train for my job, but all the toolsetters are getting is eight hours. But eight hours of training won't make you a crane driver. It's impossible, how can it? You can't learn to drive a car in eight hours. So why a bloody crane, lifting 30-ton tools across the factory floor? It's a skilled job, you're working in confined spaces. And the problem is, they're asking these men to work the cranes, but they're not doing the job regularly. If you don't do it as a full-time job you lose your feel for the equipment and you lose your competence.

And I find it so galling to find some of these youngsters doing my job and telling *me* what to do, telling *me*. And of course I end up saving their necks. I end up shouting at them, 'Don't move it that way, you'll lose your arm, you won't be sticking your hand up at the bar buying your five pints again!' But why bother? I should just shut up and let 'em learn the hard way.

The slingers and drivers lost self-esteem; many lost their jobs.[3] And the craft workers did not gain any corresponding tacit skills of their own. This process of multi-tasking, in the absence of extra time allowances, merely intensified rather than enriched the labour process. A toolmaker made the following typical observation:

The job itself has changed a lot in that we're now being asked to do far more than we used to. We have to clean the tools as they come in; the company used to employ separate workers to do that. We have to do all the slinging now, whereas previously we'd have teams of slingers doing that. We have to do a lot more machining. We have to drive the stacker trucks ourselves to move the dies around in and out of the shops. And we're now being asked to operate the cranes. So the job's been upturned altogether but with no reward. It's not been, what do they call it, 'enriching'? You're not talking about additional skills here, we're just doing other people's jobs.

The subsequent new working practices agreement represented a higher stage in the continuing process of undermining the skilled groups' defensive practices. The management sought further flexibility and efficiency in the consumption of labour power by introducing the expectation that all workers should accomplish any task for which they had the relevant skills and training. For production operators this meant working the different machines more intensively; for many skilled workers it meant performing virtually any job on the factory floor. The agreement replaced the plant's complex system of job demarcations and classifications with a simple four-grade structure. Placed into the supposedly liberating organization of teamworking, higher-graded skilled operators were expected to add the tasks of machine operation, cleaning and labouring to their routine skilled work whenever the 'needs of the business' demanded it.

Job demarcations, flexibility and seniority at CarPress were therefore governed by the traditions of shop-floor custom and practice; these in turn are a function of the prevailing balance of power between capital and labour. During the 1980s and 1990s, mass unemployment, state attacks on trade unionism and a barrage of new management ideologies combined to swing this balance firmly towards capital. Exploiting these conditions, the CarPress management sought a phased eradication of worker control over labour deployment. Ironically, this reached its highest level under the guise of 'self-management' and teamworking. The processes by which this was achieved will now be looked at in detail.

Teamworking

As indicated in Chapter 2, teamworking can be a nebulous concept, having various meanings and concrete forms in different manufacturing and technological settings. In the car industry, although it has not always been emulated, the Toyota team system represents the ideal type. At many Toyota factories, machines and labour are organized into cells to effect a redistribution and reduction of workers' motions, job cycle times, idle time and buffers. Production flows steadily and continually; labour works flexibly and more intensively (Cusumano, 1985; Oliver and Wilkinson, 1992). Much of the management literature emphasizes the development of multi-skilled labour processes as a job-enriching compensatory factor for effort intensification (for example, IDS, 1992b; Kenney and Florida, 1993), although a number of analyses of Japanese auto transplants in the UK and USA have suggested that this often amounts to little more than job rotation around a limited range of cognate tasks (Garrahan and Stewart, 1992; Kumon et al., 1994; Kawamura, 1994; Graham, 1995).

Competitive market pressures, the cost cutting interventions of key customers such as Toyota, Opel and Rover, and senior management's continual demand for more output from a leaner workforce, together compelled CarPress to gradually adopt similar work organizational changes.

The company's stated objectives varied, chameleon-like, in accordance with the different class interests at stake. Changes in working practices which intensify both work effort and management control of the labour process must be presented to workers as delusions, or as Hayter puts it, as 'promises, or moral inducements, which management hopes will secure the cooperation of workers and weaken their trade unions' (1993, p. 54). Accordingly, in the few years leading up to, and during, its plant-wide introduction in 1994, CarPress launched an ideological campaign in support of teamwork, envisaging the changes as entirely desirable and emphasizing notions of job enrichment, employee involvement in management and a new consensus between managers and workers. The discourse was often patronizingly frivolous – reflecting the management's mistrust of its workforce – as the following company newsletter extract exemplifies:

> Listen to the roar of the crowd at a cup final. That's the roar of the people who appreciate teamwork. Individual star performances blending as a team is the key to outstanding success; that's why teamwork is coming to the CarPress Group.
>
> The team members, initially, may not feel they can produce as many parts as they did under the old system and so the target is set lower. But then after a few days, one of them makes a suggestion for better working and the target can be raised. A few days later the same thing happens again. Soon the target not only reaches the original figure but begins to gallop past it to the wonderment of all concerned.[4]

Wonderment indeed. When their views were directed towards other ears the management became more candid in their convictions. For example, although the head of personnel used the terms 'empowerment' and 'ownership' quite freely in his speeches and articles for the workforce, he accepted in private that they made little sense in the practical context of the disciplines of mass-production:

> To be honest, how can you have empowerment when you've got a man dragging himself into work every morning, working five machines every day

instead of the one and then going home again? All we're doing is breaking down the demarcations, giving the man a bit of job rotation but making sure we've got all the management controls in place first. I think that's the key to it, that's what we've been concentrating on over the past year, getting the controls in place.

And 'self-management'?

It's like management pushing a boulder up a mountainside. It's hard work getting people to change, but once you get to the top the boulder can quickly fall down the other side and the whole thing runs away from you. For that reason I don't accept this idea of team autonomy. There will be no question of total self-management. The teams might not like it but they're going to need some controlling.

The senior managers agreed that, where technology permitted, team-working should be operationalized in the fashion of the Toyota model to improve shop-floor efficiency, increase output and reduce manning levels. They also sought to cement recent gains on the issues of seniority and job demarcations by institutionalizing the principles of labour flexibility and worker accountability within the team organization. In the context of the legacy of shop-floor control over labour deployment and the distribution of work, teamworking represented a union-busting strategy, a means of dismantling this legacy of control and a means of weakening the shop-floor unity upon which the factory consciousness is constituted. Even the more novel aspects of worker accountability should be viewed in these terms. In the absence of strong union organization, individual account-ability for performance represents a classic disciplinary measure; but as we shall see in Chapter 7, team accountability to the customer can potentially have a more subversive and pernicious impact on worker solidarity. As one production superintendent enthused:

The idea of accountability to the customer is important to us. I believe that operators would become more obligated and committed to the team by dealing with their customer on a face-to-face basis. You're not going to get the militancy, the continual working to rule and overtime bans that we've had in the past. Think about it. When the team members get on the phone and speak to the customer direct and the customer's complaining, 'You can't let us down, we need these parts today,' then that will start the men thinking, they'll start to get guilty about the idea of slowing production down.

CarPress also injected substantial levels of time and resources into constructing new team communications and employee involvement structures (described in Chapter 8). The company therefore established a clear 'human resource' agenda: to simultaneously boost labour productivity and secure worker commitment by significantly reshaping the technological and ideological components of production.

Prior to the plant-wide introduction of teamworking, the shop-floor workforce divided into two discrete modes of work organization: a large majority group of operators and skilled workers organized by function along classic production lines and a much smaller group organized into different teams manufacturing parts for Toyota, Opel and Honda. For the moment we will focus on the majority group, the 'backward obstructionists' as some managers liked to call them.

In fact, these workers did not reject the notion of change at the workplace. Many had experienced the icy winds of global competition and recession, the slow but continual process of shop-floor redundancy in the fashion of 'salami slicing', and the waves of factory closures elsewhere in South Wales. In these circumstances, they had been forced to accept the management's cry that in order to survive, 'you have to change your ways, think smart as well as work hard at all times'. But they also displayed a world weary cynicism here; a distrust of management's ability or disposition to introduce the types of changes that would meet their own objectives of achieving a measure of job security and a decent quality of life. As one senior shop steward remarked:

> Many of the men have worked at CarPress for 30 years or more, and you've always been told by management what your job is, you've been told what to do, to stick to the same job, your job's never changed. I feel it's not the men but the management that's been backward in coming forward. Nobody here is saying that we don't accept change. It's management that's the problem, they're always saying something and doing nothing. They've been talking about change for 20 years now but nothing ever happens.

A press operator commented on his questionnaire form:

> The management always blame the workforce for not trying to make things work. When really, the workers who have 'hands on' experience should have the opportunity to air their views. Over the years, the shop-floor workers have seen finances and resources wasted by management who seem hell bent on carrying out their ill-thought-out ideas come what may. And when

production comes to a halt through incompetence of horrendous proportions, which has happened many times, the buck is passed. The same mistakes are being made time after time, year after year. Surely somebody can see this happening?

A similar degree of scepticism characterized attitudes to the introduction of teamworking. These also reflected a clear perception and defence of basic workers' interests. Some of the replies to the first questionnaire survey (October 1994) provide an indication of this; they are summarized in Tables 6.1, 6.2 and 6.3. The different responses of the Toyota, Opel and Honda teamworkers will be commented upon later, but for the moment it is the general response that concerns us.

The proposition that no worker would suffer compulsory redundancy as a result of the changes formed an intrinsic element of the company's pro-team propaganda campaign. Indeed, the new working practices

Table 6.1 *Shop-floor workers' attitude to the introduction of teamworking in principle (Percentage by row; N = 319)*

	Support (%)	Opposed (%)	Undecided (%)
All shop-floor workers	38	26	36
Non-team operators	32	39	29
Toyota/Opel/Honda teamworkers	78	9	13
Skilled workers	39	21	38

Table 6.2 *Shop-floor workers' attitudes to teamworking and job security at CarPress (Percentage by row; N = 319)*

	Teamworking will lead to redundancies (%)	Teamworking will have no effect (%)	Teamworking will help to create jobs (%)
All shop-floor workers	59	29	12
Non-team operators	59	31	10
Toyota/Opel/Honda operators	23	42	35
Skilled workers	68	22	10

Table 6.3 *Shop-floor workers' assessment of CarPress's motives for introducing teamworking (Percentage by row; N = 319)*

	Agree (%)	Disagree (%)	Undecided (%)
Increasing job satisfaction			
All shop-floor workers	15	62	23
Non-team operators	12	63	26
Toyota/Opel/Honda			
operators	48	26	26
Skilled workers	11	70	19
Increasing efficiency and work effort			
All shop-floor workers	63	18	19
Non-team operators	61	19	20
Toyota/Opel/Honda			
operators	67	9	24
Skilled workers	71	14	16

agreement provided written assurance of this. Nevertheless, the majority of workers viewed the management's mollifying statements with suspicion and disbelief, as well they might, since a fundamental aspect of labour flexibility within team organization is the steady reduction of team manning levels through multi-tasking and 'continuous improvement'. For this reason, as Table 6.2 indicates, many believed that redundancies were inevitable, that, as one press operator put it, 'What it boils down to is that you'll be sending a brother down the road; if they start to ask you to do the job of three different people then some people will go, its obvious.' And if some operators, rightly or wrongly, regarded themselves as less vulnerable than their skilled colleagues this did not subvert the ethical basis of their shop-floor solidarity. As one female assembly shop operator expressed it:

> I will not accept teamworking. Take the toolsetting. If the foreman asks me to change the tools on my machine, then okay, I think I could do it with a bit of training. I know how to do it, I've seen it done enough times. All you're doing is lifting a tool out, lifting a new tool in, adjusting and clamping it. But when you do that you're putting another man out of work, Dai and Thomas, our toolsetters for instance. I'm just not prepared to do that. That is morally wrong.

However, as Table 6.1 suggests, the majority of the shop-floor did not oppose the general principle of teamworking. Compared to the dehumanizing fragmentation of Taylorist work organization, the idea of working in cooperation with mutually supportive colleagues carries a manifest seductive appeal. And it sits particularly well with the communitarian ethos of the South Wales valleys. As one operator remarked, 'All the steel workers and miners around here used to be teamworkers. So in that sense we have no fear of it at all, we certainly don't regard it as alien.' But teamworking becomes both alien and alienating when it is placed into the context of capital accumulation in mass-production. In these circumstances, many people on the shop-floor understood that despite its ostensible attraction, teamworking was unlikely to enhance an already limited level of job satisfaction or, indeed, to liberate the workforce from capitalist subordination under the guise of 'self-management'. As one operator commented:

> Personally, I'm cynical about job enrichment. The nature of this job is that it's monotonous work. At the end of the day, the management here want their production schedules out at fast speed and as far as I'm concerned more responsibility equals more monotonous jobs and more problems for shop-floor workers. I'm not interested in more responsibility. I just don't want it. All it means is pouring more and more of management's problems onto my shoulders.

And a toolsetter:

> Empowerment? How? There'll always be someone looking over your shoulder, someone watching you. There's nothing wrong with teamworking itself. It might be okay in terms of helping each other out and mucking in together. But it's when people *tell* you have to work in these ways that we start to get stubborn. Because the plans this management have for teamworking here don't include allowing us to be totally responsible for the job. You're joking aren't you? Somebody will always be monitoring us. They'll be monitoring our output and efficiency because at the end of the day we'll be paid on results. Somebody somewhere along the line has got to look down on you.

In an attempt to counter the concrete manifestations of this type of oppositional attitude the management had developed a deliberate political and ideological strategy of attrition during the two years leading up to the implementation of plant-wide teamworking in late 1994. This will now be examined.

The Trojan Horse Strategy

During 1992, CarPress secured large contracts to supply pressed assemblies to Toyota and Opel; two years later a similar deal was struck with Honda in Swindon. These new customers insisted on exerting a substantial influence over CarPress's shop-floor technology and work practices.

With the help of the CarPress engineering department, a team of Toyota engineers appropriated a section of the assembly shop and reorganized space and machinery into a discrete cell. They situated different manual, semi-automatic and robotic weld-assembly units around a team leader's control room and operators' self-inspection area. The section was therefore redesigned to provide a cell of strategically placed standard weld-assembly equipment on a multi-functional, single product family basis.

In contrast, Opel's German engineers required CarPress to invest heavily in 'state of the art', dedicated robotic transfer line technology designed to manufacture 300,000 car dashboards a year. This comprised a series of discrete teams of welders using the latest weld-assembly technology to manufacture various sub-assemblies which were then placed into rotary carousels feeding a fully integrated weld, paint and seal transfer line.

In both cases, the new work arrangements, by necessity, represented cell-based technological enclaves within a greater Fordist territory of more traditional work organization. But the company's attempt to reshape shop-floor social relations and reinforce management control was not driven primarily by technological change; it intended to introduce teamworking on a plant-wide basis without any substantial extra investment and, in some areas, without any significant adaptations to existing work layout. The work organizational changes demanded by Toyota and Opel were an explicit function of capitalist social relations; they accorded exactly with the CarPress management's longer-term political aims. The new technological enclaves were also political enclaves, set up in a strategic sense as centres for the wider unilateral diffusion of new working practices and worker attitudes. And in order to effect this, the management needed to do two things. Firstly, recruit workers to the teams who displayed a commitment to company objectives and a willingness to change. Secondly, if only on a temporary basis, the team-based labour processes required refashioning so that they displayed some ostensible wider appeal.

Under normal circumstances, operators would be allocated to new work areas on the basis of seniority and availability. But the traditional approach was jettisoned for recruitment to the teams. Instead, the management sought to create greenfield conditions within a brownfield setting by establishing groups of less experienced but committed workers and then shielding them from the 'contaminating' influence of the main shop-floor. Some managers perceived the latter factor as a poisonous constraint to the change process. For example, one superintendent commented:

> I took on a new man in the press shop not so long ago who initially got on really well, he actually *liked* taking the initiative and he *liked* a bit of responsibility. But what happens? This started to cause resentment amongst his fellow operators, they ended up hounding him out of the shop. I remember him coming to me in tears. I felt very sorry for him, so much so that I had to move him into the assembly shop ... So what I'm saying is, we needed to help along the new attitudes, but it had to be done in small groups. We need to keep out the influence of the trouble-makers.

The company sought volunteers off the main shop-floor and then carefully screened each individual, testing for commitment to the ethos of teamworking and positive attitudes towards the company. The chosen few were not necessarily those operators with little experience; indeed, the management was particularly keen to enlist those with a certain history of experience, as one manager enthused, 'the experienced unemployed, the people who have a real fear of it, the ones who are therefore willing to change'. As a result, nearly 50 per cent of the operators in the team areas were aged under 30 compared to only 18 per cent in the main shops; and almost 60 per cent had worked at CarPress for less than five years and only 25 per cent for more than ten years, compared to 22 per cent and 68 per cent respectively, elsewhere.

Having selected favourable human ingredients, the management introduced an induction programme to prepare the operators for the new working methods. Small groups of recruits were sent to a local hotel for three-day cathartic attitude-shaping sessions with a team of management consultants. Some of the operators out on the main shops were appalled at this blatant attempt to weaken their collective shop-floor consciousness. One cynically remarked, 'I saw one group go in, they went in normal and came out with their brains addled. They could only see things the way the company wanted them to see them, they were just totally brainwashed.' Brainwashed maybe, but the process had a seductive appeal in the context of the low-skill/no-training Tayloristic environment that most operators had suffered for years. Even an experienced shop steward, who had gone through the process himself, admitted:

> They were good fun. You'd do some exercises together, like one we had was to work out how to get a giraffe from Oldport to Scotland in a truck without using a motorway. It might all sound silly but we did build a good team spirit among our group. And you were taught team management ideas like how to organize job rotation and new tasks such as maintenance, all that type of thing. I liked the sound of it. We all did. It seemed to add a bit of interest to your job.

However, this ideological approach was not by itself sufficient to catalyse attitude changes elsewhere in the plant. People wanted more concrete evidence of job interest and enrichment under teamworking. The management provided this by taking the unusual step, in the context of past practice, of temporarily removing all management controls from the teams, particularly in the Toyota area.[5]

In many respects, the resulting style of work organization resembled Swedish group working more than Japanese teamworking. Rather than being subject to direct control, Swedish groups enjoy sufficient autonomy to influence questions such as goal formation, performance monitoring, production methods, labour allocation and choice of group leaders (Ramsay, 1992). Moreover, both Berggren (1993) and Thompson and Sederblad (1994) have emphasized the extent to which the Swedish system allows group control over work pace through the presence of buffers and the absence of supervision.

At CarPress, the teams were advised that as long as they fulfilled their customers' daily just-in-time supply schedules then they would be left alone. Consequently, although the basic labour process of operating assembly and weld machinery remained unchanged, the work underwent enlargement and, to an extent, enrichment. Team members moved from machine to machine rather than 'owning' a single machine; they became involved with inspecting and testing their work, ordering materials and inputting information into the plant's computerized stores system; and they habitually liaised with representatives of the customer, engineers and managers at the likes of Toyota in Derby and Honda in Swindon. Although the teams had their own 'informal' team leaders they were not subject to formal supervision; the day-to-day part requirements of the customer maintained the discipline and intensity of work, and even here the process was mitigated by the existence of human buffers in the form of relatively generous manning levels.

Taking into account the joint impact of the company's recruitment strategy, the new attitude-shaping courses and the concrete attempts to enrich the team-based labour processes, it was no surprise that the attitudes of the teamworkers indicated in Tables 6.1, 6.2 and 6.3 were significantly more favourable than their colleagues elsewhere on the factory floor. Brainwashed or not, many teamworkers really did feel positive about their work. One commented:

> There's no doubt that my job satisfaction has improved under teamworking. Two years ago I was working outside of the cell and the work was so monotonous. I was in a rut. But now I do get a lot of job satisfaction. Before you were just a number, a number producing parts. But now, it's not just about getting bits out the door, it's about interest. We've got these new responsibilities that make the job more interesting. It's all about total ownership.

Not all displayed such animated enthusiasm, but most did at least convey a clear sense of appreciation for the injection of an element of job conception into the previously Taylorized work routines. A young operator remarked:

> It gives you a bit more knowledge and more responsibility. So I reckon it's better than standing up pressing buttons all day long. You have to think a bit more, you have to be more cautious, because you're making parts and sending them straight out the door. And if they go out wrong then there's a come back on you and the whole team. So that's the main difference. You have to think about what you're doing.

The Trojan Horse is Dismantled

In his overview of the complexity of changes in skill patterns in the contemporary capitalist labour process, Thompson (1989) argues that rather than taking sides in a polarized and simplistic flexibility debate between, on the one hand, those who argue that multi-skilling constitutes objective skill enhancement, and on the other, those who regard it merely as low-skill task accretion, we should instead recognize that the new management techniques may represent something less rudimentary – a partial break, rather than a full rupture with Taylorist work organization.

The management strategy at CarPress provided a further twist to this argument: the political strategy of *temporary* upskilling aimed at strengthening management control in the longer term.

By the autumn of 1994, two years after its introduction, CarPress decided that self-management should be curtailed. It had served its purpose. If not displaying acceptance, the workers in the main shops had at least become accustomed to the presence of teamworking on the shop-floor; and as we shall see in the next chapter, their more overt forms of opposition became subject to undisguised managerial suppression. Moreover, the management had by now secured its new working practices agreement, and the idea of incorporating the principles of employee autonomy into the plant-wide implementation of teamworking was, in the context of antagonistic work relations, regarded as politically naive.

Therefore, different managers and engineers suddenly became interested in the performance and efficiency of their existing teams. They began asking questions that, for political reasons, were previously conveniently deferred. Although self-management contributed to each team's fulfilment of its contractual obligations to the customer, the company forfeited control over the performance of each team member, control over the extraction of surplus value. This was the principal concern. An industrial engineer put it succinctly:

> If we did a full investigation of the Toyota cell I suspect we'd probably find that they're only working a fraction of the normal working day. So are they fully utilized? Who's to say if they are or not? They won't tell you, that's for sure. And that's the problem with self-management. You've lost control.

During this period, the thorny issue of dismantling team autonomy enjoyed a clear consensus of opinion between the production and engineering functions. Many production managers and foremen deeply distrusted the operators' motives on the shop-floor. They perceived team autonomy as a recipe for shop-floor anarchy and an opportunity for workers to divest themselves of the disciplines and daily grind of mass-production. Indeed, from the standpoint of the overseer, the only pressure workers ever respond to is the dull economic compulsion of wage labour. 'Workers don't need self-management, they need real motivation, management targets and the wage incentive,' was the typical cry. But of course, self-management also threatens the tenure of traditional superintendence. Many production managers rightly regarded it as a manifest threat to the survival of the conventional machinery of production control and the supervisory role that accompanies this.

Similar concerns obtained in the engineering function. In his analysis of the labour processes of technical workers, Smith (1991), following Cooley (1987), argues that the social action of engineers may be conditioned by, *inter alia*, the coexistence of two discrete engineering ideologies: craftism and professional scientism.[6] Facets of both ideologies influenced events at CarPress. Most engineers perceived themselves as 'disinterested professionals', favouring neither managers nor workers, an identity which, as Jones (1994) argues, still aligns the engineer with corporate interests. Plant 'efficiency' was regarded unquestioningly as an objective concept; it could not embody different political interests for capital and labour. Indeed, working in an environment of mass-production, many CarPress engineers understood shop-floor workers in similar terms to those expressed by their counterparts at Smith's Cadbury's case study: as 'a flexible, efficient and malleable commodity' to be put to use for maximum production (1991, p. 194). Consequently, they repeatedly expressed misgivings over the 'inefficiencies' that resulted from their management's lax attitudes towards labour regulation within the teams. The following comment from a project engineer summed this up:

> What happens of course, if you're not careful, is that the team gets isolated from the plant. And we lose complete control over what's going on within the cell. Our Toyota team was doing everything we asked of it, the men did try to manage it, but we tended to lose track of the balance between the volume of parts that the customer required and the number of operators required for the job. So you can give them too much independence. We believe in here that they still need targets and some control. Management from above I'm afraid.
>
> You see, what's been going on inside these teams is that they've been spending too much time on non-production activities whereas their time could be more productively spent. That's what we need to be moving towards in the future. Basically, it's about measuring their production time and ensuring that in the future their working time is being used for production and not much else. I think that's the efficiency of teamworking.

For 'professional–scientific' reasons, the engineers therefore supported the company's intention to reintroduce traditional management controls. But this was not the sole reason. Additional job security interests were at stake. Chapter 4 described the process by which the engineering department was stripped of much of its design function. In response to this de-skilling, the more experienced men sought to maintain a craft component in their new project management role by colonizing shop-floor activities such as prototype 'tryout' work. In so doing, they progressively encroached upon shop-floor territory. It is in this sense that the engineers mobilized an ideology of craftism as a defensive strategy against loss of skill and status. But, in an environment of lean mass-production, craftism can be a double-edged weapon. Some men spoke of the stress and overwork that such task-enlargement entails. And although they were increasingly interacting with production machinery, it was not always on a craft basis. One tooling engineer complained:

> A lot of our time, especially overtime, is spent doing things that should be done on the shop-floor. For instance, we spend a lot of time carrying equipment about the plant, unbolting parts, fitting them elsewhere and wandering around like progress chasers. We're constantly walking around with different hats on. I'm supposed to be an engineer. But sometimes I'm an operator, sometimes I'm a supervisor. What's happening is that there's no restrictions any more on doing some of these jobs, and slowly you tend to get sucked into it, you do more and more of it. As a result, you lose more of your old technical skills.
>
> To give you an example, the other day I went to see my grandmother in my lunch hour. When she opened her front door she said to me, 'Good God John, have you changed jobs? I thought you were an office worker now!' You see, I was just covered from head to toe in grease and muck off the shop-floor. As I see things, if that's flexibility then you can stick it.

Craftism, then, had its problems. But at least it provided the engineers with work. Team-based worker self-management jeopardized these white collar jobs; it was also regarded as an impediment to productive efficiency. Elsewhere, production managers were afraid that such worker autonomy would usurp their traditional supervisory role and even subvert the shop-floor work ethic. And for senior management, the idea had outlived its usefulness once the company secured its new working practices agreement. The Trojan horse had served its purpose.

Plant-wide Teamworking

Therefore, in November 1994, industrial engineers entered the different team areas. Employing the usual work study techniques these 'objective professionals' re-balanced the lines by establishing tighter manning levels to meet the customers' increasingly demanding daily production schedules. At the same time, the teams were placed under the effective control of production supervisors. These changes reduced the level of worker autonomy previously enjoyed.

Meanwhile, in accordance with the new agreement, team organization spread throughout the main assembly and press shops. The managerial logic behind these changes was simple. Teamworking would institutionalize multi-tasking; it would engender a sense of worker accountability for team output; and, as we shall see in Chapters 7 and 8, it would contribute towards a partial fragmentation of the ethic and culture of shop-floor solidarity.

The new teams were named units. The press shop housed eight units each organized along dedicated product lines and employing as many as 50 operators. In effect, the press shop was divided into different zones containing groups of press production lines responsible for particular product families such as car doors or dashboards. By contrast, the organization of technology and the labour process in the assembly shop was more suitable for smaller-scale cellular working. Here, 15 new units were established each dedicated both to a particular product and to an external customer; they contained anything between six and 30 operators. In both shops a typical unit comprised a group of production operators, press fitters and toolsetters, technicians (including maintenance and project engineers), a fork lift truck driver (though toolsetters also performed this operation) and a quality inspector. Each unit was made accountable for its production performance in terms of meeting production targets, improving defect performance and exceeding minimum 'time delivery schedules' (governing the percentage of parts delivered to the customer on time). In addition, each was expected to generate savings in labour costs through gradual manning reductions, improving absenteeism rates and improving machine downtime.

The management originally intended to recruit a team leader for each unit from the shop-floor workforce, seeking enterprising individuals who displayed a strong commitment to company objectives. This issue proved highly contentious. In Japanese factories, team leaders are pivotal figures in the system of worker control, enjoying a pervasive power and influence over other team members and a central role in the implementation of management policy (Fucini and Fucini, 1990; Kenney and Florida, 1993; Lowe, 1993). But what really distinguishes them from the traditional foremen is their class ambiguity; their fallacious claim to represent the joint interests of management and team members in the single 'company team'. When managerial power lies in the hands of the foreman it is an overt and contestable power; the shop steward and the worker might not always regard the white coat as legitimate, but at least they can see it. With team leaders, things are different. One shop steward commented:

> The general relationship between the operators and the foremen here is okay. I mean, yeah, they represent management but they're only doing their job aren't they? And at least we know how far we can go with them. But it's different with team leaders. How can we trust them? Take Tony in the Toyota cell [one of the old 'informal' team leaders]. Everybody's thinking, can we trust him or not? Can we talk to him or not? We're all thinking, is he with us? Is he with the bosses? Or where is he?

In the event, mounting opposition from the shop stewards and the foremen themselves forced the management to back down, temporarily at least. Instead of team leaders, each unit was supervised by a 'unit manager', acting as a 'mini-superintendent' and responsible for the maintenance and deployment of labour, machines and materials and accountable for output, defect levels and general team performance. In every case, the unit managers were selected from existing foremen.

Although the management attempted to sell teamworking to the shop-floor on the basis of positive attributes such as 'empowerment' and 'job enrichment', most workers soon discovered that this supposedly radical departure from the old ways of working merely contributed to an intensification of their drudgery. In the main assembly and press shops, 81 per cent of operators felt that teamworking either had no impact on, or even reduced, their already minimal interest in the job (second questionnaire survey, November 1995). And as Table 6.4 shows, over 60 per cent of operators believed they were working harder compared to the previous year, a significantly high number for such a limited time frame.

The shop-floor workers' assessment of different aspects of teamworking, collected during the second questionnaire survey (November 1995), is summarized in Table 6.5.

Table 6.4 *Shop-floor workers' assessment of work intensification (Percentage by row; N = 471)*

	Yes (%)	No (%)	Undecided (%)
Working harder compared to one year ago			
All operators	61	24	15
Skilled team operators	59	21	20
Semi-skilled team operators	63	23	14
Original team operators	56	32	12
Technicians & maintenance staff	62	21	17

Table 6.5 *Shop-floor workers' assessment of the impact of teamworking (Percentage by row; N = 471)*

	Agree (%)	Disagree (%)	Undecided (%)
'Teamworking has given me new job skills.'			
Skilled team operators	7	86	7
Semi-skilled team operators	17	60	23
Original team operators	34	47	19
Technicians & maintenance staff	19	57	24
'Teamworking has given me more tasks to do but no real skills.'			
Skilled team operators	82	7	11
Semi-skilled team operators	55	20	25
Original team operators	46	30	24
Technicians & maintenance staff	60	20	20
'I haven't got the time to take on new tasks and responsibilities.'			
Skilled team operators	83	0	17
Semi-skilled team operators	58	19	23
Original team operators	49	30	21
Technicians & maintenance staff	63	10	27
'Teamworking has made me more accountable for the work that I do.'			
Skilled team operators	36	39	25
Semi-skilled team operators	40	32	28
Original team operators	61	24	15
Technicians & maintenance staff	40	36	24

Table 6.5 *contd.*

(Percentage by row; N = 471)

	Agree (%)	Disagree (%)	Undecided (%)
'As a teamworker, I'm no longer a number, I'm now treated as a human being.'			
Skilled team operators	7	86	7
Semi-skilled team operators	13	62	25
Original team operators	25	54	21
Technicians & maintenance staff	11	71	18

Team production operators are designated semi-skilled team operators; press fitters and toolsetters are skilled team operators; the established Toyota, Opel and Honda team operators are original team operators; and team technicians and both maintenance and toolroom workers are designated technicians & maintenance staff.

The semi-skilled team operators were so accustomed to their low-skill, degrading, Tayloristic work environment that almost *any* change in work organization might be expected to enrich the job. Yet, the majority (55 per cent) of these operators in the new teams believed that teamworking generated low-skill task enlargement rather than multi-skilling, and only 17 per cent felt that teamworking conferred new skills. Furthermore, although most respondents had experienced teamworking for just a year, a good many felt the pressure of individual accountability already. This was particularly acute in the longer established Toyota, Opel and Honda team areas; and on other issues, the workers in these original teams – who were hand-picked for their positive attitudes towards their work – were moving towards the dominant view in the main shops. The more generalized indicators of initial shop-floor attitudes towards teamworking shown in Tables 6.1, 6.2 and 6.3 do not have the same precision as those provided in Table 6.5. Nevertheless, a comparison between the two sets of statistics suggests that these original teamworkers were becoming disenchanted. One shop steward in the Opel team complained:

> I thought teamworking was supposed to be about job rotation and managing your own work. You know, being your own boss. But teamworking on the Opel section is nothing like that. Okay, we swap from machine to machine but we've got no control over it. We're still controlled by the management. So that's why we're all getting confused. I'm not so sure that we're ever going to get teamworking here. It all sounds like a bit of a con to me.

Another operator in a newly established team remarked:

> As I see it, the management have brought in all these fancy new ideas but they're all the same really. Every one is about squeezing more work out of less men. You can forget all the pretty words, they're about making you work harder, it's as simple as that.
>
> The management here are not interested in real rotation or in making the job interesting. The only thing that turns them on is getting their parts on pallets. They control the job rotation here. You get put on a machine, you go flat out until your batch is done and then they stick you on another machine and you go flat out until that batch is done.

Indeed, management was by now transparent about the company's objective: teamworking amounted to an institutional means of permanently eradicating the traditional shop-floor controls over the utilization of labour. As the personnel manager stated, 'for the majority unskilled groups it's just a realization that they have to work where their unit manager tells them to work, that no machine belongs to them any more, that they have no birthright to certain jobs because of age, experience or whatever, that they take on new tasks such as a bit of simple machine maintenance and cleaning when requested, and that they need to develop a bit of loyalty and accountability to the team'.

The low-skill groups therefore experienced effort intensification through task accretion. The skilled groups experienced something qualitatively different: effort intensification through de-skilling. The new working practices agreement introduced a simplified shop-floor grading structure which established an expectation that workers should perform any task of which they were capable, from machine maintenance to machine operating to sweeping the floor. The team technicians and craft workers in the maintenance and toolroom areas were only partially affected by these changes because the plant's low capital investment record and lack of planned preventative maintenance ensured that their traditional skills were in constant demand to keep the machinery running. They tended to float from team to team, combating the more complex technical problems and machine breakdowns as they arose – not like a new breed of 'supercraftsmen' (Turnbull, 1986) but instead, combining their accustomed specialist mechanical or electrical work with additional rudimentary tasks in other craft disciplines. By contrast, in order to both reduce idle time and improve the flexibility of production, the toolsetters and press fitters allocated to the teams found themselves routinely assigned to machine operation and cleaning during the intervening periods between machine set-up. The result, as Table 6.5 indicates, was deep disillusion with teamworking. Over 80 per cent of this group indicated that their work had undergone both task accretion and de-skilling; and 86 per cent suggested resentment at the style of management of the change process.

This is most explicitly exemplified by the management's attempt to force the toolsetters to perform production work when 'the needs of the business' demanded it. And 'the needs of the business' ensured that over the years individual targets had gradually been ratcheted upwards, 300, 400, 500 pieces an hour, and with buffers and breathers simultaneously removed. Consequently, some of the older men found themselves suddenly confronting the punishing grind of eight hours' bell-to-bell operating work on a press machine. Many of them objected. A press shop superintendent described his method of resolving this:

> I had one fitter about a month ago who refused to operate a press when requested by his unit manager. So I said, 'Right, let's have him in this office and sort him out.' He told me that he had a health problem, that his knees swelled up if he stood up all day on the presses. I ask you, if he can crawl over the presses fitting tools then he can bloody well operate them can't he?
>
> So I said, 'Well, that's just tough isn't it. I want you on the presses.' But I agreed to get external medical advice so I sent him down to a doctor in the town. The next day he comes back with a doctor's note saying that he could operate a press but only for a maximum of two hours a day. Well, that was like a red rag to a bull for me. I told him we're not having that. So I got him examined internally this time, by the company doctor. He told me that he should be able to operate a press but not for the whole shift. Okay, I said, I'll accept that. So now we've got him working for seven hours out of the eight-hour shift. Sounds tough, but that's the way you've got to fight these boys.

Textbook teamworking, according to the business writers, confers significant new skills and autonomy on an empowered workforce as well as delivering efficient working methods to capital. It is also assumed to quintessentially embody the decline of class loyalties in industry, to reflect the supposedly joint interests of capital and labour in the new enterprise culture of 'post-industrial society'. The above analysis suggests a different picture. In the enduring environment of class conflict at the point of production on a traditional factory floor, teamworking, no matter how it is dressed up by its apologists, constitutes a straightforward and rational attempt by capital to exert greater, unfettered control over labour utilization, and through this, increases in both work effort and the rate of extraction of relative surplus value. Looked at in this way, it is no wonder that in the second questionnaire survey (November 1995), two-thirds of the shop-floor said that they were 'still treated as numbers rather than human beings', that 'the factory is worse than jail' as one worker typically commented. However, this process of heightened worker subordination does not end there. At CarPress, management-controlled teamworking provided the prime levers for labour flexibility and intensification; but a further development, management-controlled kaizen, ensured that the continual refinement of the change process would only be effected on capital's terms.

Kaizen

The new emphasis upon the rights of the consumer over the past two decades has had a significant impact on the British car industry. Many companies attempted to redress the historic Fordist imbalance between quantity and quality by building quality into the production process and ensuring that marketable products were efficiently manufactured and promptly delivered to the customer. And as Jurgens *et al.* have put it, 'a new customer-oriented quality policy was proclaimed. "Quality is number one!" became the new slogan; and an appeal was made to the workers: "Produce it as if you were buying it!"' (1993, p. 126). Despite the resistance of some trade unions, the pervasiveness of this consumer ideology resulted in incremental moves towards the integration of the indirect quality function into production; operators assumed certain responsibilities for maintaining quality, such as self-inspection. Moreover, a number of companies attempted to secure a more penetrative workforce commitment to quality, and indeed, wider corporate goals, by introducing – often with mixed results – 'Japanese-style' practices such as quality circles and briefing groups. Rover was one such company. During the late 1980s, as part of its 'Working With Pride' campaign, it introduced a package of measures aimed at greater employee involvement in process quality and related matters (Smith, 1988; Storey, 1992).

At CarPress, the workers' experiences of these developments under the previous Rover management and their lack of trust in the current regime had a major influence on their attitudes towards new quality programmes. Although Smith (1988) argues that Rover's zone (quality) circles eventually failed due to a combination of trade union opposition and worker apathy, the Oldport shop stewards recalled that they also collapsed under the weight of management indifference and incompetence. Few supervisors were trained in the arts of discussion management; few details of the principles of quality circles were ever communicated to the workforce; and few production managers felt obliged to turn their attention away from moving parts out of the factory gates.

Furthermore, the shop-floor believed that most Rover and CarPress managers had only a minimal appetite for offering them the trust that accompanies worker involvement in the management of production. In the past, some operators did attempt to mobilize their own experience in suggesting improvements to work organization, but they were invariably rebuffed. The result was a consistent cynicism amongst the workforce summed up by one press operator who complained that 'any suggestions we ever make to the company, for example, improving your work or improving your working environment, they just don't want to know. So we've given up. Nowadays, we just walk in the gate, clock in and leave our brains at the clocking station.' Essential factory-based class divisions and attending fears and conflicts over status and reputation partially accounted for this. As another press operator sardonically remarked:

> We're the ones with the experience. We know what the real problems are on the shop-floor and we have the answers. But the management won't listen to us, they never do. They don't even think that we should have the knowledge. You see, they're afraid of us, they just can't handle the idea of us having some input, some control. They know nothing. It's like barrow boys trying to run a supermarket ... And you know the shop-floor managers are just the same. They're afraid to ask us to sort out their problems because they know their own bosses will start to ask questions, start to ask why they hadn't sorted the problem out in the first place. These people will never come to us because they know that they'll end up getting their own arses kicked.

This comment raises a further point. It implies that rather than constructing a sense of identity and dignity by paradoxically giving up their own little 'parcels of knowledge' in the interests of the continuous improvement of management control (Garrahan and Stewart, 1992), if given the chance workers may instead attempt to maintain their dignity by challenging the legitimacy of such control. Partly in reaction to the alienation of Taylorization but also out of contempt for the perceived inaptitude of their managers – and a firm conviction they could do things much better themselves – many CarPress workers were prepared to become involved in continuous improvement (or kaizen) in the belief that it offers a route into self-management and greater shop-floor influence. Although many workers sought extra pay for this influence and would never countenance the idea of participation in kaizen groups in their own time, over half of those questioned in the first survey (October 1994) indicated their support for continuous improvement in principle. But not on management's terms. Worker after worker commented on the lack of congruence between the objectives of the management and the shop-floor, that 'teamworking will be introduced by *them* but it will not succeed until their ideas come into line with *ours*', that, as another pointed out, 'in past years we've pulled the company out of trouble by hard work when the management said the factory was going to close but we've got together and made the job work for us, it wasn't the managers it was the workforce, we did it on our own', and that, therefore, as another wrote, 'I would be in favour of having meetings to criticize management, or of meeting regularly to discuss ways of improving management.'

Of course, this was not management's idea of kaizen at all. Firstly, the shift in the balance between product quantity and quality was not so great as to counter to any extent the principle that most shop-floor workers are employed to perform productive labour for the direct creation of surplus value rather than walking off the line to participate in discussion groups. The pressures of lean production militated against the idea of full worker involvement in the kaizen process. The personnel manager explained:

> I must admit, a lot of the earlier ideas we were looking at were based on the idea that everybody would be encouraged to spend time off production on kaizen activity. But I'm afraid that's not reality is it? Life isn't like that. We still want involvement from the shop-floor, but our 100 per cent priority, and I stress 100 per cent, must be making parts. Therefore, the direction we're moving in now is that the team leaders, the unit managers, will be the problem-solvers and they will just involve team members in more of a consultative manner through more effective communications with the employees.

Secondly, just as the CarPress workers had no faith in the ability or intent of their managers to protect shop-floor interests, the management in turn had no real belief that their workforce might begin to act in support of the employer's interests. As one industrial engineer – who had a keen interest in this conflict – triumphantly observed:

Look, supposing kaizen awareness was high in a cell. And let's suppose you had a three-man team and suddenly one man says, 'Hold on a second boss, we could do that job with two men if we tried it this way.' That's how kaizen and improved efficiency is supposed to work isn't it? But I tell you, it will just never happen here! The attitude is, 'That's my job, I do that and nobody else touches it.' I've been working on continuous improvement for years, that's really what my job is about, and the operators have always viewed me as the 'big bad wolf'. You don't really imagine that they'll become the 'big bad wolf' themselves do you? They will never take on a labour-saving attitude. So they need some sort of control, it's as simple as that.

Consequently, although the new working practices agreement stipulated full employee involvement in kaizen activity, the idea was eschewed – in the short term at least – in favour of management-led kaizens. Following the practice of a good number of the Japanese transplants in the South Wales survey, and indeed, many other manufacturers in the UK (IDS, 1990b) along with Japanese transplants in North America (Fucini and Fucini, 1990; Milkman, 1991; Rinehart et al., 1994), production and engineering management took full control of the process of reorganizing and continually improving manufacturing practices, job assignments and cycle times in the quest to eliminate waste and idle time.

The business consultants have coined a new euphemism for this management-driven process – 'reengineering'. Essentially, teams of engineers accountable to the demands of senior managers select core processes for reorganization and set about performing value-added analysis to eliminate non-productive tasks and waste. And despite the claims of its proponents that reengineering enriches the labour process through the creation of new polyvalent skills and 'multidimensional work' (Hammer and Champy, 1995, p. 65), in fact, as Conti and Warner have observed, this approach to continuous improvement more often results in ' "downsizing" and cost reduction, combined with increasingly Taylorist job designs for operating the redesigned processes' (1994, p. 101).

The kaizen activity at CarPress eventually followed similar principles. The management prioritized key organizational problems and then directed cross-functional teams of engineers and production supervisors to 'brain-storm' their way towards cost-cutting solutions. In this way, top-down kaizen transferred any notions of 'ownership' from the worker to the controlling engineer. As the engineering director put it, 'our engineers do regard many of these cells as "their baby", they do regard themselves as owners'. So they did. And they also ensured that the ideologies of craftism and professional scientism combined to exclude their shop-floor subordinates from any aspect of the 'ownership' process. A robotics engineer:

> Kaizen is inbred into this department ... On the Opel line, for instance, we hold weekly meetings between engineering and maintenance to discuss things like kit performance and efficiency levels, looking at ways to push efficiency up, 60 per cent, 61 per cent, 62 per cent, and discussing improvements over the week and searching for new ideas. So this thing kaizen is not new to me. But to be honest it will always be unlikely that we'll suck the operators into the process. In my opinion, if you get these people around a table, okay they'll talk, but it won't get you anywhere, it would just be a forum for waffling. These things need to be controlled by experts who know what they're talking about.

The second questionnaire survey (November 1995) explored the impact of this approach on a group of experienced operators in the assembly shop. One section in the shop, employing around 40 operators and producing car doors for Rover, consistently fell below the plant's average efficiency levels. To resolve this, the management engaged the services of a leading industrial consultant, the Kaizen Institute of Europe. Working in conjunction with a team of CarPress engineers, which included the token involvement of just two carefully selected operators, members of the Institute executed a transformation of the old Rover production line. Different weld and assembly machines were reorganized into semi-circular cells; line-side store compounds were dismantled; non-value-added process steps were reduced; full flexibility enabled manning level reductions and increases in production targets; and operators were cajoled into performing continuous self-inspection routines to cut down waste and defect levels. The reorganization decreased the superfluous expenditure of quantities of objectified labour in the form of wasted materials and low machine utilization rates; it also maximized the consumption of labour power and the extraction of surplus value.

Table 6.6 summarizes the impact of these changes on the workers concerned. Whether considering questions of work effort, skill levels, worker accountability, worker involvement or relationships with management, the statistics indicate that these 'kaizened' operators suffered more subordination and degradation than their colleagues elsewhere on the shop-floor. Two-thirds of this group felt that they were working harder; three-quarters confirmed that teamworking merely increased the number

Table 6.6 *The impact of reorganization on operators in the kaizen area (Percentage by row; N = 471; kaizen operators = 35)*

	Yes (%)	No (%)	Undecided (%)
Working harder compared to one year ago			
All operators	61	24	15
Operators in kaizen area	64	18	18
'Enough time for inspecting and approving your own work?'			
All operators	14	73	13
Operators in kaizen area	3	92	6

	Agree (%)	Disagree (%)	Undecided (%)
'Teamworking has given me new job skills.'			
All operators	19	59	22
Operators in kaizen area	6	69	25
'Teamworking has given me more tasks to do but no real skills.'			
All operators	56	21	23
Operators in kaizen area	75	19	6
'Teamworking has made me more accountable for the work that I do.'			
All operators	43	32	25
Operators in kaizen area	50	28	22
'Management would take no notice of my suggestions to improve plant performance.'			
All operators	60	18	22
Operators in kaizen area	71	20	9
'As a teamworker, I'm no longer a number, I'm now treated as a human being.'			
All operators	14	64	22
Operators in kaizen area	3	84	13

of tasks to be completed rather than offering new skills; and virtually all respondents had insufficient time to complete extra tasks such as self-inspection. Ironically, in the context of the ethos of employee involvement associated with managerialist descriptions of kaizen, over 70 per cent of these operators also maintained that their managers would ignore worker suggestions to improve plant performance.

One protagonist in the kaizen movement has argued that its philosophy is a benign way of thinking and acting that constantly improves our quality of life, to the extent that, 'the moment we start talking about kaizen, the whole issue becomes breathtakingly simple. First of all, nobody can dispute the value of improvement, since it is generic and good in its own right. It is good by definition. Whenever and wherever improvements are made in business, these improvements are eventually going to lead to improvements in such areas as quality and productivity' (Imai, 1986, p. 9). The results shown in Table 6.6 expose this seductive doctrine as mere euphemistic managerial ideology designed to obscure the fact that 'improvements made in business' tend to be very much one-sided in nature. The 'kaizened' operators at CarPress ended up working harder, working more intensively, working without buffers and informal breaks, suffering multi-tasking rather than multi-skilling, suffering the stress of individual accountability rather than autonomy, suffering a rejection of their knowledge rather than its incorporation, and suffering virtual imprisonment in the new forms of work organization rather than liberation from the old.

From labour's standpoint, then, kaizen is not so much a 'benign corporate philosophy' encouraging the improvement of quality by all, but a straightforward management technique for furthering efficient capital accumulation by intensifying the rate of labour's exploitation. And looked at in conjunction with lean production control, bell-to-bell working and teamworking, this process of work organizational change at CarPress amounted to a cruel denial of the enriching and empowering ideologies propagated by employers and their agencies. The shop-floor experienced disempowerment rather than empowerment. Not just because, as Ramsay puts it, 'part of the attraction of job reform, as distinct from some other forms of participation, is that it is "soft on power", affording little or nothing in the way of concessions on business decision-making and carrying little danger of getting out of hand' (1985, p. 74), but also in a more detrimental sense. Over a period of five years, distinguished by a combination of incremental and occasional radical changes to the labour process, the workforce lost a number of its collective and individual controls over day-to-day working time, labour deployment and both effort and skill levels. The outcome was further worker subordination, more extensive managerial prerogatives and an inevitable intensification of the work process.

These developments in the organization of work, labour regulation and shop-floor power relations at this brownfield factory therefore bore certain similarities to the management practices and levels of managerial control identified within the Japanese manufacturing transplants in South Wales. The extent to which the changes were matched – and indeed facilitated – by shifts in CarPress's personnel and industrial relations policies is considered in the next two chapters.

Notes

1 'The Way Forward': Team Working and Continuous Improvement Policy Agreement, CarPress Ltd, 1994.
2 See for example Blyton and Bacon's (1997) description of the hierarchically structured, seniority-determined occupational culture at British Steel.
3 During the 1970s, the plant employed around 40 drivers and slingers per shift. By 1994, most shifts employed just four drivers.
4 'It's a Team Spirit that Makes Teams Work', *CarPress Group News*, Summer 1994.
5 Self-management was less advanced in the Opel teams where the complexity and cost of the automated technology necessitated a good degree of supervision from the maintenance and engineering functions.
6 The craft ideology is characterized by a more cooperative, fluid relationship between engineers and shop-floor workers. Smith suggests this is a reflection of a number of factors: the historical origins of engineering as a practical craft; the wage labour condition of engineers and their common bond with other workers and differentiation from management; and the apprenticeship method of training, which supports a definition of engineering as a holistic, integrated labour process, with cooperative manual and mental components that are not easily divorced.

The more Taylorian professional-scientific ideology reflects the integration of engineers into management and support for capitalism; the professionalization of engineers through indirect, university-based training systems; and the development of new technologies such as CAD which facilitate the Taylorian fracturing and compartmentalization of the holistic engineering labour process. (Smith, 1991, pp. 190–1)

7 THE NEW INDUSTRIAL RELATIONS

The foregoing analysis described how the installation of a lean production regime at CarPress represented an essentially disempowering and exploitative restructuring of factory work. What it did not consider, however, was the potentially double-edged nature of such restructuring. That is, the creation of new labour process conditions which significantly disadvantage workers through job displacement and labour intensification but also conditions which generate promising circumstances for the execution of industrial action against the employer.

In other words, in the context of the fragile, contingent nature of lean production arising from a heightened dependency on the shop-floor worker, the traditional weapons of collective labour organization, such as the strike, the work to rule and the overtime ban, can have immediate and damaging consequences for capital. Consequently, many writers argue that the dynamic of restructuring at work must also address the employment relationship to secure both a transformation of shop-floor attitudes and the curtailment of independent trade union activity. If, as Turnbull (1986) puts it, the managers of lean production 'require the positive application of discretion, initiative and above all *effort* on the part of the workforce if labour productivity is to be improved' (p. 196) and if through new management techniques such as teamworking, 'the production system itself is to be the principal work motivator rather than the payment system' (p. 199), then 'Japanizing' companies may seek to eradicate those aspects of traditional British labour organization which threaten both the production of goods and the production of worker commitment.

The preceding three chapters underplayed these problems by deliberately abstracting the process of work organizational change from its industrial relations context. Such an approach enabled a more focused analysis of the impact of change on the labour processes and work attitudes of different groups of CarPress employees. This chapter helps complete the picture by incorporating the politics of industrial relations into the enquiry. It addresses the different ways in which a 'spirit of opposition' on the shop-floor assumed concrete forms of both individual and collective resistance which itself prompted managerial suppression and an attempt to fashion a more accommodating variety of trade unionism.

The chapter also analyses this conflict in the context of the distinctive economic and political conditions of the 1990s. It considers how particular manifestations of these conditions have significantly constrained shop-floor resistance to the 'management of change'; in particular, the state's multifaceted anti-trade-union laws, enduring mass unemployment, and the new power relations which bind suppliers to their customers in contemporary manufacturing industry.

Managerial Incorporation and State Control: The Beginnings of a New Industrial Relations

When CarPress's Oldport plant formed part of BL and Rover, its management–labour relations were marked by a combination of low trust and guarded mutual respect. Although the factory was not especially militant in respect of its record of official strikes, the shop-floor unions still exerted considerable control. In the post-war British car industry, the growth of trade union power, and in particular local shop steward power, was based on buoyant employment levels and a high consumer demand for cars. Shop stewards and rank-and-file members were able to exploit this as they became accustomed to management's obsession with *avoiding* strikes (Marsden et al., 1985). Managers were forced to make concessions on questions of fair wages, parity and 'job property rights' in return for high output, the costs of which were passed on to the consumer. Accordingly, as one CarPress convenor commented, the real power of the unions lay in their ability to exploit their collective organizational strength by keeping the rank and file *in work* and maintaining control over their work by periodically executing the 'in-house strike', that is, the go-slow, the work to rule, the overtime ban or the brief sectional walkout.

In March 1989, the new owners of Rover, British Aerospace, sold the Oldport plant to CarPress. The old Rover management gave way to a qualitatively different regime; the new style was more assertive, more aggressive and more congruent with Fox's (1974) ideal type of unitarist management. The concept of bargaining and negotiating with trade unions was abandoned in favour of minimal consultation. The shop-floor responded in appropriate fashion with a series of short strikes and walkouts over job security, pensions rights and union recognition. Then, in February 1990, again with only minimal negotiation, the CarPress management introduced a new agreement which harmonized Oldport's basic wages and conditions with those operating at the company's other UK plants. This had the effect of reducing most basic rates and cutting back on redundancy terms, pensions payments, overtime premia and sick pay.

This distinctly 'macho' management therefore intensified the low-trust relations inherited from Rover. Attacks on union rights and working conditions generated increasing militancy. A war of attrition continued until September 1993, when CarPress recruited a new operations director and personnel manager whose single objective was to secure a radical overhaul of shop-floor working practices.

These two new men were guided by principles which embody the contradictions inherent in contemporary 'human resource management' theory. They regarded any challenge to their right to maintain control and order on the shop-floor as anathema, yet they were also keen to build a new ethos of shop-floor cooperation and participation with an emphasis upon joint interests between manager and worker. In other words, they envisaged an industrial relations of 'sophisticated unitarism' (Scott, 1994) aimed at inhibiting rather than suppressing any dissension. From this standpoint, the social relations inherited on the CarPress shop-floor appeared to be on the point of inducing insurrection. The personnel manager:

> When I first arrived here I couldn't believe it. I found worker militancy, the site came under total trade union control and the managers were continually walking on shells. As far as I was concerned, the site was completely out of control. My goal was to change the culture of the place and bring in the new working practices necessary for the site to survive.
>
> But I've got to admit at first I was quite taken aback. I didn't think the things that were going on in this place really happened any more, I thought I'd walked back into the 1970s. Virtually as soon as I stepped into my office I was faced with immediate unofficial industrial action, what we call 'throwing your teddies into the corner'. And I knew that my first job was to force the unions to behave legally.

Even if it were possible, the new management had no intention of dismantling the plant's existing machinery of collective bargaining;

instead, the objective was to ensure that the machinery worked in the company's interests. As we shall see, this represented a 'partial union exclusion policy' which aimed to maintain some form of plant union organization whilst seeking to consolidate a *de facto* redistribution of power to the employer (Smith and Morton, 1993, p. 108).

The managers were faced with an autonomous rank-and-file control, which, as Hyman has argued, provides the means for workers to more effectively resist the intensive exploitation of labour which develops from the 'rationalization' of management in modern capitalism. In these circumstances, formal bargaining and disputes procedures can deliver important advantages to capital by effectively disarming and demobilizing trade union members and imposing a 'peace obligation' which leaves management the prerogative of initiative (1975, p. 159). Resurrecting the 'peace obligation' required a number of managerial actions aimed at different levels of the union organization. Incorporating the senior stewards came first.

Traditionally, the senior stewards maintained a distant relationship with their full-time officials, a situation that reflected the delimited 'factory consciousness' shaping social action on the CarPress shop-floor. Working with a union bureaucracy sometimes means complying with constraining rules and regulations, complying with policies on trade union law for example, that undermine rank-and-file control. The new managers desired a shift in attitudes here. They became agents for building a new tripartite cooperation between the company, the senior stewards and their officials. Regional officers were drawn into a regular dialogue with senior management; meetings were organized between officers and stewards to enable discussions on matters such as national agreements and legal procedures for taking industrial action; senior stewards participated in management workshops; and as a result of such activity, the officers and stewards were drawn together towards management's agenda for securing the survival of the plant.

In this way, incorporation into management accompanied incorporation into the union bureaucracy; and for a senior steward, the act of making positive contributions towards company performance and responding favourably to the manager's viewpoint involves the reshaping of more than one social relationship. Unlike his predecessors, the CarPress personnel manager began meeting the stewards on a daily basis, sometimes for formal negotiating sessions but more often for informal discussions and 'friendly chats'. This subtle process of soliciting for union cooperation had the effect of usurping rank-and-file democracy and reversing the steward's line of accountability. CarPress sought a new style of shop steward: somebody who was prepared to act as a transmission belt for management policies and who had the determination to maintain control over the rank and file. In other words, a shop steward representing something akin to business unionism. The personnel manager summarized the effect of this:

> We inherited a group of senior stewards who used to be a law unto themselves. They spent too much time doing what the members wanted and they ended up becoming their members' mouthpieces. They failed to carry out their responsibility of member management. But over time, they've become more committed to the management's viewpoint.
>
> Previously, the stewards used to come up to meet me in this office and it would all end up in a slanging match with a lot of shouting and hot air. They used to get a lot of flack from us and we used to get a lot of flack from them. So there would be arguments all right and then they'd go back to their members parading their victories. But nowadays there's less argument up here and much more downstairs between the stewards and their members.

'Downstairs' on the shop-floor the senior stewards did not exactly warm to these changes. Despite a series of Conservative government measures aimed at weakening union membership densities during the 1980s and 1990s, virtually 100 per cent of the CarPress shop-floor belonged to a union.[1] These 600 members annually elected 17 TGWU and 13 AEEU shop stewards to the Joint Shop Steward's Committee (JSSC), a steward–member ratio of one to twenty.[2] The JSSC then elected four convenors or senior stewards. Since the Oldport plant opened in 1962, this local union hierarchy provided the lines of accountability and democratic rank-and-file control which so disturbed the new management's vision of a trouble-free industrial relations. The company's attempt to fracture it placed the four senior stewards in a difficult position. Their hearts remained close to the members but they realized they would have to make unpopular decisions if they were to stay within the law, stay within the management's agenda and fight for the survival of the plant. Three of them, Barry Edwards, Gethin Rees and Neil Rolfe, discussed this with the author:

Neil:

> The members have always viewed us with some suspicion, mind. That hasn't changed. But yeah, things have got worse. We're placed in a difficult situation. The members think that we're the bastards who sit up here, doing

> nothing, just sat on our arses. And they think we've all been bought off. So we can't do right can we? We're wankers whatever we do.

Gethin:

> That's right. And we're now having to police our members a lot more and keep them in check with respect to the law. Many of our members still want to walk out at the drop of a hat whenever there's a problem. But you can't do that anymore and we have to tell them. I know they don't like it but we have to tell them that we're putting ourselves at risk.

Barry:

> But don't forget there's been dramatic changes around here. For a kick off the plant capacity is down from a peak of 2,000 to 800 and that affects your strength. And the government's legislation has attacked us. But we still have to try and work within it. That's just the reality of it. We have to be careful to protect the union and to protect the members' jobs as well and make sure that the union organization survives.
>
> All three of us have got kids at school. And I for one would not like to see any of them employed in some of the cowboy outfits around Oldport where the conditions are terrible. CarPress is one of the few major employers left, and if it went down it would have a disastrous effect on the town.

Protecting jobs, protecting the union and working within the system. These responsibilities have always characterized the ambiguous position of Britain's senior shop stewards: they are dependent on management, they operate against the background of managerial power, and to keep their jobs manageable they have an inevitable interest in 'orderly' industrial relations (Hyman, 1975, p. 168). Nevertheless, in the current context of 'the Japanization of work', it is misleading for some authors to argue (for example, Bratton, 1992, p. 217) that determined managerial attempts to incorporate shop stewards represent no real threat to their authority or to their trade union organization; as if it were the mere existence of organization that mattered rather than its qualitative nature. The CarPress rank and file were all supportive union members, but many perceived their own unions as increasingly impotent in the face of the management's introduction of new working practices aimed at increasing the rate of exploitation. In the first questionnaire survey (October 1994), 59 per cent of the workforce indicated a belief that their unions were ineffective. Many commented on this during interviews and informal discussions. A toolmaker complained:

> The unions here just don't support us any more, especially the AEEU. All they're doing is looking after the company's interests. They sign agreements with the company without consulting the members at all.
>
> You see I thought everything was supposed to be negotiated, but nothing is these days. Now if the company wants changes to any of our agreements then they change it. All they do is give us ten days' notice and it's done. That's it. Full stop. The union just has no power.

And an assembly shop operator:

> The Tories have taken a lot of the rights away from your union. These days, before you can take any action the convenors we've got in the plant just put the fear of Christ into you before you take a vote. It's not their fault, they're forced into it. They have to tell us before we vote that under the law the company can sack you, the company can do this, that and the other to you. And of course it puts the fear of God into the youngsters.

Some advocates of 'a new industrial relations' attempt to fashion benign alternatives to such disillusion by presumptuously arguing that business unionism and innovations such as 'no strike deals' are becoming popular with trade union members and employers alike because they offer a measure of job security and the prospect of stable, consensual industrial relations (Bassett, 1987; Trevor, 1988). The problem here is that such arguments tend to ignore workers' accumulated experience of the stark, concrete nature of exploitation in capitalist mass-production. As Hyman comments, 'strikes are, quite simply, a challenge to the autonomy of managerial control. They are the means by which labour refuses to behave merely as a commodity (1972, p. 151). Accordingly, in the first CarPress questionnaire survey (October 1994), although 46 per cent of the small groups of specially recruited young teamworkers supported the idea of 'no-strike deals', only 12 per cent of all other shop-floor workers did so; 74 per cent opposed the idea. During discussions on these issues, different shop-floor workers articulated strong convictions that particular manifestations of this 'business unionism' represent a transparent threat to customary collective safeguards against the commoditization of labour. As one worker typically put it, 'it all means that you jump on your shovel, you do what they tell you to do, and you lose your liberty'.

Nevertheless, the point was also consistently made that the whole debate is becoming academic: in the workers' own experience, the state had effectively provided British capital with a nationwide 'no-strike deal' through the cumulative obligations contained in the last Conservative government's employment and trade union reform law (most of which will remain in place under Tony Blair's Labour government).[3]

Of course, some writers would reject such a notion. For example, drawing primarily on different sets of quantitative data, both Edwards (1992) and Marsh (1992) suggest that the impact of the legislation could be limited compared to determinants such as the business cycle, the political climate and changes in the occupational structure. Conversely, Brown and Wadhwani (1990) maintain that, although the laws governing strike ballots force union leaderships to act more judiciously than hitherto, the widely perceived legitimacy of a positive result often strengthens the hand of organized labour. However, such arguments only consider part of the picture; in particular, their reliance on quantitative analysis obscures the qualitative impact of the changes.

Firstly, they overlook the implications for workers of the highly restrictive definition of what constitutes a legal trade dispute in the 1990s. Secondary action, solidarity action, political action and crucially, in the context of worker attempts to maintain customary local controls over their work, unofficial action, are all outlawed.[4] Moreover, the sheer complexity of balloting regulations is increasingly making the strike weapon both prohibitive in terms of costs and an impractical means of resolving the many problems that demand immediate action (Labour Research, 1993a; 1993b). Secondly, as Nichols argues, just because the laws are not used regularly – in the sense of daily appearances of trade unionists before the courts – does not mean that their impact is slight. Injunctions against some of Britain's most powerful unions and the sequestration of funds might be rare events, but when they do occur they make a 'public clatter', so much so, that just the threat of using the law can have a critical psychological effect on organized labour (1990, p. 45).

These factors inform us of the need to take into account the impact of the anti-union legislation on social action on the shop-floor. In the case of CarPress, it denied workers access to resources of collective power (Smith and Morton, 1993, p. 100) and it also engendered feelings of impotence and defeatism, to the extent that many workers believed the intervention of the state had provided management with a decisive set of controls over formal collective resistance. The following remarks were repeated consistently throughout the factory. A press shop operator:

> I support the unions and I always will do but these days their powers are non-existent. These days we're all governed by the law, aren't we? Everything

must go through procedure, and even when we've managed that we can't win, the stewards just bring in the full-time officials and they never do anything. All these laws, they're all on the company's side.

An assembly shop operator:

I believe every individual should have the right to strike. It's a basic right. But nowadays strikes seem to be a thing of the past. Not because they are wrong but because there are so many procedures you have to go through before you're allowed to go out. I mean with these government laws the management just can't be touched, everything seems to be in management's favour. If you put a foot wrong they can seize all your union's assets. It just seems like taking action now is virtually impossible.

Defeatism in some quarters converted into a caustic, trenchant anger in others, an anger which would soon spill over into more 'unofficial' forms of opposition. One worker complained that, 'The management in this plant are nothing but industrial thugs. They've got the law on their side and they use it to the full.' A woman in the assembly shop was more discriminating: 'We've got no union any more, what with the stewards being bought off and with all Thatcher's laws. There just doesn't seem to be anything we can do about it, we've got nothing left. What we've got here is not Victorian times, it's bloody Thatcher times. All the management are just Thatcher clones.'

Shortly after his arrival, the CarPress board of directors considered a proposal from the new personnel manager for a pendulum arbitration-type 'no-strike deal'. In a mirror image of shop-floor sentiments, the board rejected it, believing that the combination of strong management and supportive employment legislation is more likely to provide the prized 'stable industrial relations' than a pendulum that can swing both ways. However, by themselves, these conditions do not completely suppress resistance, they only reshape it into alternative forms. The CarPress management soon realized that fostering a more pro-company, law-abiding attitude amongst the senior stewards would be ineffectual without also addressing the plant's historical legacy of rank-and-file control on the shop-floor. The senior stewards represented the members during the formal collective bargaining process, but the members and their local stewards exerted their own controls on the production line. It is in relation to this more informal wielding of collective power that many CarPress workers were keen to stress that, 'We are the union – not the officials or the stewards – the shop-floor is the union.'

The new operations director provided his own commentary on this tradition by spelling out his preference for an alternative trade unionism that would function more in the company's interests:

> In my view, there's nothing wrong with unions, what's wrong is the people who join them. The officials and the senior stewards work well with the company and are on our wavelength. But the normal stewards strut around as if they own the place. They're power mad.
>
> But I don't think there's a need to introduce Japanese industrial relations here. Let's face it, we are where we are – we're not a greenfield site. Ideally, I'd like to have one union and one bloke to speak to. But the problem is not the union, it's the individual members. They think it's a malingerer's charter. In saying that, people do need some organization to represent them. Many do feel insecure. Indeed, I'd rather have a decent union here than no union at all. Because you have to remember that when people sign an agreement here they're generally loyal and they'll stick to it. The agreements just need managing properly, that's what's been missing in the past.

In the winter of 1993, the company inserted into the annual wage-bargaining process the package of new working practices. The management was confident of dissipating senior shop steward resistance to these innovations through careful, assiduous negotiating, but it recognized that it faced a serious oppositional challenge from the rank and file, chiefly from the more experienced workers. Chapter 6 described the processes by which the general resistance to teamworking was partially eroded by the astute introduction of work organizational changes on a piecemeal, sectional basis. However, a change in shop-floor attitudes of a more substantial nature was needed to secure compliance with the new production regime. Drawing on the plant's historical traditions of low-trust relations and conveniently leaving aside its pretensions to 'sophisticated unitarism', the management opted to induce this change through a mobilization of fear, and in particular, by publicly punishing a number of individual scapegoats for the shop-floor's 'spirit of opposition'.

Trust, Treachery and Class Struggle at the Point of Production

First and foremost of these scapegoats was an assembly shop senior steward named Ieuan Thomas. Ieuan had been a TGWU representative in the plant for 23 years, culminating in eight years as a convenor. He came to union activism out of an intense concern for the health and safety of his workmates. In the 1960s and 1970s, compensation for industrial injury in manufacturing tended to be restricted to the more tangible and immediate impairments; slow-developing injuries, such as those associated with continual limb movement or work on constantly vibrating machinery, often went unreported. Ieuan became increasingly disturbed about the rising incidence of recurrent debilitating limb conditions amongst his colleagues, conditions such as vibration white finger and repetitive strain injury, and he resented the cynical way in which his shop-floor managers turned a blind eye to this. He became a health and safety representative, immersed himself in the fine print of the laws and regulations governing industrial injury and compensation, and then commenced filing claims on behalf of his members. Over the years he achieved many notable successes through a combination of scrupulous research and personal representation at meetings with management and union lawyers and with doctors at medical appeal tribunals.

This was the original basis of Ieuan's union activism, a resolute attachment and sense of duty to his members and his class, a relationship that was sustained during his later role as a shop convenor. It provides the quintessence of something that Beynon (1984) refers to as a dialectical social process involving the construction of strong mutual bonds of respect and understanding between the steward and the member. He attracted none of the cynicism recently encountered by other senior stewards in the plant, indeed, many members revered him, variously describing him as, 'a clever man, just too clever for this management, but also too good for them', 'a man you could depend upon, he would always look after your interests', and, 'a real shop steward, someone who stuck up for all the members in the plant, not just his own'.

In the context of the company's attempts to insert a divide between the senior stewards and the more militant rank and file – by incorporating the former – Ieuan Thomas presented a problem for management. He was able to mobilize principled and authentic legitimizing arguments in the negotiating process which consistently opposed company interests. This was not the new 'business unionism'. Management's idea of a virtuous union activist is now any individual who is prepared to break the link of accountability between the member and the representative. In contrast, Ieuan's motives, interests and personal vocabulary fully corresponded with the rank and file's; he perfectly encapsulated the model shop steward, an individual who is able to act in spontaneous rapport with his constituents (Armstrong *et al.*, 1981, p. 36). This conflict of interests came to a head during negotiations over the new working practices.

As we saw in Chapters 5 and 6, a number of elements in the company's proposals were antithetical to shop-floor interests. As well as further eroding conditions of employment such as sick pay and holiday pay, the company proposed to substitute continuous bell-to-bell working for payment by results, it proposed to introduce management-led kaizens to continually improve rates of labour exploitation and it sought a deepening and widening of the labour flexibility process, primarily through teamworking. As the latter practice represented the most significant change, the management spent all of 1993 pursuing the consent of the senior stewards through informal discussions and joint management–union workshops on the subject. This strategy proved effective for some but it had little impact on Ieuan Thomas. He understood that teamworking amounted to little more than the redistribution of additional tasks amongst fewer workers. This knowledge erupted into angry confrontation during a negotiating session in December 1993:

> I remember facing up to the managing director, head on, nose to nose. I tell you, a cigarette paper couldn't have separated us. There was this real heat being generated between us. And I remember saying to him, 'I'm telling you straight, teamworking is not coming to this plant if it hurts my members. I'm not selling my members' jobs.' And that's how it ended. The MD just stood up, smiled, held out his hand, shook mine and said, 'It's been a pleasure doing business with you Ieuan.' The next thing I knew I was given an ultimatum – stand down or be sacked.

The following day, an indignant shop-floor held a mass meeting and voted overwhelmingly for strike action. But this threat was soon incapacitated in the face of authentic management warnings of widespread dismissals, the lack of support from some other senior stewards, and crucially, Ieuan's personal reluctance to place his members' jobs in jeopardy. He therefore decided to stand down from office. Despite this, many of his sympathizers in the assembly shop maintained an unofficial overtime ban for three months.

Six months later, in the early summer of 1994, after a long period of intensive negotiations, the senior stewards felt confident enough to recommend a draft working practices agreement to the membership. However, both TGWU and AEEU members rejected it by four to one and attempted, section by section, to implement a plant-wide, unofficial overtime ban. The new management was incensed at this explicit rejection of its authority, but it also realized that without the support of the senior stewards and the union bureaucracy the fragmentary, disorganized nature of the shop-floor's resistance rendered them easy meat. The operations director belligerently explained:

> They didn't have the brains to come out and have a go at the company en masse. If they'd done that we wouldn't have known what to do. But instead they came to us in groups. The maintenance group came to us saying they were refusing to work to the new contract and threatening to implement their overtime ban. So we immediately turned around and gave them a 15-minute warning to withdraw the threat or they'd be sacked. Of course they all capitulated.
>
> Then what happens? The toolroom workers came in, they came out with the same threats and so we gave them the same 15-minute warning and they capitulated. Consequently, the operators were left by themselves and they had to give up because their strategy was to leave it to the skilled groups to come out and halt the whole of production. But I'm afraid the skilled groups were stupid enough to raise themselves above the parapet and they got their heads shot off.

The company then turned the screw decisively. The group's managing director spent a week at the plant 'counselling' small groups of workers and urging them to abandon their resistance; representatives of Rover threatened the shop-floor with the withdrawal of work and immediate redundancies; and finally, with the connivance of some regional union officials, the plant management sent to the home of every employee a written ultimatum to sign the new labour contract or face instant dismissal. The workforce had no choice but to submit. The agreement was signed in August 1994.

The company's problems did not end there, however. Signatures placed on contracts under duress do not denote support for their contents. Workers in many areas of the plant remained bitterly resentful at the management's dictatorial stance. This manifested itself in a variety of different forms of informal resistance: some sections maintained discrete 'go-slows' and 'work to rules'; individuals might refuse to work overtime on the basis of sudden personal or medical problems; machines would develop mysterious disabling faults; quality defects would go unreported; and so on. The management created a cycle of discontent by responding in kind with frequent threats of dismissal and the repeated use of the disciplinary procedure.

In consequence, manufacturing performance deteriorated. As we noted in Chapter 5, the plant used a 'break even' gross efficiency benchmark figure of 133 per cent as a basic performance target. By October 1994, this figure had fallen to 128 per cent for the first time in many years. CarPress decided to act swiftly to reverse this decline.

CarPress had expropriated Ieuan Thomas's union position, yet he retained a significant influence. In his own assembly shop, many members still came to him for advice and to discuss ways of combating management's actions. He remained a kind of 'champion of the rank and file', if no longer an elected one. As well as causing continuing displeasure in management circles, Ieuan's sway and popularity on the shop-floor generated resentment amongst some senior stewards. For example, during an official union enquiry into the circumstances surrounding Ieuan's removal from office, two of these stewards complained that his continuing participation in union affairs was resulting in their being 'hounded by the membership to secure concessions which were almost impossible'. This rank-and-file pressure clearly caused problems for management, yet its severance from the union hierarchy, something the management had assiduously cultivated, also provided propitious conditions for the isolation and destruction of its protagonists.

The problem of overtime provided the flashpoint to precipitate this. Beynon (1984) observed that on the assembly lines of the 1960s and 1970s, the allocation of overtime became an important aspect of the conflict of control between the shop steward and the supervisor. Put crudely, workers in general needed their extra hours for extra money to help control domestic debts; foremen also needed extra production hours but they liked to exercise control over who worked it. In many plants, this contradiction was subsequently managed through informal agreement and evolving custom and practice. However, the same conflict of control has again become acute in the 1990s. Whilst the contemporary mass culture of credit card consumerism intensifies worker debt and the general demand for overtime, the simultaneous trend towards a more immediate factory production for consumer demand places a higher premium on managerial control over the allocation of working time.

Prior to the new agreement, overtime on the CarPress shop-floor was distributed on a rota system managed by the shop stewards. In normal circumstances, no production operator could be offered more than 'two shots' of extra working during any one week, thus ensuring general equity and protecting individuals from overwork. Management disliked this system for three reasons. Firstly, it interfered with managerial prerogatives; secondly, it prevented foremen from choosing their favoured, most productive workers; and thirdly, it frustrated the new principle of working extra time – just in time – for immediate market requirements.

Accordingly, the new working practices agreement placed overtime allocation firmly back into management's hands. And as a result of this, extra working hours became the exclusive property of both the 'blue-eyed boys' and other more reluctant workers who, against their will, were routinely requested at short notice to work on at the end of their shift.

During the last week of October 1994, the rank and file tried to put a stop to this development by implementing another unofficial overtime ban. By midweek, the management responded in turn by asking all individuals on the shop-floor to indicate in writing whether or not they were prepared to comply with their new contract of employment. In the resulting indecision and confusion, a group of 105 assembly shop operators decided to hold an impromptu shop meeting. There was nothing unusual in this. Historically, whenever the shop had a specific problem, the operators would meet together to openly discuss it. In some circumstances the company might sanction either a paid or unpaid meeting in advance but far more common was the unofficial, spontaneous assembly where the members would finish their business in a matter of minutes and then send their senior steward to gain retrospective managerial authorization for an unpaid meeting. By giving their tacit consent to this tradition, the shop-floor managers became assimilated into it, to the extent that they could read the minds of their operators, they always knew when a meeting was likely to be called. Things were no different on this occasion, they fully expected the operators to gather together. What was abnormal this time, however, was that the management was rather pleased to see it happen.

An amendment to the Trade Union and Labour Relations Act introduced in 1992 established that an employer wishing to dismiss an employee who is taking part in unofficial industrial action no longer has to be concerned about selective dismissals or re-engagements.[5] As Income Data Services have confirmed, 'he can select those employees he considers to be organizers of the strike or general trouble makers in order to get rid of them. Furthermore, there is nothing in the Act to prevent him from deliberately provoking unofficial industrial action in order to bring these dismissals about.' The same amendment also prevents unions from defending members dismissed in this way by removing immunity from proceedings in tort in respect of industrial action.[6]

These changes became ingrained in the minds of certain CarPress senior managers, particularly so since they also came to realize that, under the terms of the law, the shop-floor's tradition of holding short informal meetings was a form of unofficial industrial action. The time had arrived to translate this knowledge into action.

Two minutes after the CarPress assembly shop operators assembled together, the head of production suddenly arrived on the scene and demanded that they go back to their machines. As they began doing so he bellowed out instructions for all 105 operators to go home under suspension. Over the following three days they were each called for interrogation before a disciplinary hearing in a local hotel. As a result of this 'kangaroo court' – as many workers described it – the management decided that the decision of some workers to exercise their traditional right of collective discussion for just two minutes constituted both unofficial industrial action and 'gross misconduct'. Forty-seven workers, mainly shop stewards, rank-and-file dissidents, women and disabled workers were dismissed; the remaining 58 were handed final warnings.

The workforce was stunned. Not surprisingly, Ieuan Thomas was one of the dismissed. A week later he told the author:

> This was a management set up – it was an entrapment. I hate to use the word but I was watching a programme on the telly last night about prostitution, and the word entrapment kept being used, it hit me in the face, that's what happened with us. It was like policemen catching prostitutes by asking favours, asking for sex. The management knew the concerns of the plant, they knew our traditions and they knew people would respond with a meeting. It was all over in two minutes. The management set us up, they pounced and sent us home in disarray.

The personnel manager was interviewed during the same week. In normal circumstances, these managers of factory politics tend to act as 'dealers in ideology' (Nichols and Beynon, 1977), seeking to obscure the harsh fact of capitalist exploitation by coaxing their listeners into believing that life in a factory is essentially harmonious and trouble-free. But on this occasion the factory had reached a state of crisis; nerves were on edge, adrenalin was flowing and the mask dropped:

I know you outsiders think that these disputes happen by accident, that they're all the result of individuals making unfortunate mistakes. But you're wrong I'm afraid. They're often planned. We plan these battles and so do the other side. I tell you, some of the operators down there are anarchists, they believe that they are the ones to control the shop-floor. We were determined to take these groups out. I don't like talking about industrial relations as if it's a war, but this *is* a war as far as we are concerned. And this was the big one, this was the big battle, it was the final Alamein for both sides. And we had to win.

This wasn't any accident. It was planned strategy, we were planning it and so were the anarchists. This factory is not a mini police state, but it was absolutely essential that we got rid of the militants, the obstructionists. You cannot implement change, you can't have progress with these people around.

We knew they'd go off on an unofficial dispute, and of course we knew that their union officials couldn't support them on this any more. And they're fools. If it were an official dispute we could still have sacked them but we would have been forced by law to sack the lot of them. And maybe we would have done. But the laws on unofficial action allow you to select who you want back and who you want to dismiss. And we don't have to say why! They're all fools, and they walked right into it. But I'll tell you something. It's concentrated minds down there all right. We've got the bastards working at last!

The 47 dismissals were subject to a final appeal procedure. The company appeared to prejudge this by immediately employing 60 young temporary workers, who, after a two-week period of intense coaxing and heavy-handed supervision, were proclaimed in Stakhanovite fashion as paragons of effort and high productivity. Needless to say, all 60 were shunned as 'scab labour' by the rest of the workforce. During this period, 21 appeals failed. CarPress reluctantly re-employed 26 workers in order to dissipate the potential for strike action and, since a good proportion of these were women, to avoid tribunal applications for sex discrimination. However, it made sure that the remaining 21 were useful scapegoats. Ieuan Thomas headed these. They also included four shop stewards and some of the more vocal dissidents amongst the rank and file. Others were workers with an absenteeism record due to intermittent disabilities sustained by the continuous operation of heavy metal-finishing machinery for most of their working lives.[7]

As little as ten years ago, such an attack on the shop-floor's moral order would have been countered by immediate strike action. But this is not 1984, it is 1994. If you are a trade unionist attempting to defend yourself, 'Big Brother' really is watching you. Two days after the initial sackings, a meeting of the plant's TGWU membership voted overwhelmingly for an all-out strike if any one of the appeals failed. But the intimate collectivism of the mass meeting is qualitatively different to the loneliness of the secret ballot. The essential logic of current strike balloting law is to debilitate the collective power of the mass and extinguish the immediacy of workers' anger. It removes men and women from the collective security of the mass meeting and places them, after a suitable cooling-off period, into individualistic insecurity, into the domestic environment of the debt-ridden consumer.

The cumulative practical ramifications of the legislation ensured that the CarPress rank and file would not get their legally sanctioned, heavily scrutinized, individualized vote for nearly three months. Firstly, the legal imposition of postal ballots in 1993 placed decisive time-consuming state and employer controls over union organization and strategy.[8] Secondly, support from the regional union bureaucracy was, in any case, lukewarm. The TGWU officials were well aware that the union faced possible fines and the sequestration of funds since the law no longer gave immunity against organizations supporting workers who are dismissed for taking unofficial action. Moreover, the AEEU Executive Committee decided that since none of its 200 members were sacked they could not offer any traditional solidarity action.

During the second week of December 1994, the plant's 421 TGWU members had their first secret ballot. In keeping with contemporary management's perverse notions of what counts as legitimate workplace democracy, the membership was bombarded with continual warnings of the likely loss of contracts and jobs in the event of a strike. Immediately before the vote, each member received a personal letter from the CarPress chairman threatening the loss of Rover contracts and instant dismissals if any strike went ahead. And it was Christmas. Ieuan Thomas was pessimistic:

> These laws are so clever. You'll have the members receiving their ballot forms at home, they'll have their wives and husbands looking over their shoulders, they'll have their kids bawling for Christmas presents and they've got their mortgages. And worst of all they've got fear.

Despite these intense pressures, a small majority of members voted to strike. But it counted for nothing. The state-approved scrutineers discovered that some ballot forms had been despatched to a number of retired members. The result was nullified. In a rearranged ballot in mid-January, a full three months after the sackings, a dispirited CarPress TGWU membership produced a tied stalemate; 83, by this time apathetic, members did not even bother to vote. Amidst anger, despair and resentment at what many activists perceived as growing evidence of collusion between union officers and management, a relieved union bureaucracy announced that the dispute was over.

Structural Impediments to Collective Resistance

We have seen how the capitalist state can profoundly influence the processes by which employers seek advantageous shifts in the nature of contemporary employment relations. Most conspicuously, the sheer weight of state legislation has created an ideological power sufficient to decisively reduce worker self-confidence whilst its particular concrete interventions may seriously undermine rank-and-file attempts to maintain a sense of moral order on the shop-floor.

However, this is not a solitary influence; anti-trade union legislation can be debilitating because it is exploited within distinctive contemporary political and economic conditions which are advantageous to capital in so many ways. These same conditions also provide the framework for an interplay of important additional factors which together may further influence the outcomes of class conflict in capital's favour. At CarPress, the most significant of these were management's manipulation of the perpetual fear of unemployment in South Wales; the political ramifications of the new customer–supplier relations; and both the political isolation of, and divisions within, the shop-floor rank and file. Starting with the latter, these factors will now be briefly considered.

Isolation and Division

Virtually since the CarPress plant opened in 1962, the shop-floor's ideology of resistance derived exclusively from the practical experience of local class conflict, local struggles over work rates, seniority, discipline, and so on. It represented a classic example of Beynon's (1984) 'factory-class consciousness', bolstered by expanding product markets and the self-assurance that comes with job security. Autonomous shop stewards ruled the roost, they felt no need to build relationships with the union bureaucracy, with external political organization, or even with shop stewards in other plants.

This sense of separateness was given a further twist by its Welshness. For example, during one interview, Ieuan Thomas reminisced about the activities of senior stewards on the old BL/Rover combine committees in the 1970s and 1980s and how the Oldport stewards would sometimes communicate privately with each other in the Welsh language to prevent their English colleagues from eavesdropping on their independent strategic discussions; when the members donated money to the miners during the 1984 strike many were essentially supporting Welsh miners; and when the new CarPress managers arrived in 1989, they were not regarded as typical agents of control but as something more alien, as 'English barrow boys', as people who, as another operator put it, 'being English have no regard for the Welsh and its culture'. These Welsh identities were therefore built on a strong sense of difference as well as pride. As one woman commented when asked about teamworking: 'all that is putting worker against worker. The bosses don't understand that we're not like that in Wales. We're real workers, we're Welsh workers and we stand up for ourselves!'

In consequence, when its rights at work and union organization came under management attack in the more competitive and insecure market conditions of the 1990s, the Oldport workforce found itself isolated; it had no established means of securing solidarity support in any decisive form from outside the factory gates. Crucially, the Joint Shop Stewards Committee failed to build constructive links with stewards at other CarPress plants in England. Moreover, its customary rejection of close relations with the union officialdom in South Wales and beyond was only eventually reversed on management's terms, yet as Spencer (1989) argues, contemporary political and economic conditions dictate that shop-floor organization will not successfully engage in struggle without the support of official union structures, despite the political constraints involved. The corollary of this was that solidarity support was restricted to the well-meaning petitions and speeches of local Labour MPs, local-authority dignitaries, trades councils and church leaders. But as the miners discovered in 1991, an outbreak of public moral indignation is no substitute for action.[9]

Taking these wider political consequences into account, it can be seen that this factory-class consciousness weakened the shop-floor's ability to maintain effective collective resistance. And the latter was further undermined by the existence of intra-factory divisions. The two work-force attitude surveys (October 1994 and November 1995) detected attitudinal differences between older and younger workers and, particularly, between workers with different lengths of service, on issues associated with seniority, teamworking and industrial relations. Less-experienced workers tended to be less oppositional; and although their attitudes rarely completely contradicted those of the more experienced workforce, a relatively higher number of 'undecided' respondents amongst this group reflected a greater degree of apathy and passivity towards change. The view of a young Honda teamworker was both typical and instructive here:

> I think there's one big difference between younger people like myself and the older workers at CarPress. The older men are all too set in their ways. They've been used to coming here for three basic reasons: marriage, kids and mortgages. They've been used to nothing else, nothing's ever changed in their lives for twenty years or more. But me, I'm young, I'm not interested in that crap, I'm interested in other things, you know? The three things I'm interested in are cars, beer and women. That's all. So to tell you the truth, I don't worry about changes at work here, it really doesn't bother me. I'll do anything to get the money into my hands. The only thing that bothers me is that I'm able to spend it to have a bit of fun before it's too late!

Such values reflect the relative lack of class awareness amongst young people in the 1990s which in turn is a function both of contemporary adolescent youth cultures and the growth of youth unemployment (Bradley, 1996). Of course, these values also create a new set of headaches for managers; but their immediate problem, in the brownfield context of the management of change, is to separate the 'experienced obstructionists' from the 'inexperienced submissives'. The CarPress toolrooom manager commented:

> Of course it's easy for them [the Japanese] with their teamworking on greenfield sites, they're working with new, young, green people who will do what they're told to do. But in the older factories people will feel part of the old workers' culture with all the demarcations that go with it. And I don't believe it's a case of bad individuals necessarily, it's really the case of the type of factory that these individuals walk into which then changes them.

The management therefore purposively created age- and experience-based shop-floor divisions by concentrating recruitment on young people, whether on a permanent or temporary basis, separating these workers off into discrete teams and then nurturing pro-company, pro-customer attitudes by, as one quality manager put it, 'coaxing them all the time, bringing them along, keeping our eye on them, making sure they are looking at the customer's needs'.

The historically fragmentary nature of autonomous shop steward control contributed to further divisions. Craft and seniority demarcations, the disparities of piecework and the different personal qualities and political positions of the stewards, together impart different degrees of local control over work. At CarPress and elsewhere in the auto industry it created a situation where 'work groups were thus competing against each other to maintain their pay positions as well as against managerial control, so that their aspirations were sectional and fragmentary' (Marsden *et al.*, 1985, p. 145). For example, the divide between the CarPress assembly and press shops was not merely technological or spatial. The press shop workers tended to display a more macho image and looked down on their assembly shop colleagues, 'the press shop employs real men, we're handling 800 tons of steel a week', one operator typically explained. Increasing labour mobility was beginning to undermine this divide, but even so, the two groups rarely communicated with each other. This even extended to union organization. Although both groups of operators were TGWU members, for historical reasons they insisted on maintaining two separate union branches. One senior steward commented that, 'sometimes it's like a "Berlin Wall" between the two branches'. Political divisions such as this continually hindered the attempts of the more progressive shop stewards to mount effective plant-wide campaigns.

Management by Fear

Shop-floor isolationism and division therefore frustrated the construction of a disciplined, broad collective resistance necessary to oppose managerial prerogatives and particular acts of management aggression. But the attendant discord and defeatism were also a consequence of an environment of fear. CarPress exploited two particular aspects of this: a fear of the dole and a fear of the customer.

Chapter 4 began with an account of the restructuring of employment opportunities in Oldport. The town had suffered consistently high levels of unemployment for nearly two decades. The fear of job loss, particularly among CarPress's young workers, was acute. Hardly an interview or more informal conversation went by without the subject being raised in one form or another, particularly in relation to managerial attitudes. A toolmaker characteristically remarked:

> Yeah, unemployment's had a real impact here. As far as we see things the days of full employment are going fast. A lot of the youngsters in Oldport have never had a job at all. We've been lucky here, mind, but we're fighting to keep ours now. And really all these changes and practices that have been forced upon us all boil down to that. They all boil down to the threat of unemployment. That's how the company has got away with it.

CarPress exploited local labour market conditions in a number of ways in its attempt to secure a compliant workforce. Firstly, although for some the fear of unemployment may remain abstract for as long as the jobless remain outside the factory gates (Fevre, 1989), attitudes change if the gates are opened. Following the example of a number of Japanese transplants in the region by increasingly utilizing young temporary workers, CarPress harnessed the fears and hopes of Oldport's 'experienced' young unemployed whilst simultaneously undermining the security of its permanent workforce in the pursuance of higher labour productivity. Secondly, the proposition that any workers displaying the temerity to oppose managerial prerogatives would be likely to join the ranks of the unemployed became part of the natural vocabulary of the shop-floor supervisors. In some respects, this was little different to the employers' use of Roy's (1980) 'fear stuff' tactics to prevent organized labour opposition in the American South, twenty years ago. As one woman in the assembly shop said, their habitual retort that 'you either work the way I tell you or it's down the road for you – there's another 500 where you came from' tends to sap shop-floor self-assurance when repeated often enough, especially inside factories that are continually fighting for survival. Thirdly, this is particularly so when management has sufficient confidence to prosecute the threat. As another worker commented on his questionnaire (November 1995):

> Since the termination of employment of 21 individuals the company has ruled by fear and is inflicting a dog-eat-dog atmosphere on the shop-floor. All attempts to make the operator feel more a part of the company are an affront to our intelligence. You are a clock number full stop. When they shout 'shit!' you jump on the shovel.

Product markets also connect with managerial control strategies in ways which restrain worker resistance. Since CarPress's Oldport plant opened in 1962 its organizational ethos was built around the belief that 'quantity is king'; success was measured in terms of consistent fulfilment of a weekly quota of parts to Rover's main car assembly plants. Intense global competition, contractualization and a more accurate synchronization of product supply with demand undermined this ethos and placed a new onus on the 'needs of the customer'. The impact of these changes on work organization and the labour process is described in various parts of this thesis. Here, we consider their impact on worker consciousness. It was profound. The CarPress personnel manager:

> If we'd sacked 21 operators from this plant as near as 12 months ago we would have seen an all-out strike here, with a 100 per cent vote, there's no doubt about that. It just shows how attitudes have changed. We really have worked on that. We've made the shop-floor far more aware of what it means to break your employment contract. And I think we've successfully bred a new culture of customer awareness, we've made the shop-floor aware of where the customer lies in the chain and we've made them start to think about being responsible for their actions.

Chapter 4 described how final assemblers in the chain of mass production intervene in the management of their first-tier suppliers in order to secure maximum quality, minimum prices, acceptable working practices and, crucially, a risk-free, continuous supply of parts. If the latter is placed in jeopardy, their interventions may become more threatening. For example, during a number of the overtime bans described above, Rover sent teams of purchasing, supplies and logistics personnel to the CarPress plant to organize contingency plans for maintaining production. These personnel also spent time on the shop-floor cajoling operators into submission, warning them they were placing their jobs at risk. During the crucial new working practices dispute in 1994, Rover managers suddenly arrived in the press shop and threatened to permanently remove their press dies. This decisively affected its outcome. One operator told the author:

> The management told us that unless we accepted the package on the same day our pay rise and jobs would be taken away. And they'd done a good job, you see, bringing the Rover boys down. They were really putting the frighteners on. We've taken on about a hundred new young lads here and they threatened them all with the dole.

So the strike-breaking interventions of the customer can have a sobering effect in particular circumstances. But such actions are merely single, albeit unfamiliar, manifestations of a more pervasive and malignant customer influence. Many CarPress workers blamed management's aggression, its introduction of new working practices and their own inability to frustrate this on the new customer prerogatives. Indeed, as one inspector intimated, the ramifications of the contemporary imbalance of power between the producer and the customer were embedded in the shop-floor's collective consciousness:

> Attitudes have changed on the shop-floor all right. There's this real realization that if you go on strike your customer will get hit and just get up and go somewhere else. This is a real change. There's definitely a strong awareness of this especially among the younger workers on the line.

Moreover, the construction of an additional, more intimate social relationship between the teamworker and the customer provided another corrupting influence on shop-floor solidarity. CarPress sought to pervert customary notions of workplace democracy and instil a new sense of personal discipline by substituting team responsibility to the customer for traditional collective accountability. The views of two young teamworkers supplying Honda and Toyota reflected the success of this strategy amongst some groups:

> I've built up a sort of loyalty with Honda, I don't know, it just seems to come down to pride. I am much happier here, I'm more involved. And loyalty makes you feel guilty some times if you make a mistake, it kind of makes you feel more responsible for the job.

Another:

> Oh yeah, we're directly involved with the customer all the time. I mean if there's quality problems with the parts the Toyota management might ring us up direct, senior management sometimes, and we might ring them. And they call us by our first names. So this makes you very careful about the job. You don't want to let them down. You're always watching what's going on, watching what you're doing, because it's obvious, it's your job that's on the line.

This ideological dimension to the enhancement of management control in industries subject to 'Japanization' has been noted elsewhere (Delbridge *et al.*, 1992; Oliver and Wilkinson, 1992; Newsome, 1996) although its efficacy may by no means be complete in every case (Roper *et al.*, 1997). Moreover, it is not in itself especially new. For example, Pignon and Querzola's analysis of work organizational changes in the American telecommunications industry two decades ago discerned evolving team-based principles aimed at modifying the social form of work in ways which both provided workers a measure of trust and induced a new accountability to the customer. In this environment, 'employees are no longer confronted with the boss as the person they are responsible to but rather with their customers and with the market' (1976, p. 75). However, qualitative ideological differences emerge when these new relationships are placed into the highly disciplined, closely supervised, low-trust social relations of lean mass-production. As the above examples testify, a worker's perception of the customer may take on a new dimension in the context of the different ways in which contemporary customer–supplier relations act to circumscribe shop-floor resistance. Significantly, despite the plant's immediate legacy of a classic Tayloristic culture, 81 per cent of CarPress's shop-floor workers indicated in the second questionnaire survey (November 1995) that they thought about the requirements of the external customer as they carried out their work; 52 per cent indicated 'most of the time', only 13 per cent indicated 'never'. Perhaps this does denote the emergence of positive attitudes towards product quality, but such customer awareness also reflects the power of a new alienating hegemony on the shop-floor: a customer hegemony thriving on fear of retribution as much as customer satisfaction. The participative ideology of TQM may seek to obscure these processes, but it is this real fear and insecurity which underlie the current fashion for 'customer care'.

This chapter provides in-depth qualitative evidence of the conflictual nature of the contemporary employment relationship which stands in stark contrast to the picture of consensus presented in official UK industrial dispute data. In so doing it highlights how the restructuring of capitalist work is rarely unproblematic. If the new management initiatives contain a repertoire of techniques aimed at intensifying rates of labour exploitation then we must expect worker resistance, including traditional collective forms.

The social relations of this change process, therefore, contain a paradox. Whilst lean production regimes may ultimately depend on cooperation and high-trust relations through such practices as teamworking and kaizen, workers' actual experience of effort intensification, stress, fear and insecurity will ensure the reproduction of the same antagonistic relations inherited from conventional Taylorist work organization. The next chapter considers the methods by which CarPress sought gradually to mitigate these inherent tensions by mobilizing ideologies of consensus and shared interests. However, the company also came to realize that in the short term, securing shop-floor cooperation does not always require trust-building measures; 'cooperation' through coercion may suffice, provided environmental conditions are favourable. The distinctive economic and political conditions of the current period provided such an environment. It allowed management to exploit the different processes of shop steward incorporation; the legal interventions of the capitalist state; pervasive job insecurity; the new customer relationships; and internal class divisions, all in ways which profoundly weakened shop-floor resistance.

The 'management of change' at many brownfield plants progresses on this basis. For a good number of workers, this is the reality of 'Japanization' and the 'New Industrial Relations'. It may involve a systematic suppression of rank-and-file dissent, and for those who do not respond to this treatment, the removal of certain basic rights: the right to participate in decision-making at work, the right of freedom of association and even the right to work. Until the balance of power between capital and labour begins moving towards the latter, some collective forms of working-class resistance to these changes will remain critically restricted, whilst other, more covert forms will emerge. In the meantime, the underlying managerial tensions that accompany the contradiction between the contemporary ideology of 'worker empowerment' and the harsh reality of labour exploitation in lean production will continue:

> All changes have been forced through in an atmosphere of threats, intimidation and above all, fear. All talk of teamworking, co-operation, etc., has proved to be nothing but empty rhetoric. The sad fact is that management now behave in a way that is draconian, dictatorial and anti-union. This of course they are able to sustain with the support of oppressive labour laws and with a workforce that is captive owing to mass unemployment. The sad fact is that a management that is unchallenged will be unchallenged in making bad decisions. (Press shop operator, Questionnaire comment, November 1995)

Notes

1   Different Conservative governments executed an assault on the closed shop in the 1980, 1982, 1988 and 1990 Employment Acts. It is now illegal (Marsh, 1992). The Trade Union Reform and Employment Rights Act (1993) attempted to reduce both membership densities and union finances by forcing unions to secure their members' approval for continuance of check-off payments every three years. The government assumed that some members would stop paying because of administrative shortcomings, apathy or personal finance problems (Labour Research, August 1993c).

2   The number of trade union members per union representative in British workplaces varies directly with the size of the establishment. In 1990, stewards in establishments with 500–999 employees represented, on average, 27 employees (Millward *et al.*, 1992). The 1:20 ratio at CarPress reflects the strength of union organization of the plant.

3   The more debilitating components of the legislation governing ballots, picketing and industrial action have been endorsed by Tony Blair's new Labour government and are likely to remain firmly in place (Barratt Brown and Coates, 1996; The Labour Party, 1997).

4   The 1990 Employment Act seeks to prevent unofficial industrial action by forcing unions to take positive steps to bring such action to an end. In addition, the 1990 Act and, as we shall see, more detailed amendments to the Trade Union and Labour Relations Act, allow employers to selectively dismiss individual employees who participate in such action (Welch, 1991; IDS Employment Law Handbook).

New definitions of a legal trade dispute established in the 1980, 1982 and 1990 Employment Acts outlaw secondary, solidarity and political action. Together these constitute the most devastating of the Conservatives' legal changes. The total prohibition of solidarity action is in breach of the International Labour Organization's Conventions on labour standards and is unique in the Western industrialized countries (Hendy, 1991).

5   Section 237, Trade Union and Labour Relations (Consolidated) Act 1992.

6   IDS Employment Law Handbook, Series 2 No 7: *Industrial Action.*

7   Many of this group were metal finishers. Different individuals suffered from vibration white finger, cervical spondylitis and carpal tunnel syndrome. These injuries were sustained by, in some cases, working for over 30 years with constantly vibrating, heavy hand tools, such as linishers, orbital sanders, 20lb mop machines and pneumatic hammers. Despite the fact that the most common prescribed industrial disease, vibration white finger, can involve painful paralysing attacks, the state rarely assesses individuals as being 14 per cent or more disabled which qualifies them for industrial injuries benefit (Labour Research, 1996). Of the 21 workers dismissed, eight were metal finishers with 8–10 per cent registered disability.

8   As Labour Research (1993a and 1993b) describes, the Trade Union Reform

and Employment Rights Act (1993) places significant new constraints on unions: all ballots must be postal; employers must be notified twice before a ballot is held (the first being the formal notice of intention to ballot, the second being a copy of the ballot form); employers must be notified again after the ballot to give them at least seven days' notice of when the strike will take place; this notice must also inform the employer whether the union's action will be 'continuous' or 'discontinuous', thus virtually giving away all of its action strategy; unions have to appoint expensive independent scrutineers to oversee the ballot; and finally, following a later ruling from the Court of Appeal, unions now have to provide employers with the names of members being balloted.

9   The local media were particularly sympathetic to the plight of the sacked workers, as were local politicians who made a number of attempts to intervene on their behalf. For example, in December 1994, the local Labour MP, the local vicar, mayors and other leaders of local councils sent letters both to the CarPress managing director and the head of its parent company in Germany appealing for a gesture of 'Christmas goodwill' and 'an act of imagination and generosity' by reinstating the workers with no strings attached. Their pleas were rejected.

The Oldport Trades Council also pledged unanimous support for the CarPress workers, stating that 'the management were attempting to destroy the trade union movement, sack the activists and castrate [sic] those remaining members'. The Trades Council also said it was mindful of the fact 'that the attacks on the Trade Union movement would continue and that an injury to one is an injury to all'. Despite these bold words, no practical support was offered.

8 THE DISCIPLINARY IMPACT OF HUMAN RESOURCE MANAGEMENT

The introduction of lean production control and associated new management techniques at CarPress undermined the shop-floor's traditional defences against the imposition of managerial prerogatives. The last chapter explored how the company responded to the attendant worker resistance by embarking upon a process of incorporation of union officials and senior stewards and by mobilizing a number of explicitly coercive measures against the rank and file. The efficacy of this strategy depended upon a propitious external environment of control. However, this factor alone meant that a sole reliance on coercion could be self-defeating in the longer term; the distinctive economic and political conditions which made the strategy possible would not hold indefinitely. Moreover, the required investment in the various concrete mechanisms of coercive management control can be both prohibitive and inefficient compared to measures aimed at building worker commitment. As Thompson and McHugh put it, domination by coercion requires 'constant reinforcement of coercive pressures and extensive monitoring of reactions to them. Domination of the individual through self-limitation and constraint is far more effective. This is engendered through individual assimilation of, and accommodation to, dominant workplace cultures and ideologies' (1990, p. 294).

Most managerial analyses of work restructuring emphasize this more sophisticated form of worker subordination. For example, Oliver and Wilkinson argue that 'many Japanese-style manufacturing practices require *willing* cooperation, not mere compliance, on the part of the workforce' (1992, p. 175), a willingness to perform extra tasks and take on new responsibilities. These authors argue that the introduction of Japanese practices into the UK will be problematic unless employers simultaneously mobilize new, employee-centred strategies based on the kind of principles outlined in Guest's (1987; 1991) paradigm of human resource management.[1] Similarly, Kenney and Florida (1993, p. 274) maintain that

Japanese 'innovation-mediated production', involving wider worker responsibilities as well as more intensive basic labour processes, relies on various managerial instruments of social control and socialization to secure workers who identify as closely and completely with the company as possible.

Theoretically, therefore, creating authentic worker commitment and loyalty constitutes an important facet of any lean production regime. Yet, the survey of personnel policies in the South Wales Japanese transplants demonstrated something less straightforward than this facile functionalist fit between 'soft' HRM policies supporting 'hard' production-control techniques. New workplace cultures and ideologies did obtain in many of these firms; but these were not built upon the principle of extensive employee participation, and through this, a close attachment to the enterprise. The pace and intensity of lean production rarely provide the time, space or material conditions for anything so adventurous. Instead, the various social control and socialization measures employed, such as distinctive recruitment procedures and direct communication techniques, were designed primarily to maximize individual and team performance, to secure accountability for performance and to engender an awareness of responsibility and commitment to the customer. These measures contributed to a dominant workplace culture which aimed to build a collective understanding of the relationship between performance in production and the disciplines of the capitalist market.

This chapter investigates the extent to which the same ideological processes of social control took hold at CarPress, once again focusing on their impact on the workforce. Following a similar pattern to Chapter 3, it considers recruitment, selection and equal opportunity policies; job security and labour retention policies; employee involvement, new communications and single status; and finally, worker loyalty and trust.

New Recruitment Policy: The Pursuit of Commitment

Recruitment and Selection

When it acquired the Oldport plant in 1989, CarPress inherited a casual, unsophisticated recruitment system reflecting management's perception of labour as a cheap commodity to be recruited or discarded in accordance with the immediate demands of product markets. These principles held for many traditional British firms operating in Wales (Morgan and Sayer, 1988), where managing numbers took precedence over monitoring individual performance and attitudes.

The plant utilized a recruitment method called the 'family' or 'community' system. Labour requirements would be posted up on notice boards so that names of potential recruits could be submitted by the workforce. These would invariably be family members or close friends living in the vicinity. The system relied upon the intimate connections that characterize close-knit communities and entailed minimal administrative costs for the personnel bureaucracy. It was also, of course, effectively controlled by the shop-floor.

The restructuring of work under the new CarPress management placed fresh demands on the workforce: greater effort, a willingness to work more flexibly and a willingness to take on extra tasks when requested. As we saw in the last two chapters, the management attempted to create the conditions for compliance with these changes both by fostering pro-company attitudes amongst the less experienced members of the workforce, some of whom were separated off into discrete teams, and by gradually breaking down the resistance of the experienced majority. In quantitative terms, this segmentation of experience was heavily skewed towards the latter more 'troublesome' group.[2] Consequently, in late 1993, following a dispute with the plant's TGWU membership, the company succeeded in taking back full control of the recruitment system and commenced selecting only those individuals who, by virtue of their age or employment history, had little experience of working in a traditional unionized firm.

A lack of personnel resources prevented CarPress from using the same cautious and scrupulous selection techniques utilized in Japanese auto transplants located in the UK and USA.[3] Instead, the personnel department initially screened basic biographical data on application forms. Candidates then performed three aptitude and manual ability tests and attended just one interview with production and personnel management. Apart from employment history, the most important selection criteria were manual ability, physical ability, attitudes towards flexibility and change at the workplace, and above all others, attitudes towards absenteeism. Successful candidates were closely monitored for performance and attendance during a three-month probationary period.

This important shift in recruitment strategy took a further turn after the sackings dispute described in the previous chapter. The proposition that manufacturing firms are beginning to exploit temporary labour in a more coherent, systematic manner continues to attract doubts from some academics (see for example, Pollert, 1988; 1992; Marginson, 1989; Fowler and Bresnen, 1991; and Cumbers, 1996). Yet one recent survey of union representatives in 1,000 establishments found that whilst temporary contracts continue to be used to manage fluctuations in product demand, 52 per cent of firms were increasing their numbers of temporary workers *at the expense* of permanent jobs (Labour Research Department, 1995). Another report from the TUC estimates that between 1992 and 1995 the number of permanent jobs in the UK fell by nearly 300,000 while temporary jobs increased by 320,000 (TUC, 1997). Moreover, the survey of Japanese transplants in South Wales demonstrated that the use of temporary contracts facilitated many of these firms' lean manning strategies whilst simultaneously providing a cheap and effective screening mechanism for new recruits. CarPress began using temporary labour in a similarly strategic fashion.

Since they left school, many of the 60 young temporary workers employed during the sackings dispute had drifted from one meaningless training programme to another, from one low-paid job to another. When they walked onto the CarPress shop-floor they recognized an opportunity for engaging in something potentially much better than this sordid cycle of human waste, and they worked as if their lives depended on it. The management was impressed. The personnel manager commented at the time:

> It's been marvellous! You know the Mini door section in the assembly shop? Everyone knows that it's the easiest job in the shop. The men have always reached their targets with ease and of course they've always been the older men due to the effects of the seniority system. Well guess what. Of the 105 operators we suspended, we managed to include every operator from this section and we were then able to replace them immediately with temporary labour, young kids the lot of them. And now, after just three weeks on the job, those boys have broken all productivity records. They've literally beaten every record set by the older men, men who have been in this plant for 30 years some of them. And that's just after three weeks!
>
> Not only that, the fitters have told us that mysteriously these kids never get any machinery breakdown times, even though they're working the same line and the same machinery as the older men used to. Machinery downtime has virtually disappeared on this section. Now doesn't that say it all?

The unions had a long-standing agreement with the company that any temporary worker employed for more than three months must immediately be offered a permanent contract. The agreement was important because it provided the shop-floor some protection against wage-cutting and job insecurity. Accordingly, in the summer of 1995, after already conceding one three-month extension, the shop stewards insisted that the company make the 60 youngsters up to permanent employees or release them. Amidst much public acrimony, in which the unions received most of the blame, the company cynically dismissed all 60. But it also exploited this episode to replace the agreement with a new policy. From January 1996, every new recruit would be employed as a temporary worker. Labour contracts could be cancelled or extended at the whim of management whilst individuals who showed themselves to be outstanding performers with pro-company attitudes might be taken on permanently, workload permitting. In preparation for this, CarPress advertised for nearly 200 new temporary workers towards the end of 1995.

Fevre (1989) argues that in the loose labour market conditions of South Wales and other depressed regions in the UK, temporary workers' attitudes are shaped by the disciplinary experience of temporary employment as well as unemployment. They possess the certain knowledge that they are likely to become unemployed again in a short time: 'they are always looking for work, and always act as if they are outside the factory gates, hammering to get in, even when they have employment' (p. 151). Indeed, more recent Labour Force Survey data show that for such workers this temporary-employment/no-employment cycle has virtually become a permanent feature of their labour market experience (Gregg and Wadsworth, 1997).[4] In these circumstances, they will always constitute an acquiescent and malleable pool of labour. Moreover, in offering a minority of carefully selected workers the tantalizing prospect of breaking out of this life of relentless job insecurity, CarPress, and many of the neighbouring Japanese transplants, are able to exploit the large pools of unemployed labour in the region for purposes additional to maintaining their lean manning strategies or boosting labour productivity. That is, the careful selection of prime candidates for permanent work formed an important component in their construction of new corporate cultures of cooperation and compliance. Therefore, attempts to categorize different workforces simply in terms of segmented core and periphery groups (Atkinson, 1985) conceal some of the internal ramifications of a firm's flexible employment policy. CarPress embarked upon a strategy of using periphery temporary workers to *interact* with the core not merely to produce a disciplinary effect but to help catalyse changes in attitudes and culture within the core itself.

Equal Opportunities

In keeping with the currently pervasive corporate ideology of granting respect and opportunity to all employees, as enunciated by literally thousands of company mission statements throughout the country, CarPress claimed to be an equal opportunities employer. In practice, the company employed no ethnic minority workers;[5] as we saw in the last chapter, it readily dismissed disabled workers with inferior absenteeism records in a quite amoral fashion; and as we describe below, rather than encourage the employment of women workers, it relentlessly victimized them.

At the end of 1994, the company employed just 45 women out of a total workforce of 767. None were managers, supervisors or engineers; 27 were clerks and administrators; the remaining 28 were employed on the shop-floor as semi-skilled operators. Although no longitudinal data were available, the management admitted that this represented a substantial decline. One operator remembered that in past years there could be over 50 women employed in the press shop alone, an area where the manual work was particularly arduous.

The macho culture that often accompanies heavy metalwork partly explains this decline. For many of CarPress's male managers, engineers and shop-floor workers, this was 'real men's work'; working lives were dominated by the continual lifting and shaping of heavy steel sheet and by the grime, noise and rhythm generated by giant metal presses and welding machinery. In this sense, the men had appropriated the technology for their masculinity, the work had become gendered (Cockburn, 1985). As an MSF representative commented:

> I'm not against equal opportunities, but it's difficult in some environments. This is a predominantly masculine workforce, many of the machines are historically masculine if you see what I mean. The thought of my wife hauling bits of steel around doesn't exactly fill me with joy. She'd end up with arms of Samson. In fact there are few women in any significant position here. It's sad, I've no doubt some of the women are sharper than the men, but even in the offices there's a strong male culture. We all swear a lot. We all like our men's talk, you know? There's nothing wrong with that is there?

Although these attitudes provided the cultural context for gender inequality at the factory, they do not fully explain why this inequality deteriorated further. In the past, some women had survived and even thrived in this masculine environment. As a clerical worker, who eventually moved off the shop-floor, reminisced:

> I tell you, in my day, the shop was far more physical than it is now. I used to work on the Morris bonnet assembly lines, and in those days you were dealing with thick steel, not the flimsy stuff you get nowadays. And us girls were faster than the men. I was faster and I had to work out of necessity. I needed the work and I worked hard, I can tell you. We all worked faster than the men, so don't tell me women can't do it.

Despite the fact that women were perfectly capable of performing many tasks on the shop-floor, most CarPress managers remained reluctant to employ them. When quizzed about this, these men offered a number of excuses. Women workers were incompatible with the new flexibility because they were 'physically incapable of performing the more arduous jobs'; too many women displayed 'a pin money mentality'; or, since the Equal Pay Act came into force, the company enjoyed no advantage in employing women who possessed the 'wrong temperament for heavy factory work'. Even the senior stewards were not particularly sympathetic. One remarked:

> To be honest, looking at things from management's point of view, this is not the sort of place where you can come in sick. You have to be on your toes all the time or you'll end up having a serious accident. That's the problem for the women. They're different aren't they? Their bodies are different for a start. They've got the monthly problem and they can't keep going out sick every time.

Thus, the men in different positions of authority defined women in terms of domesticity. Following similar processes to those identified by Cockburn's (1995) recent studies of gender inequality at the workplace, women's 'natural' attributes were articulated with domestic ties and maternal responsibilities and then constructed as drawbacks in the sphere of production. Once these ideological assumptions were placed into the material context of capitalist rationalization, de-manning and consequent lean production – where maximum labour utilization, attendance and effort were at a premium – then, for many managers, the retention of women became a 'problem'. A number commented that women were no longer suited to the stress and speed of work on the shop-floor. And if any women complained, they were not likely to receive sympathy. As one superintendent said:

> We have to tell them straight, 'You're all supposed to be into equal pay aren't you? If you can't do the work then you'll have to get out, it's as simple as that. I'm supposed to be running a press shop here not a kindergarten you know.'

Sex discrimination law prevented management from overtly selecting women for redundancy. However, to maintain its lean manning strategy, CarPress operated a long-running voluntary redundancy scheme. In response to the increasingly harsh treatment from their foremen and managers, and an indifference to their problems from many senior stewards, a good number of women left the company. Those who remained needed an especial toughness and tenacity to preserve their hold on a living wage. For example, some were sectioned off into an area that the shop-floor appositely named 'Bosnia'. It was cold, it had no proper heating system, winter draughts would blow through cracked windows and roofing sheet, and yet in this environment the women were expected to perform rapid light assembly work with targets of up to 1,000 pieces per hour. One 'Bosnian' woman protested:

> We've been fighting for years to get heating, but the management have ignored us just because we're women. If it gets cold in the main shops, the management bring in the heater cannons for the men. But not here. Not likely. Some winters I've been working in here wearing four jumpers at a time, and we're always wearing them out. Sometimes we even work in our coats. Can you imagine it? It got so bad, I was off sick last winter with chilblains. I could have got bloody frostbite! But the management didn't care. They didn't believe me. My boss rang me up and told me to come in immediately or I'd be sacked. It's just like slave labour.

The exigencies of capitalist mass-production combined with managerial patriarchy to abuse women's bodies in the main shops as well. Annette, another 'Bosnian' woman who transferred out of the press shop, spoke at length about this:

> When we worked the big presses some of the metal guards would quite regularly spring up and hit you on your breasts if you didn't have your wits about you. It could give you a real nasty knock with bruises to show for it. And just as often we'd be put on machines which were too difficult for us to

operate. We couldn't reach into the tools [dies], we just weren't tall enough. So we'd complain to the foreman but all he would say was, 'If you can't do the job then we don't want any more women in here do we?' Then he'd have a good laugh at us. It used to feel degrading. Sometimes you actually had to bend right into the machines and the men standing behind you on the line would be laughing and cat-calling while you were on tiptoes trying to reach in.

And we've been involved in some nasty accidents too. Some of those presses can develop faults. Sometimes they go into a double cycle with no warning at all so that the safety bar would come up the first time when you're expecting it but then suddenly spring up for a second time when you're not. And it knocks you right back. The bar will then knock you in the chest and give you some right nice little bruises.

These women were not seeking preferential treatment or even 'positive action' on the shop-floor; they merely demanded protection from the harmful concrete ramifications of a managerial system that is obsessed with production, output and profit. They were, of course, refused.

Such managerial behaviour constitutes the antithesis of equal opportunity policy. Lean production can be a highly efficient, low-waste system of surplus extraction and capital accumulation demanding workers who are most likely to consistently fulfil the strict attendance and performance criteria of the employer. As we discovered in Chapter 3, the interaction between capitalist social relations and gender relations in the Japanese electronic transplants in South Wales ensured that these workers may be young women with the necessary dextrous skills who also display the 'commitment' that naturally accompanies their need for a basic family income. And at factories like CarPress, increasingly, they may be the 'experienced unemployed', men with the obligatory stamina for continual production work on heavy machinery who similarly display the 'commitment' that follows the desperate quest for a first decent job. Either way, questions of equal employment rights, parental leave, sick leave, the needs of women, the needs of older workers and special measures for disabled workers become marginal matters. Lean production regimes enlist ideologies of equality which often mask enduring forms of structural disadvantage for many workers. Their recruitment and selection techniques may be more proceduralized and scrupulous than hitherto, but these will not necessarily incorporate the principle of equal opportunity at work.

Married to the Company, in Sickness and in Health: Labour Retention and Job Security

Between the years 1978 and 1985, as in many UK manufacturing firms, the BL/Rover workforce was butchered; a series of rationalizations and plant closures caused the combine's employment to fall by 114,000 (Williams *et al.*, 1994a). During the decade following 1981, as part of this process, the number of workers employed at the Oldport factory was reduced by a half. In this context, the author's attempts to discuss with different employees Japanese notions of 'jobs for life', were plainly inopportune. Job security was central to the workers' concrete interests, yet in the barren environment of mass unemployment it remained merely an aspiration, a desire for a basic right that could be cruelly manipulated by management's demand for change. A press shop operator:

> Look, we're all in the same boat here, we're no different to anybody else. If you're a worker you've got the same interests wherever you are. You go to school, you try to get yourself some qualifications, you try and get yourself a job, you go to work and then you want your job security. You need job security in order to plan your life, to get a home for your family, to get a car and other things in life. They're the concerns of all of us. And because of that, the fear of losing these things, the fear of losing the dignity that you have in work, the real fear of redundancy, they're in your mind all the time.

One quality inspector knew only too well the effects of managerial manipulation here:

> The management are clever. They'll often issue a redundancy notice just before the annual pay talks start up and then they don't tell you who's got to go. So it's issued as a general threat, to sober us up, you know what I mean? It leads to a lot of uncertainty. Then the management will wait a few months and they'll re-issue the same redundancy notice. Again, no names, so it creates greater uncertainty. It's all about playing on your nerves. It's the company playing with your life all the time. It becomes a life of fear. You can't plan for anything. You can't plan for a home, for your mortgage, nothing. So what do you do? I'll tell you what you do. You either give in or you turn into a militant.
>
> I used to be a toolmaker. Do you know, during my time in the toolroom I received 11 redundancy notices in 6 years. Notices telling me I'll be outside the gates in a couple of weeks' time. Then at the last moment they're suddenly withdrawn. Now how can you live like that? Me, I did end up a

militant. And the company repaid me. I got thrown out of the toolroom and dumped on inspection.

The new working practices agreement attempted to temper shop-floor opposition with a commitment of no compulsory redundancies. However, like the Japanese transplants in South Wales, and indeed, Japanese transplants in North and South America, workers were forced to trade an acceptance of greater numerical and functional flexibility in return for a job security that market conditions could periodically undermine (Kenney and Florida, 1993; Black and Ackers, 1994; Humphrey, 1994). As the plant's chief production manager commented:

> There's no God-given right for anybody in any company to have a job for life. We all hope for the best of course, many of us hope for a long stay at CarPress, but nothing in life is forever. And if there is such a thing as 'jobs for life', it's only there if the company is making a profit. We're not a registered charity, you know.

Nevertheless, during the 1990s, CarPress did eschew the traditional 'hire and fire' employment methods inherited from Rover. Instead, by means of voluntary redundancy programmes and natural wastage, the ageing core of the workforce was only gradually reduced and then replaced by judiciously recruiting younger, less-experienced workers; higher workloads were maintained by the redistribution of tasks; whilst the exploitation of temporary labour helped the company manage product market fluctuations.

Moreover, as we saw in the last chapter, management succeeded in appropriating the distribution of overtime from the shop stewards. Now, production variations could also be realized by extending working time, without hindrance from the unions. Although overtime premia costs prevented management from extending hours on a continuous, plant-wide basis, particular groups of process operators and skilled workers did experience acute labour intensifying pressures in this way, none more so than the plant's maintenance fitters.

Between 1984 and 1994, cost-reducing labour flexibility measures caused the plant's skilled maintenance staffing levels to fall by 50 per cent; in addition, all general hands and fitters' mates were made redundant. Manufacturing and maintenance labour costs were further reduced when the plant moved from a standard three-shift to an alternating days/nights plus twilight shift system in 1994. At the same time, as we saw in Chapter

5, the plant's worn-out machinery was consistently pushed beyond the limit to meet customer demand in an environment of continuous production and low buffers. The combination of frugal resources, no preventative maintenance, perpetual machine breakdowns and managerial coercion forced many of the remaining maintenance staff to virtually double the length of their working week. In such circumstances, these workers enjoyed a funny sort of 'job security'. Two electricians angrily reflected on this:

> In the last six months the press shop's been operating flat out. It's been going all day, all night just keeping up with the customer's requirements.
> Everything is driven by the customer these days. That takes precedence over everything else. So you've got your maintenance staff working an extra three hours every day to cover overtime on production. Then on Saturdays we're working from 6.00 in the morning to 6.00 in the evening. On Sundays we're doing the same and often straight through to the night shift.
> Some of us have been doing this for six months continuously. And things are getting so bad with the manning that we're only getting two electricians on each shift. So, on average, the maintenance people now, we're working 65 to 70 hours per week. And it's all virtually compulsory. If you say no you get threatened with the sack.

Another:

> And these alternating days and nights. It's fucking terrible. I'm never at home, my wife never sees me. I've got no social life whatsoever. The alternating shifts are bad enough. But when the plant has been on a three-shift system for 20 years then those shifts become part of your working life. Your body gets used to it. And now we suddenly get taken off it and forced to work one week days, one week nights, plus an extra 30 hours on top! You end up with health problems. Sometimes it just gets unbearable.

In more favourable external labour market conditions, many workers subject to such stress and pressure would seek alternative employment elsewhere. However, in the mid-1990s, these conditions favoured capital not labour; they reinforced the high level of labour retention necessary for CarPress to successfully operate its system of continuous, lean production.

Labour retention has other facets as well. Although the plant's labour turnover was low, the absence of generous manning levels and high buffers exposed poor labour attendance as a potential threat to production. Therefore, like its neighbouring Japanese transplants in the region,

CarPress placed a high premium on reducing absenteeism. To this end, the management introduced new disciplinary measures against absence due to both sickness and injury.

In 1990, CarPress diminished the sick pay scheme inherited from Rover by setting payments below basic rate earnings and restricting these to 40 days in any one year (the Rover scheme paid basic rates for a full year). Furthermore, the company sought worker accountability for absence by introducing measures such as strict return–to–work interviews and regular home visits. Although, on the surface, this latter approach was little different to contemporary management practice elsewhere,[6] CarPress followed it with an especial determination. A production superintendent:

> The control of sickness is a perennial problem here. For example, I was called in recently by my director to discuss deteriorating absenteeism in the assembly shop. Now, I had to explain to him that for some reason an unusual number of my operators were off sick with a variety of broken bones. Legs, arms, shoulders, you name it, they broke it. God knows what they'd been up to. None work-related, but real sickness, nevertheless. The response of this director was to say, 'Well you'll have to go out and sack the lot of them!' And he was serious! Now I can be quite hard but I have a heart. Some of our directors have no logic and no heart either.

The operators were not sacked in this case, but they received a severe reprimand upon their return to work. Individuals suffering work–related injuries – and these were habitual at CarPress – were treated in similar fashion. The most common injuries were lacerations from handling sheet steel (some of which could be severe); knocks, bruises and sprains from the press safety bars; damage to eyes from metal splinters and welding flash; and general welding burns. More serious injuries such as fractures and amputations occurred much less frequently. An AEEU health and safety representative commented on the company's safety record:

> The problem we've got is that half the machines in this plant are falling to bits. Some of them are in a terrible state. In the old days they always used to be repaired and maintained at weekends, but now that's all stopped because of lack of money. These days we're told everything's down to the customer. Nothing must get in the way of meeting the customer's needs. So yeah, the customer rules here all right. But all this talk about a customer philosophy, it can actually end up hurting people. People get hit. But I don't think the management are bothered, to be honest. They're totally obsessed with production, it's all they think about.

This managerial obsession extended to treating absence through injury as a threat to production rather than a consequence of it. Stage by stage, the management introduced measures which forced all but the most seriously injured to report for alternative work. This culminated in a detailed procedure which established that 'a collective effort must be made to ensure that employees are not sent home from their workplace whilst they can be gainfully employed in work outside their normal range of duties'.[7] A good number of workers provided personal anecdotes of how they or their colleagues were forced to report in for light production duties with severe lacerations, damaged eyes, even broken limbs. And this was not just a matter of managerial vindictiveness against certain individuals; it was another manifestation of a coercive management control on the shop-floor. CarPress was intent on sending out a more general message that absenteeism would no longer be tolerated.

The success of this strategy is reflected in the factory's accident statistics. Both the total number of accidents (averaging 2,200 per year) and the number of accidents per employee (averaging just over three per year) remained fairly constant between 1991 and 1995. In contrast, the lost time accident rate – the rate of absenteeism through industrial injury – declined by a dramatic 74 per cent. Moreover, the company's personnel department confirmed that overall absenteeism also fell by 50 per cent: from 12 per cent in the late 1980s to around 6 per cent in 1994.

These statistics, and the actions which prompted them, demonstrate that analyses which stress novel aspects of Japanese management practice, such as the disciplinary effect of peer pressure and management attempts to capture this to the benefit of the employer (Oliver and Wilkinson, 1992, p. 309), sometimes miss the more significant impact of the conventional. As Edwards and Whitston (1993) discovered, there is little empirical evidence to support the idea of a move towards 'self-discipline' at the workplace. Instead, shop-floor discipline, order and attendance are currently maintained through a mix of measures, including, in the contemporary context of loose labour markets and weak trade unions, a return to more traditional, coercive forms of managerial authority.

Employee Involvement: Maintaining a Deficit in Worker Participation

So far, then, CarPress's HRM strategy consisted of 'hard' measures aimed at building a more acquiescent, malleable and disciplined workforce. Even the benefit of improved job security came with a sting in the tail in the form of a relentless pressure and stress that accompanies labour intensification in the 1990s. However, in parallel with this approach, the company introduced ostensibly 'softer' socialization techniques aimed at cementing a more durable form of control by incorporating the shop-floor into managerial doctrine. Essentially about building trust, acceptance and conformity, the impact of different employee involvement measures such as open communications and single status will now be considered.

The New Communications

During the 1980s, the practice of direct communications between management and employees became increasingly common in British firms (Townley, 1989; IDS, 1992a; Marchington et al., 1992). Although the rationale for this was more complex than many business writers suggest (Townley, 1989), things were more simple at Rover. Management perceived direct communications as the only way 'to win the hearts and minds of the men at all levels' and to bypass the company's more militant shop stewards (Edwardes, 1983, p. 87). Malcolm Edwardes instigated the practice of sending letters direct to employees homes and regularly issuing factory briefing sheets. Later in the decade, as part of its 'Working With Pride' programme, Rover introduced more refined techniques such as zone (team) briefings. However, as Smith (1988) discovered, the limited, top-down nature of the communications system soon engendered disillusion and disinterest on the shop-floor.

'Working With Pride' had perished by the time CarPress acquired the Oldport plant. The new management's communications style was both *ad hoc* and minimalist. Team briefings became more infrequent, management cascades were only used in exceptional circumstances and company newsletters petered out; the notice board became the principal official means of communicating information whilst the 'grapevine' remained its most fruitful source. Although, by the time of the first questionnaire survey (October 1994), the company had reintroduced a site journal, 84 per cent of employees indicated their dissatisfaction with company communications. This was not just a function of the paucity of information, it was also a consequence of a widespread distrust which some workers believed was inherent in British industry. A toolmaker typically commented:

> We get nothing from head office, they tell us nothing about how the company's doing, new investments and that sort of thing. And when they communicate at the local level, well, there's so much distrust, you just don't know whether the management are misleading you or not. Because at the moment, the way things are, what's always at the back of your mind when your local manager makes some announcement is that he's lying again.

And a cranedriver:

> I don't think there's any British company in this country which is really copying the Japanese. I mean, getting changes through that are pushed up from the bottom to the top. And I'm not blaming that on British workers. It's the fault of the middle and higher classes. They'll never change in this country ... if anything, the best management communications policy for this bloody place would be distributing books on stress at work.

This antipathy to management was not a matter of lack of interest in the company *per se*, or in change at the workplace. After all, CarPress provided work and a livelihood; it established the context and organization for different activities which shaped the lives and identities of every one of its employees. Another driver reflected the position of many on the shop-floor in aspiring to become more involved, to utilize his skills and knowledge, to enrich his working life in ways which might form a radical departure from the passive drudgery and discipline which accompanied direct management control over the capitalist labour process:

> I don't know anything about teamwork. The management here are shocking, they won't involve you with anything. As I see it you've got one team up there and one team down here. Okay, they might have all the qualifications going, you know, their 'O' levels, 'A' levels, degrees and the rest of it. But we've got our hands. It's hands that do the work in this place. We know how to make things in the plant, we know all about the problems you get with changing the jigs and tools. But they wouldn't dream of asking us. They're too scared too ask us for one thing, and in any case, they think they know it all.

During the war of attrition which preceded the shop-floor sackings in October 1994, CarPress realized that incorporating its senior stewards would enjoy limited success without also addressing independent rank-and-file militancy. It sought a more pervasive process of incorporation. Accordingly, management devised a new direct communications strategy of 'employee involvement' to complement the introduction of teamworking. It was implemented in the immediate aftermath of the sackings dispute.

Strategically planned monthly team-briefings formed the linchpin of the new policy. Every month, a subcommittee of the board, comprising representative directors and senior managers, drew up a cascade of company and customer information which would form the basis of team discussion. At each team-briefing, unit managers fed their teamworkers a wide range of company statistics and general information concerning plant performance; plant profit levels; part reject rates; performance in fulfilling customer time delivery schedules; absenteeism rates; lost time accidents; new projects; kaizen activity; and customer visits to the plant. The personnel manager also stressed that, 'employees are made particularly aware of the needs of the customer, of areas of work where CarPress is failing to meet the customer's needs, and its possible consequences'. At the end of each presentation, time was set aside for questions and answers and shop-floor input.

The company also established Quarterly Business Reviews which provided the same type of information but in more depth. Forty individuals attended each review in a plush management presentation area. These comprised 20 permanent representatives from management, the unions and non-steward shop-floor workers, along with 20 different shop-floor and office volunteers.

The author visited CarPress a number of times during this period and encountered a quite profound transformation in the quality of public displays of information. Each team had its own large display board providing different team performance parameters; each provided photo-graphs of team members and their task/NVQ credits;[8] the longer-established teams even included birthdays and hobbies. The press and assembly shops also housed two much larger displays containing colourful graphical presentations of plant performance, absenteeism, defects, sales, and so on. In addition, the company began installing 'Toyota-style' overhead electronic displays of daily team performance.

Along with the plethora of posters and other displays urging maximum performance, ostensibly, this new approach to information management exemplified both strands of Townley's (1989) analysis of contemporary employee communication programmes: communication as a process of education and communication as a strategy of commitment. CarPress sought to dampen rank-and-file aspirations by inculcating a bit of 'economic reality' and understanding of market discipline; it also aimed

Table 8.1 *Three main sources of information at work, all employees N = 384 (1994) and 514 (1995)*

	Percentage of respondents citing this source of information	
	1994	1995
Immediate supervisor	39	49
Team briefing	5	59
Quarterly Business Review	–	3
Company notice boards	44	28
Company newsletter	9	4
Trade union	47	30
The 'grapevine'	79	66
Other	5	3

to build greater employee commitment to corporate objectives in respect of company performance.

Analysing changes in the prominence of different sources of information at work provides one measure of the impact of the new policy. In both the 1994 questionnaire survey – which was completed immediately before the changes – and the 1995 survey – completed a year after – shop-floor and office workers were asked to select their three main sources of information concerning 'what is going on at work'. The results are summarized in Table 8.1.

Although the numbers relying on the grapevine remained high (and in most large social organizations this will always be the case) and the Quarterly Business Reviews made little impact, there were major shifts towards supervisors and team briefings as salient sources of information. At the same time, the relative impact of union communications significantly deteriorated, a decline which could also be attributed to the incorporation of a number of senior stewards.

However, what appears to the outsider as a considerable improvement in the quantitative and qualitative provision of company information may not be regarded in quite the same way by its recipients on the shop-floor. Many CarPress workers remained both frustrated and discontented. In the second questionnaire survey (November 1995), although 29 per cent of shop-floor workers felt that company communications had improved, 35 per cent believed they were no better whilst 36 per cent felt they had actually deteriorated. In the same survey, 58 per cent of shop-floor

Table 8.2 *Shop-floor workers' replies to the question, 'What impact do you think your team briefings have had on the following?' (Percentage by row; N = 471)*

	Increased (%)	Decreased (%)	No change (%)
The amount of useful information you receive about the company	41	7	52
Your understanding of management decisions	18	21	61
Your commitment to the company	25	11	64
Management's openness	13	32	55
Opportunities for you to have a say about what's going on at work	18	22	60

workers indicated that they did not believe most of the information they received from management. A similar picture emerges when we look at the particular impact of team briefings. Table 8.2 summarizes this for shop-floor workers.

Although a substantial minority of respondents felt that team briefings improved the provision of useful company information, and a smaller minority believed they had increased their commitment to the company, the overall impact was negative. The already low levels of understanding of management decisions, of perceptions of management's openness and of opportunities to have a say about changes at work, all deteriorated further. One foreman, now unit manager, wryly admitted:

> Listen, these briefings are a fucking joke, even I'll admit to that. My manager gives me a written brief, I'll read out a load of figures and that's it, it's all over. Figures such as latest profits, sales, monthly defects and plant efficiency. All interesting stuff, eh?
>
> When we started the briefings there was some interest from the boys at first. You'd get some sort of dialogue going. But that's because it was new. Now they're bored stiff with it. You read out your brief, look up, and you're confronted with a sea of blank, bored faces. Nobody ever asks you a question. But with these briefs, what do you expect?

Most CarPress workers, therefore, were not fooled by these new developments. Many had little time for a policy which under the benign rubric of 'employee involvement' represented a distinctly 'top-down' approach to communications, a one-way transmission belt for both instilling a sense of discipline in production and promoting capitalist market ideology and the employer's interests. And they had little time for a mechanism which frustrated the propagation and advance of their own interests.

Single Status

The new working practices agreement committed CarPress to creating 'a single status company' where all distinctions between monthly staff and hourly paid employees would be ended. However, as the personnel manager admitted, 'this doesn't mean that we're going to get caught up with moving everyone up to the staff level ... there's going to have to be compromises'. Indeed there were, for the concrete benefits of this commitment proved hard to identify. For example, a year after the new agreement was implemented, clocking distinctions between monthly and hourly paid employees remained, whilst the rationalization of grades and the introduction of credit transfer did not prove particularly popular on the shop-floor. Neither did management's approach to the harmonization of sick pay which insisted that shop-floor absenteeism fall below 4.5 per cent, and remain there, before the operators could enjoy the same sick pay as their office colleagues.

CarPress was more interested in mobilizing the idea of single status as a flimsy and spurious ideology of benevolence rather than as a mechanism of reducing real class inequalities at the workplace. And in the context of antagonistic management–labour relations, the policy represented an extraordinarily weak facade for disguising the concrete manifestations of labour exploitation in capitalist production. This is exemplified by the group chairman's message to his employees in 1995:

> My view of what a good company looks like is one - that attracts the best people; that pays the top rate for the job; that offers the best working conditions; where *everyone* is involved in achieving continuous improvement; where all stakeholders, employees, shareholders and customers are satisfied.
>
> For this, managers should not have the attitude of wanting the most out of employees for the least pay, nor should employees strive to get the maximum out of the company for the least effort. I see a future where harmony and consensus reign in an environment in which everybody wins. I want responsibility and authority devolved to the extent that *everybody* feels involved in the decision making process relative to their function in the company. Why shouldn't CarPress be like that?

> A better question is, which of us are going to actively work towards achieving this and which of us are going to obstruct the process? I ask every CarPress employee – which camp will *you* be in?[9]

The second questionnaire survey (November 1995) reversed this assertive challenge by asking respondents whether managers and workers should be members of the same team, and secondly, whether they thought their own managers believed they were in a separate team to the workforce. The results are summarized in Table 8.3.

Table 8.3 *Shop-floor workers' assessment of managerial 'team spirit' (Percentage by row; N = 471)*

	Agree (%)	Disagree (%)	Undecided (%)
'I believe that all managers and employees should be members of the same "company team".'			
All shop-floor workers	76	12	12
'I think that the management here believe they are in a separate team to the employees.'			
All shop-floor workers	88	5	7

The figures speak for themselves. Invariably, when the subject of single status was raised with shop-floor interviewees it would be met initially with a quizzical look, then amusement, then anger. When they eventually expressed themselves, these workers demanded far more substantial changes in both material and class-relational terms than that provided by mere managerial platitudes or the superficial benefits of single-status canteens, car-parks and the like. A cranedriver:

> All single status means for management is that I don't have to clock in and that type of thing. But does that make us all equal? Yeah, I understand the fact that you need leaders, but if it's real single status then why can't we have the same money? If the general manager and the manufacturing manager, and the rest of 'em, didn't turn up for work today, would the factory stop running? Of course it wouldn't. It would keep going. But it would stop like that if the shop-floor didn't turn up. It's the workforce who should have the top status here. And the management should come down to our status, then they might see for themselves what we've been suffering over the years. No, the production workers are the real breadwinners for the company. All these others are just hangers-on and pussy cats.
>
> In any case, all this talk about single status, it's a dream, man, it's a dream!

> You don't think the Japs have got single status do you? All they've got is fucking canteens and uniforms. And they'll tell you that, 'right, lads, we're all equal now!' But some people are more equal than others. Believe me, we need a revolution here. And it will come.

Many workers spoke in similarly trenchant terms about their aspirations for more dignity and equality at work. But aspirations they remained, for few believed that management at CarPress, or elsewhere for that matter, would be prepared to dilute its status, power and control. A woman from the assembly shop said, 'We should all be on the same rates and benefits, but if you're talking about getting rid of "us and them", I can tell you the "them" would never give up their status;' in the same vein, a foreman commented, 'I really think single status is an impossibility here. Our managers strive to become one of "them" rather than one of "us" and they'll defend it to their death;' and a toolmaker felt, 'There is, there's a definite class distinction here and in British industry generally. And I think over recent years the distinction's got worse, we've gone into reverse.'

These shop-floor workers well understood the duplicitous nature of the single-status rhetoric that has become fashionable in business circles. They recognized a confidence trick when they saw one. And on occasions they could also mobilize their collective humour to 'get even' with management. A press shop operator recounted a recent example of this:

> Single status? That's a laugh! Not so long ago we had a mass communications meeting with senior management about the introduction of the new agreement. After a while, one of the managers starts to talk about single status and he started everyone off sniggering. Then Mervyn, one of my mates on the next table, stands up and shouts, 'I tell you what, if we've got single status coming here, you can take my Honda 50 and I'll have one of those management Rovers out there.' We all roared with laughter at this and banged the tables, and of course, the management quickly moved on to another subject. Angry they were too. But d'you see what I mean? Single status is one big joke in this factory.

Drawing together the egalitarianism and equal involvement in decision-making commonly associated with single status, and the participative workplace democracy which is assumed to be embodied in teamworking and the new communications policies, CarPress's shop-floor workers were asked in both questionnaire surveys whether they felt they had 'enough say' in decisions made at work affecting different levels of the

Table 8.4 *Shop-floor workers' assessment of employee involvement (Percentage by column; N = 316 (1994) and 471 (1995))*

	Percentage 1994	Percentage 1995
'Enough say on decisions made about your own job and working conditions?'		
Yes	16	24
No	84	76
'Enough say on decisions made about the running of your department/section?'		
Yes	11	13
No	89	87
'Enough say on decisions made about the whole factory?'		
Yes	5	7
No	95	93

organization. In this way, the surveys provided a rudimentary indicator of the overall impact of the new employee involvement initiatives a year after their implementation. The results are summarized in Table 8.4.

The results demonstrate the presence of a profound democratic deficit on the shop-floor of the 1990s. Workers' say over changes to their own jobs and working conditions improved only moderately, and even this result was distorted by the length-of-service factor: in 1995, 80 per cent of the majority group of workers with more than ten years' service indicated that they did not have enough say on decisions made about their own job and working conditions compared to 69 per cent of workers with less than five years' service. And as Table 8.4 shows, their involvement in the decision-making process at the sectional level – which teamworking and the team brief are supposed to especially enhance – remained abysmally low; whilst at the factory level it was almost non-existent.

These statistics should surprise nobody. The exigencies and driving logic and intensity of contemporary capitalist mass-production do not provide sufficient margin for anything approaching meaningful worker autonomy. More than ever, CarPress workers remained subordinated to management, to the customer and to the machine. What is surprising is that some managers really believed that their programmes of specious employee involvement, of ideological control, would actually deceive their subordinates; some were even seduced by it themselves. But on the shop-floor, where only the hard experience of capitalist social relations counts, real 'empowerment', 'enrichment' and 'autonomy' remained both abstract and elusive.

Trust, Loyalty and Commitment

High-trust management–labour relations in contemporary capitalist production are often assumed to arise from a post-Taylorist work organization which induces a new common purpose between managers and workers. Trust, loyalty and commitment may then develop through the processes of joint problem-solving, sharing information and devolving discretion, responsibility and autonomy (Fox, 1985). To put this another way, 'a Taylorite factory de-skills blue-collar workers and removes the need for trust; an un-Taylorite factory would tend to improve worker skills such that workers could be trusted with a higher degree of responsibility for both the design and implementation of the production process' (Fukuyama, 1995, p. 234). Unconsciously or not, these writers use the same kind of arguments which, ironically, Frederick W. Taylor himself employed to support his vision of cooperative and participative employment relations in factories organized on scientific management principles. Taylor believed that low-trust relations and antagonism in industry could be dissolved by securing a complete mental revolution on the part of both managers *and* workers: 'the great revolution that takes place in the mental attitude of the two parties under scientific management is that both sides take their eyes off the division of the surplus as the all important matter, and together turn their attention toward increasing the size of the surplus until this surplus becomes so large ... that there is ample room for a large increase in wages for the workmen and an equally large increase in profits for the manufacturer' (Taylor, 1947, cited in Bendix, 1956, p. 276).

Notwithstanding these ideological similarities, using the managerialist theses of Ohno (1988) and Womack *et al.* (1990), Fukuyama goes on to place his analysis into the context of Japanization. He argues that 'un-Taylorite' Japanese production methods, and in particular teamworking, are dependent on the commitment, participation and knowledge of the workforce and that the experience of working in teams itself engenders trust, loyalty and commitment. For these reasons, Japanese lean production represents a more 'humane, communal factory system'. Therefore, without digressing into the possibility that wider cultural and political supports may also determine worker commitment (which in any case, some writers refute[10]), the main emphasis is placed upon the relationship between contemporary shifts in the nature of the capitalist labour process and changing shop-floor values.

At CarPress, although the reorganization of work offered affected employees little meaningful autonomy, they nevertheless worked in teams, they worked more flexibly and they were expected to use their initiative for the benefit of the company. The preceding four chapters have placed most emphasis upon the shop-floor's reaction against the consequent loss of traditional controls over the labour process. However, the research also enquired whether these significant changes were accompanied by the emergence of new, more individualistic, even enterprise-based shop-floor values, built upon the trust that the business writers associate with teamwork.

The 1994 and 1995 questionnaire surveys contained a number of questions aimed at assessing this. For example, all employees were asked to select from a list of eleven options, three aspects of work which they felt were most important to them and three which were least important. These are listed in Table 8.5.

In both years the majority of respondents clearly prioritized 'decent working conditions', 'good pay' and 'job security' as being most important, which is not in itself surprising. But they also shunned options more associated with the pro-enterprise values of teamwork such as 'getting on well with supervision', 'plenty of overtime', 'good promotion prospects', 'having responsibilities at work' and 'opportunity to use initiative'. Therefore, the data provided no evidence of any initial shift in workers' values following CarPress's 'un-Taylorite' work reorganization.

Both surveys also explored the question of trust. In 1994, respondents were asked whether or not they agreed with the statement that 'the Company treats me with trust and respect'. Seventy-one per cent of shop-floor workers disagreed; 40 per cent strongly disagreed. In the second survey, a year after the introduction of teamworking and the various accompanying instruments of ideological control, although the question was operationalized in a slightly different way, this low-trust relationship clearly hardened; 89 per cent of shop-floor workers indicated low levels of trust existing between managers and the workforce. The data from the second survey are displayed in Table 8.6.

Teamworking, the new communications, single status and other management initiatives together, therefore, failed to dent the traditional,

Table 8.5 *Aspects of work most and least important to all employees (N = 383 (1994) and 498 (1995))*

	Percentage 1994	Percentage 1995
The aspects of work which respondents felt were most important to them.		
Decent working conditions	56	62
Getting on well with colleagues	23	22
Getting on well with supervision	4	5
Good pay	83	80
Having an interesting job	21	21
Having responsibilities at work	7	6
Job security	76	73
Plenty of overtime	5	6
Opportunity to use initiative	6	7
Good industrial relations	14	12
Good promotion prospects	4	5
The aspects of work which respondents felt were least important to them.		
Decent working conditions	6	5
Getting on well with colleagues	18	18
Getting on well with supervision	40	39
Good pay	3	3
Having an interesting job	14	19
Having responsibilities at work	32	25
Job security	1	3
Plenty of overtime	72	65
Opportunity to use initiative	18	24
Good industrial relations	16	21
Good promotion prospects	59	57

Respondents were asked to choose three aspects of work which were most important to them and three which were least important.

low-trust values of instrumentalism on the CarPress shop-floor. Moreover, the cynical, but trenchant and emphatic, worker denials of the notion that things could ever be different suggested that the low-trust management–labour relations which accompany the intensification of labour exploitation in lean production would endure in the longer term. A press fitter typically commented, 'This factory is just a place of work, nothing more. It's just a place where we happen to come into work and

Table 8.6 *All employees' assessment of the level of trust existing between management and the workforce (Percentage by row; N = 533)*

	Complete trust	Trust most of the time	Not much trust	No trust at all
All operators	2	9	35	54
Skilled operators	1	1	40	58
Semi-skilled operators	2	12	34	52
Staff	2	23	56	19

where management dictate to us all the time. You've got no rights here any more.' When asked about loyalty to the company, workers replied that the only loyalty they extended was their allegiance to the pay cheque every Thursday. And an assembly shop operator spoke for many when he replied:

> No, it's not the British way, it's not in our culture. And in any case, management here don't actually want loyalty. All they want is for us to work harder. It's the same old Tory philosophy: 'if the rich man works harder pay him more, if the poor man works harder pay him less'... And I'm not loyal to this lot anyway. They seem like a bunch of crooks to me.

Even some of the more recent recruits felt the same way. A press shop operator:

> No mate, I'm telling you, there's been no change in attitudes here. It's as bad as ever. I've only been here for two years. I used to be keen when I started, mind, I wanted to get on. But now I've learnt, what's the point? The company never invests in new machinery. These presses are 30 years old, they're clapped out. They're always breaking down. But the company doesn't care. As long as they're making money out of us, that's the only thing they care about. We can never make money out of them. No. I've had it up to here. My attitude now is 'fuck the lot of 'em'. Nowadays, every morning I just clock in, keep my head down and try and earn a wage. I don't think about the job, I just turn off. When my eight hours are up I just clock off and go home.

If anything, these comments suggest a reinforcing of the instrumentalist base of worker 'commitment' with absolutely no evidence of the emergence of pro–company attitudes which many business writers tend to emphasize. However, we cannot leave the matter there. Certain other facets of traditional shop-floor values were slowly changing. This study emphasizes the increasingly harsh nature of labour exploitation which was intrinsic to CarPress's implementation of 'Japanese-style' management initiatives in the 1990s. Nevertheless, in earlier times, stress and drudgery also characterized the labour process, despite the presence of local rank-and-file controls. But at least this human degradation was mitigated by a communitarian shop-floor culture which incorporated the values of mutual help, comradeship and, crucially, humour. At various times, different workers provided their own fond anecdotes of manifestations of this. To provide just one example, Ieuan Thomas remembered the antics of one character in the assembly shop who came to be known as 'the Mohican':

> I remember, not long after I started in 1964, the metal finishers used to have their benches arranged in lines, row after row of them. And no kidding, at the end of every line, without exception, you'd have a foreman watching over you all the time. Real bowler-hatted stuff. There used to be hundreds of 'em. One man, I can't remember his name, he got really pissed off with this. One night, he went home and had the whole of his head shaved, except for a line down the middle. Just like a Mohican. The next day, he came in to work with a pick axe. Then, no word of a lie, he chopped up his bench into firewood with his axe, put the wood into a neat pile and, no kidding, he stripped off bollock naked, lit the wood and danced around the fire waving his pick axe around like a spear. And he was chanting, 'Too many chiefs, not enough Indians! Too many chiefs not enough Indians!'
>
> We couldn't believe it. We just stood there laughing our heads off. Next thing, the superintendent comes along and screams, 'Fuck me, what's wrong with him? Someone take him away!' So they did. He ended up in a mental hospital for a couple of days for observation! Mind you, he was soon back at work.

Notwithstanding the partly myth-like quality of the narrative – which is an inevitable function of the passing of time – we have here a somewhat idiosyncratic form of resistance to management control which embodies a distinctively working-class comic humour. One difference between life on the shop-floor during this era and the present is that contemporary management will no longer tolerate any form of worker insubordination, irrespective of the shape in which it comes. And in particular, it will not tolerate insubordination that questions the method of operation or rationale of capitalist mass-production. The new management techniques, therefore, do not allow for 'Mohicans' or other manifestations of working-class opposition. Neither do they respect the more communitarian values of working-class solidarity. At the end of one interview, Annette, a woman from 'Bosnia', delivered the following parting shot of dejection:

> The way things have turned out here now, this continual fear for your job, it's resulted in a situation where we're all competing against one another. We're all saying, 'Yeah, I could do this job, I could do that job.' But there's no longer any consideration for others. What about those who can't do the hard jobs anymore, those who can't keep up with the speed and the pressure? In the old days we'd help them out, but I'm afraid it's not like that any more. The company has made sure that we're all on our own, that we're by ourselves. There's just no togetherness any more.
>
> This factory used to be a happier place. There used to be a time when we all mucked in and helped each other out. But now we're all forced to rush our own jobs. We rush every job. And some men are struggling with nobody there to help them any more. Personally, I try to help people out, I'm still striving to get this better atmosphere, but to tell you the truth it's all gone. Most people in this factory now hate the place. They come in for the money and get out as soon as they can.

This poignant commentary on the shifting nature of shop-floor social relations in the 1990s injects a final human element into this chapter's analysis of the different management techniques that may be employed to build new corporate cultures of cooperation and market awareness. Like many of the Japanese transplants in South Wales, CarPress was not so much interested in quixotic notions of 'worker loyalty' and 'total commitment' to the firm but more in securing personal responsibility, personal discipline and a sense of obligation to production, the market and the customer. The case study demonstrates that in fact, a pervasive mood of compulsion and fear on the shop-floor can drive these sentiments rather than any sense of true commitment.

Moreover, as a number of the above comments testify, the same pressures are forcing workers to substitute the principle of individualistic self-protection for the ethic of mutual support. This raises the possibility that although shop-floor instrumentalism remains dominant, other aspects of the customary 'factory-class consciousness' are now under threat. In a penetrating climate of fear, and a wider economic and political environment which itself critically undercuts effective rank-and-file resistance, the imposition of managerial and customer prerogatives – aimed at maximizing surplus extraction and capital accumulation – is acting to pervert the virtue and integrity of traditional shop-floor solidarity. This process of change, which some call 'Japanization' but which might just as appropriately be termed 'unfettered capitalism', therefore, impairs not just the material condition and collective strength of those who labour but also their human spirit.

Notes

1 Guest (1987; 1991) provides four central HRM policy goals: integrating HRM issues into corporate strategic plans; attaining both high employee behavioural commitment to pursue agreed management goals and high attitudinal commitment towards the enterprise in general; raising both the quality of management behaviour towards employees and the quality of employees' skills and qualifications; and finally, introducing workforce functional flexibility and an organic, organizational flexibility capable of meeting the challenge of market-led changes.

2 Of the 533 respondents in the second questionnaire survey (November 1995), 63 per cent had more than ten years' service with the company and 78 per cent were aged 31 or above. Only 26 per cent had five years' service or less.

3 At Toyota's new vehicle assembly plant in Derby, the selection process can take from two to six months. It comprises a daunting series of interviews, psychometric tests, observation quizzes and different days spent at an assessment centre (Bailey, 1995). Similar techniques allow Japanese auto plants in the USA to weed out 'troublemakers' and dissidents to select group-oriented workers who identify with the company (Fucini and Fucini, 1990; Kenney and Florida, 1993).

4 Using the 1994 Labour Force Survey data, Gregg and Wadsworth found that the stock of jobs available to unemployed workers has changed substantially over the past two decades: 'the full-time job is in secular decline and is being replaced with either part-time, or self-employed and latterly temporary working opportunities' (1997, p. 73). Temporary jobs are now heavily over-represented in the stock of entry jobs (defined as those held by respondents who are in a job with tenure of 12 months or less and who were out of work one year earlier). Temporary jobs are also heavily over-represented in job-to-job moves (defined as a move by respondents with tenure of 12 months or less and who were also in employment with a different firm one year earlier) (1997, p. 69).

5 At the time of the 1991 Government Census, members of ethnic minority groups comprised only 0.4 per cent of the total residents in the Oldport travel-to-work area. Despite this, at the end of 1994, the CarPress Personnel Department confirmed that a small number of the 1,000 job applications in

the firm's 'waiting file' came from members of these groups. However, they had never been considered for interview.

6 A recent IDS Study based on CBI data found that many employers are currently focusing their attention on employee absenteeism because of the costs of both sick pay and disruption to production. Many are attempting to secure worker accountability for absence using measures such as the return-to-work interview more scrupulously than hitherto (IDS, 1994a). Another recent TUC survey of 171 workplaces found that employers were reducing the costs of sickness absence by tightening their absence control policies and sick pay schemes and taking health more into account in the recruitment process. Women, older people and disabled workers suffered particular discrimination here (Welfare at Work, 1996).

7 'Employees Sustaining Injury at Work Policy', CarPress Ltd, 7.2.95.

8 The company's new shop-floor grading scheme corresponded with the operators' NVQ ratings. At the bottom end of the scheme, all Grade 4 operators (the majority) were assessed at NVQ Level 1, and at the top end, Grade 1 skilled workers were rated at NVQ Level 4. At the time of the research, the company had embarked upon major investment in training its semi-skilled operators to NVQ Level 2. This involved limited technical skills training; it was more an exercise in changing attitudes. For example, different units covered customer–supplier relations, involvement in communications, teamworking skills, presentational skills and 'self-analysis', 'a kind of continuous improvement of the self', as one NVQ facilitator expressed it. In the second questionnaire survey (November 1995), only 10 per cent of shop-floor respondents believed the NVQ programme was introduced to 'develop technical skills'; 13 per cent felt it 'served no useful purpose at all'; 18 per cent believed it was introduced to 'develop more positive attitudes to change at the workplace'; whilst 45 per cent believed the programme was merely 'window dressing put on to impress the customer'.

9 Extract from 'The Chairman's Platform', *CarPress Chronicle*, Summer 1995.

10 As noted in Chapter 1, Dohse *et al.* (1985) argue that the weakness of Japanese trade unions, the dependence of Japanese employees on a single employer, and their dependence on both the individualized wage system and the goodwill of the supervisor, together constitute the more decisive factors in the 'committed worker' syndrome.

9 CONCLUSION

Throughout most of this book, the analysis has investigated the impact of Japanese-style management innovations on the interests of shop-floor labour. The author makes no apology for this. Industrial sociology is becoming consumed by managerial questions; for example, the extent to which new management techniques in the UK are different from old management techniques; or different from practice in Japan and other competing capitalist economies; or, whether the emerging restructured work organizations are fully functional, part-functional or dysfunctional. Such a managerial bias is a corollary of the academic world's current tendency to exclude labour from society. The notion that a fundamental conflict of interests between capital and labour remains central to the organization of work in the factories of the 1990s has succumbed to the new egalitarian ideology of 'empowerment'. Consequently, both the articulation of separate class interests and the mobilization of working-class resistance in its various collective and individual forms are no longer subjects of interest. Where the standpoint of labour is considered it is more often placed into an analytical framework of advanced modernity rather than advanced capitalism; here, subjectivity and conflicts over individual identity count for more than conventional resistance against a subordinating capitalist class.

In contrast, the research described in the foregoing chapters demonstrates that by putting labour back into industrial sociology and recognizing that the essential conditions for resistance and misbehaviour are still present at the workplace (Thompson and Ackroyd, 1995, p. 629), we find that the process which some call 'Japanization' at work is not unproblematic. If the new management initiatives constitute rational capitalist attempts to intensify rates of labour exploitation, then we must expect worker resistance, including traditional collective forms.

Analysts who are primarily interested in management systems and organization theory would discover much material in this book to reject the universalistic, paradigmatic approach to Japanization followed by many business school writers. Pure JIT/TQM/HRM ideal types have no factual basis because, *inter alia*, the existence of different corporate logics, different sectoral traditions, different technological constraints, different product markets, different labour markets and different industrial relations traditions together produce diverse, often more mundane work organizational outcomes. However, when the management innovations are looked at from the standpoint of the many individuals who bring their labour power to the shop-floor of 'Japanizing' factories, then taken together, the transplant survey and case study data reveal a more uniform, significant, and indeed, pernicious series of changes. In particular, once the impact on labour's *interests* – rather than management system – becomes the focal point of the analysis, then a marked congruence emerges between the different management practices, modes of work organization and human resource management strategies followed in both the Japanese transplants in South Wales and in CarPress.

Operating within an economic environment of intense competitive pressure, the managers of lean mass-production in these firms were not particularly interested in enriching the lives of their employees; during many discussions with the author on this subject they regarded the notion that assembly line workers could enjoy meaningful 'empowerment' and 'self-management' as nonsensical. Their labour control priorities were somewhat more mundane than this, reflecting the timeless capitalist exigencies of efficient surplus extraction and capital accumulation. But from the workers' perspective, these priorities represented a fundamental threat to traditional forms of rank-and-file control and shop-floor autonomy. It is in relation to this order of change that a 'model' of Japanese practice begins to emerge. This is summarized in Table 9.1.

Whether organized on the basis of cells, teams or conventional long assembly lines, the work of most production operators was intense, limited in skill, and lacking in autonomy. The gradual dismantling of rank-and-file controls over the labour process in the British case study, and their suppression in the greenfield Japanese transplants, imposed stricter managerial prerogatives and a more flexible and productive consumption of labour power. And this distinctively disciplined approach to production was matched in the ideological sphere. The different firms in this study displayed little interest in cultivating new, innovative and enterprising workforce attitudes. Instead, they sought to instil something more prosaic but fundamental to the needs of the 'capitalist spirit'. That is,

Table 9.1 *A 'Japanese model' of labour control in South Wales*

Organization of the labour process

Lean production control: workers more completely subordinated to the machine and to the intensive pace of production by reducing production line buffers, stocks and work-in-progress; by more accurately synchronizing output with customer demand; and by the maintenance of strict bell-to-bell working.

Labour flexibility and teamworking: labour utilization maximized and idle time minimized by dismantling/prohibiting traditional job and skill demarcations; maintaining a fragmentation of tasks; and enlarging jobs by task accretion, either within team organization, or by management-controlled flexibility on conventional assembly lines.

Worker accountability and teams: workers organized into 'teams' or groups to create manageable units for accountability to both management and the customer.

Industrial engineering: trade union and rank-and-file influence over conventional processes of job design and work measurement eradicated.

Supervisory control: strict, close supervision of the production worker, and where appropriate, direct customer surveillance.

Continuous improvement: labour productivity systematically raised by operating strictly management-controlled kaizen schemes with limited worker participation.

Socialization process

Employee recruitment: exploitation of sophisticated recruitment techniques and/or temporary labour to build workforces sufficiently malleable to meet the strict demands of lean producton.

Job security: job security philosophies – rather than guarantees – offered in return for worker cooperation and compliance. Job security for core workforces maintained on the basis of lean manning; labour intensification; reduced absenteesim by attacking workers' sick leave rights; extended working hours; and perpetual job insecurity for temporary workers.

Direct communications: unidirectional employee communications techniques used to undermine independent trade union information; to instil an understanding of economic and market discipline; and to develop employee commitment to corporate objectives.

Single status and equal opportunity policies: used to promote corporate egalitarian ideology rather than address concrete inequalities at the workplace.

Industrial relations policy: promoting non-adversarial industrial relations by subverting conventional trade union democracy. Involves incorporating trade union officials and shop stewards within company councils or more informal bargaining arrangements; and both fragmenting rank-and-file resistance and weakening traditional values of shop-floor solidarity.

a sense of responsibility in production and accountability to the customer, and this, as a stark substitute for those facets of working-class loyalty and solidarity which threaten capitalist interests.

This uniformity of practice did not emerge naturally or by accident. A number of different catalysts and forces came into play to connect the process of change at CarPress with the various labour-control techniques operating in the Japanese transplants both in South Wales and elsewhere in the UK.

The first of these is the effect of the sheer density of Japanese transplant activity in South Wales. Although only one firm operated in the same sector as CarPress, the collective presence of so many salient factories – a good number of them large employers – in such a relatively small industrial area impacted upon the consciousness of management. And particular local activities and encounters strengthened this. For example, the Welsh Development Agency, different Training and Enterprise Councils, different Chambers of Commerce and other similar agencies regularly organize seminars, conferences and more informal meetings which bring together managers in Japanese and British plants with the explicit purpose of facilitating the diffusion of ideas.

Moreover, this contact, in a region of high unemployment – which plays on the fears of managers as well as workers – heightens the ideological threat of Japanese competition. Many writers emphasize the symbolic significance of the Japanese model in Britain which managements often mobilize against workers in pursuance of traditional agendas of labour intensification (Elger and Smith, 1994b). Notions of 'the Japanese productivity miracle' and 'factory survival' are central here. But perceptions of Japanese superiority also impact upon managerial consciousness and social action, to the extent that, as we saw in Chapter 4, many CarPress managers genuinely believed that a more fundamental restructuring of shop-floor work organization and social relations was necessary if their factory was to successfully compete.

The intensity of market competition, on a global scale, is therefore central here. The new relationships between Japanese 'customer' assemblers and their suppliers in particular product markets constitutes an important facet of this. The de-industrialization of the British economy over the past two decades has left surviving British suppliers in cars, electronics, and other sectors, desperate for new contracts with the incoming inward investors. So desperate, in fact, that they are forced to concede to Japanese transplant management influence and direct intervention over their labour costs and labour control strategies. As we saw in Chapters 4 to 7, this 'rule of the customer' had a profound impact on both the reorganization of work at CarPress and the shop-floor's ability to resist this. It also, of course, increases the density of interaction between managers in British component suppliers and Japanese assemblers, a factor which helps sustain the process of change.

Lastly, the distinctive contemporary economic and political environment oils the wheels of the diffusion process in a number of ways. The introduction, into a brownfield, unionized car plant, of many aspects of the new labour control and exploitation policies described throughout this book would have been unthinkable twenty years ago. During the 1970s, organized labour in British industry was not in a position of control, despite the alarm and foreboding of many right-wing political commentators at the time of the 1979 General Election. However, the balance of class forces was more in its favour at that time than at any subsequent period. Indeed, during the 1980s and 1990s, the cumulative effect of de-industrialization, mass unemployment, anti-trade-union legislation, and the high-profile defeats of such seemingly invincible groups of workers as miners, shipbuilders, steelworkers, carworkers, dockers and printers, has left an indelible mark on the spirit of resistance of British workers. In this context, many British managers have acquired sufficient confidence to effect a restructuring of work which significantly shifts the frontier of control on the shop-floor in capital's favour.

The British state has also played a more particular and interventionist role here, despite the *laissez-faire* ideology of successive Conservative governments. As we noted in Chapter 4, at the regional level the Welsh Development Agency now acts both as broker in matching British suppliers to different inward investors and as management consultant in helping the former introduce acceptable working practices. At the national level, the state has offered substantial financial incentives to Japanese firms who locate in the UK. Hiding under the benign cloak of dynamic 'job creation', the Thatcher regime of the 1980s was more interested in using Japanese inward investors to catalyse significant changes in British industrial relations. Thus, mobilizing the symbolism of the no-strike deal, and the dominant perception of consensus-based relationships between workers and managers in Japanese firms, the Conservatives sought to decisively weaken the bargaining power of British unions by explicitly supporting Japanese enterprise unionism (McIlroy, 1988).

It has become fashionable in the 'post-labour' labour process debate to de-emphasize and even marginalize the different strategies of managerial control over labour power. As Thompson (1989, pp. 231–4) has observed, some writers reject the privileged moment of extraction of surplus value in the circuit of capital, whilst others question the idea of control strategy completely, stressing instead the salience of managerial contradictions, complex contingencies and 'negotiated preferences'. This author's analysis of both management practice in Japanese transplants and the political process of change at CarPress demonstrates that such postmodern obfuscation and obsession with appearances should be disregarded. When asked the appropriate questions, the managers at CarPress enunciated an explicit discourse of labour control. They talked incessantly of their inability to shape and control the views of older workers; they became obsessed with undermining traditional rank-and-file controls over labour allocation and the pace of work; they wistfully reflected upon the efficacy of Japanese control strategies on greenfield sites; their constant fear of losing control determined their exclusion of the principle of self-management from the practice of teamworking; their fear of losing control also determined their rejection of full worker participation in kaizen; the introduction of bell-to-bell working constituted an emphatic direct control over workers' time; their new industrial relations policies embodied their resolution to dissipate rank-and-file control; and their various socialization practices were aimed at cementing a more endurable labour control. Managerial social action was saturated in the politics of control.

Of course, this was not control for its own sake. As Thompson points out, those who criticize the emphasis upon control confuse 'the *goals* of firms and managers with the *means* of achieving them. Control is seldom relevant to the former, but essential to the latter' (1989, p. 234). Thus, at CarPress, and in the Japanese transplants, different techniques of control over labour power merely ensured a more efficient process of surplus extraction and capital accumulation.

The model of labour control summarized in Table 9.1 is notable for the comprehensive repertoire of techniques applied at the point of production. However, external forces are also important here. Just as economic and political developments facilitated the introduction of these measures, they also help sustain their effective operation. Indeed, as we shall now discuss, once the politico-economic elements of both the state and the rights of the consumer are incorporated into the analysis, then these Japanese and 'Japanized' management regimes take on distinctly hegemonic characteristics.

Burawoy (1985) periodizes developments in the process of capitalist production on the basis of changes in the political apparatuses of production, that is, the shifting role of the state in reproducing the social relations of the labour process through the regulation of struggles. This periodization comprises three phases: despotic regimes; hegemonic regimes; and hegemonic despotism.

In the first phase, Marx's (1976) conceptualization of factory despotism, under which workers are subordinated to the merciless dictates of the foreman and the machine, is supplemented by the dull force of economic compulsion – the worker's dependence on cash earnings for a livelihood. This 'market despotism' was, therefore, a wholly coercive system of labour exploitation. In the face of crises of under-consumption and periodic worker resistance, it gave way to the second phase of the hegemonic regime in which the mobilization of the labourer's consent to continuing exploitation prevailed over coercion. Here, two forms of state intervention broke the ties binding the reproduction of labour power to productive activity in the workplace. Firstly, social insurance legislation provided workers with a guaranteed minimum income independent of their participation in production. Secondly, the state placed limits on managerial domination and coercion by establishing a legal framework of workers' rights. Burawoy argues that in these new conditions, management could no longer rely on the economic whip of the market to sustain factory discipline; instead, 'workers must be persuaded to cooperate with management. Their interests must be coordinated with those of capital' (1985, p. 126).

Burawoy characterizes contemporary developments in capitalist production in terms of a transition to hegemonic despotism. According to this analysis, the state regulation of factory conflict in a context of global capitalism eventually laid the basis for a further crisis of profitability. The emergence of new, coercive factory regimes in semi-peripheral regions of the global economy exposed the costs and rigidities of Western hegemonic regimes. At the same time, Western multinational companies could more easily exploit the large pools of cheap, malleable labour in both peripheral countries and peripheral regions in the advanced countries. These global operations became possible because the fragmented labour process can now be effectively coordinated and reintegrated by exploiting advanced transport and communications technologies. Burawoy argues that, as a result of these structural changes, worker consent under hegemonic regimes gives way to the coercive pressures of hegemonic despotism. The tying of workers' interests to the survival of their factories leaves them defenceless against the new challenge of global capital. Workers are forced to make concessions on wages and employment conditions in order to maintain relative plant profitability and to limit the possibility of a transfer of operations. Thus, the new hegemonic despotism is 'the "rational" tyranny of capital mobility over the *collective* worker .... The fear of being fired is replaced by the fear of capital flight, plant closure, transfer of operations, and plant disinvestment' (1985, p. 150).

The interaction between the political apparatus, market relations and the Japanese control techniques summarized in Table 9.1 established a distinctive variant of this new despotism in the factories of South Wales. During the 1980s and 1990s, the state enforced a series of policies which together established a quite pervasive and coercive climate of fear. Workers' rights came under a ruthless assault from successive Conservative regimes. Effective minimum wage provisions in the form of Wages Council settlements, unemployment benefits, social security benefits, strike benefits and so on, were either discontinued or significantly cut back. For many workers, such employment protection rights as safeguards against unfair dismissal and victimization also disappeared. At the same time, as the events described in Chapter 7 exemplify, different governments significantly undermined trade union rights and immunities, a process which is unlikely to be reversed by the current New Labour regime. And both capital and the state used the new anti-union legislation to prosecute a number of significant victories against some of Britain's most powerful unions.

The state also played a central role in both creating and sustaining mass unemployment throughout most of this period. In South Wales, as we saw in the last chapter, employers are able to adroitly exploit large pools of young, more acquiescent workers both to manage their new lean manning strategies and to weaken traditional shop-floor solidarity.

These quite profound state interventions partly repaired the ties which bound the reproduction of labour power to the labour process under market despotism. However, a new development in the form of close, 'cooperative' customer–supplier relations has added a further twist to this picture of market coercion at the workplace. Burawoy's conceptualization of hegemonic despotism emphasizes the ability of footloose global capital to sap the confidence and weaken the resistance of collective labour. In contrast to this, although the outcome is the same, different capitals in the lean production chain are now quite prepared to commit themselves to their suppliers and customers – and to their workers and local communities – on a long-term basis. But this commitment only stands provided their workforces are also prepared to submit themselves to the dictates of market relations *within* production. That is, as we have seen in various parts of this book, those workers who resist in the supplier factories of lean production may soon find themselves subject to the job-threatening interventions of the customer. And many of those who labour within the final assembler in the production chain are also subject to the dictates of the consumer as embodied in the unrelenting pressure of just-in-time assembly.

We have arrived, therefore, at a 'Japanese model' of labour regulation in South Wales bolstered by distinctive politico-economic conditions which critically constrain labour resistance. It constitutes a particularly coercive form of hegemonic despotism which sits in stark contrast to the spurious business ideologies of worker empowerment and autonomy. However, this author is not suggesting that these developments in coercion and control have effectively banished resistance from the shop-floor of the 1990s. The case study material in Chapters 4 to 8 provided a wealth of evidence of the tenacity of different forms of worker opposition to the new management techniques. And although the CarPress management eventually succeeded in putting into place its work organizational controls by mercilessly sacking workers and thereby defeating general rank-and-file opposition, the resulting shop-floor defeatism did not translate into total submission. If the introduction of new management techniques is a function of the dynamic of class struggle, then so is their continuing application. As Holloway comments on the 'new reality' of the car industry epitomized by Nissan in Sunderland, 'but for capital, the struggle to subjugate and exploit labour is endless. And oppression by capital daily meets resistance from labour. The world of Nissan is suffocating, but occasionally a scream of protest breaks the silence' (1987, p. 163).

At such brownfield plants as CarPress, the organization of 'screams of protest' remains central to the politics of production. Six months after the process of sackings and shop-floor demoralization described in Chapter 7, the CarPress management attempted to implement a pay deal which involved a minimal pay rise, a worsening of the hourly paid sick pay scheme and a withdrawal of the unions' temporary workers agreement. The rank and file rejected this in a secret ballot by 22 to 1 and, against their shop stewards' recommendations, voted by 4 to 1 for a strike ballot. In customary fashion the management then threatened to close the plant and sack the first person to go on strike. After regional union officers beseeched the membership to back down – again in customary fashion – the members voted narrowly against a strike.

The significant point here is that despite their despondency, despite their lack of effective leadership, and despite their knowledge that management was likely to win this particular fight, these workers were still prepared to display overt defiance. Their actions demonstrate that although the new forms of shop-floor regulation in capitalist production exact from labour a more complete subordination to management and, through this, an intensification of its exploitation, this new despotism still cannot suppress the worker resistance and conflict which remain inherent to the capitalist labour process. The dynamic of class struggle in capitalist factory organization – including too, struggle initiated from above – ensures that the restructuring of work and employment relations will always be problematic. And it follows that the process of change will be subject to more fundamental tensions, inner contradictions and open conflict once the current imbalance of class forces begins to move in the opposite direction.

Appendix: Research Methodology

The research investigated the process of restructuring work and labour relations in South Wales by exploring the nature of new management techniques operating in local Japanese manufacturing transplants and the effect of similar techniques within an emulating British firm. In an attempt to redress industrial sociology's current managerialist bias in the analysis of contemporary change at the workplace – described in Chapter 1 – the research placed particular emphasis upon both the microdynamics of factory politics and the impact of restructuring on shop-floor workers. To operationalize this, the research design was divided into three unequal phases, which although discrete, involved some overlap in time periods:

- Initial exploratory phase (November 1993–January 1994)
- Survey of Japanese transplants (January–June 1994)
- The CarPress case study (January 1994–November 1995)

Initial Exploratory Phase

This initial phase had a number of objectives. Interviews were sought with representatives of different state and industrial agencies in South Wales to help construct a rudimentary industrial profile of the region; to procure their views on the impact of Japanese Foreign Direct Investment; and to gain an understanding of the roles of the different agencies in the change process. In addition, interviewees were invited to discuss their own experience of dealing with particular Japanese transplants and emulating British firms. Through this, the author also gained an appreciation of the problems of access; a recognition of the most appropriate firms to approach; and an initial *ad hoc* list of individual contacts within these firms.

Interviews were carried out with ten senior managers and directors from the Welsh Office; the Welsh Development Agency; different South-Wales-based Chambers of Commerce; the Confederation of British Industry; the Engineering Employers (Western Association); a South Wales Training and Enterprise Council; and a South Wales County Council Economic Development Unit. Each interview lasted two hours on average.

Survey of Japanese Transplants

This phase of the research aimed to establish the incidence and nature of any distinctive managerial innovations in the organization of the labour process and employment relations inside Japanese transplants operating in South Wales. It therefore utilized a survey method incorporating the collection of both quantitative and a limited amount of qualitative data.

At the time of the research, the South Wales region contained 17 Japanese transplants employing more than 25 workers. Following an arduous process of limited-access negotiation, 15 of the 17 firms agreed to participate in the survey. Of these, ten consented to plant visits – in some cases, multiple visits – including both interviews with managers and shop-floor observations, whilst the remaining five agreed to complete a survey questionnaire followed up by extended telephone interviews.

In all, 18 managers were interviewed for, on average, two hours each. Interviewees comprised: 11 human resource managers; a deputy managing director; a site manager; a TQM manager; a product assurance manager; a production control manager; a finance manager; and a manufacturing manager. In addition, interviews were carried out with the GMB Regional Secretary for South Wales – who was responsible for trade union members at AIWA, Diaplastics, Matsushita Electric and Star Micronics – and with a group of GMB shop stewards. A two-hour session with the General Secretary of the Welsh TUC was also incorporated into the survey's examination of new industrial relations strategies.

Interview schedules, questionnaires and factory observations were used to collect data on the following: products and product markets; factory output figures; workforce profiles, including employment of temporary labour; hours worked, overtime and shift systems; shop-floor labour processes; nature of technologies employed; production control systems; labour deployment and flexibility practices; TQM practices; employee recruitment techniques; equal opportunity policies; job security policies; employee communications; single-status policies; pay, job grading and job evaluation policies; training policies; and industrial relations issues.

The Case Study

The final – and longest – phase of the research comprised an in-depth enquiry into the process of introducing new labour regulation and HRM practices at the British case study. This involved monitoring developments at the CarPress company's Oldport factory over a period of nearly two years.

A number of preliminary interviews with different managers, shop stewards and shop-floor workers were completed in the late winter and spring of 1994. Following this, the bulk of the interviewing, the first questionnaire survey and many shop-floor observations and informal discussions took place between September and December 1994. Further groups of workers and managers were interviewed during 1995, culminating in the completion of the second questionnaire survey during November of that year. I also paid separate off-site visits to the sacked union convenor, Ieuan Thomas (a pseudonym), during 1994 and 1995.

Nearly 150 CarPress shop-floor workers, office workers and managers were interviewed in total. These comprised company directors; senior managers; line managers; production superintendents and foremen; production operators; toolmakers; press setters and fitters; electrical and mechanical maintenance fitters; project engineers; tooling engineers; industrial engineers; a robotics engineer; a CAD engineer; different quality assurance personnel; different administrative and clerical staff; senior shop stewards; staff union representatives; health and safety representatives; and the site safety officer.

The author prepared 16 different interview schedules appertaining to the various functions and jobs involved. All schedules raised the issues of teamworking; labour flexibility; bell-to-bell working; labour intensification; kaizen and other TQM practices; company communications; single-status and equal opportunity policy; company loyalty; and industrial relations. They also contained a number of prompts to initiate discussions about job satisfaction; job security; the impact of unemployment; the impact of Japanese firms in South Wales; and finally, the extent to which both the job and CarPress had changed over the years. Additional questions varied in accordance with the nature of the interviewee's occupation. For example, industrial engineers were asked a series of questions on the nature of workstudy in the 1990s; foremen were prompted to discuss the problems of policing bell-to-bell working; and so on.

Both the management and the Joint Shop Steward's Committee refused to sanction the taping of interviews for fear of inducing a walk-out of suspicious shop-floor workers. I therefore minuted each interview by taking detailed notes. Apart from this, in most cases full facilities were provided in terms of time off for interviewees and secluded interview rooms where individuals could talk openly and freely. Some employees were interviewed in small groups, some in pairs and others singly.

The first survey questionnaire was distributed during October 1994. Initially, a good majority of recipients declined to complete it, some because they believed that senior managers were likely to vet all responses and trace these back to individuals, others out of a refusal to participate in any company-approved survey. Eventually, following, amongst other measures, a three-day process of careful persuasion – during which the author visited every machine and virtually every dayshift worker on the shop-floor – 387 questionnaires were returned from a distribution of 572: a 68 per cent response rate.

Although the same milieu of suspicion prevailed during the second questionnaire survey in November 1995, out of 630 questionnaires distributed 533 were completed and returned, an improved response rate of 85 per cent. The rate on the shop-floor reached 87 per cent; in office areas it was lower at 69 per cent.

BIBLIOGRAPHY

'A Cowley Worker' (1993) 'The Unions and the Closure', in Hayter, T. and Harvey, D. (eds), *The Factory and the City*. London: Mansell.

Ackroyd, S., Burrell, G., Hughes, M. and Whitaker, A. (1988) 'The Japanization of British Industry'. *Industrial Relations Journal*, **19**, 1, 1–23.

Alford, H. (1994) 'Cellular Manufacturing: The Development of the Idea and Its Application'. *New Technology, Work and Employment*, **9**, 1, 3–18.

Amin, A. and Smith, I. (1991) 'Vertical Integration or Disintegration? The Case of the UK Car Parts Industry', in Law, C. (ed.), *Restructuring the Global Automobile Industry: National and Regional Impacts*. London: Routledge.

Anglo-Japanese Journal, **6**, 1 (May 1992).

Armstrong, P.J., Goodman, J.F.B. and Hyman, J.D. (1981) *Ideology and Shop Floor Relations*. London: Croom Helm.

Atkinson, J. (1985) 'The Changing Corporation', in Clutterbuck, D. (ed.), *New Patterns of Work*. London: Gower.

Bailey, E. (1995) 'On the Planet Toyota'. *The Electronic Telegraph*, 28.3.95.

Barratt Brown, M. and Coates, K. (1996) *The Blair Revelation: Deliverance for Whom?* Socialist Renewal No.11. Nottingham: Spokesman.

Bassett, P. (1987) *Strike Free: New Industrial Relations in Britain*. London: Macmillan, Papermac.

Beaston, M. (1993) 'Trends in Pay Flexibility'. *Employment Gazette*, September.

Bendix, R. (1956*) Work and Authority in Industry: Ideologies of Management in the Course of Industrialization*. London: Chapman and Hall Ltd.

Berggren, C. (1993) *The Volvo Experience: Alternatives to Lean Production in the Swedish Auto Industry*. London: Macmillan.

Beynon, H. (1984) *Working for Ford*. Harmondsworth: Pelican Books (2nd edn).

Black, J. and Ackers, P. (1994) 'Between Adversarial Relations and Incorporation: A Study of the "Joint Process" in an American Auto-Components Plant', in Elger, T. and Smith, C. (eds), *Global Japanization? The Transnational Transformation of the Labour Process*. London: Routledge.

Bloomfield, G. (1991) 'The World Automotive Industry in Transition', in Law, C. (ed.), *Restructuring the Global Automobile Industry: National and Regional Impacts*. London: Routledge.

Blyton, P. and Bacon, N. (1997) 'Re-casting the Occupational Culture in Steel: Some Implications of Changing from Crews to Teams in the UK Steel Industry'. *Sociological Review*, **45**, 1, 79–101.

Bradley, H. (1996) *Fractured Identities: Changing Patterns of Inequality*. Cambridge: Polity Press.

Bratton, J. (1992) *Japanization at Work: Managerial Studies for the 1990s*. Basingstoke: Macmillan.

Braverman, H. (1974) *Labour and Monopoly Capital*. New York: Monthly Review Press.

British Standard 3138 (1979) *Terms Used in Work Study and Organization and Methods (O&M)*. London: British Standards Institution.

British Standard 3375: Part 3 (1985) *Work Study and Organization and Methods (O&M), Part 3. Guide to Work Measurement*. London: British Standards Institution.

Broad, G. (1994) 'Japan in Britain: the dynamics of joint consultation'. *Industrial Relations Journal*, 25, 1, 26–38.

Brown, W. (1973) *Piecework Bargaining*. London: Heinemann.

Brown, W. and Wadhwani, S. (1990) 'The Economic Effects of Industrial Relations Legislation since 1979'. *National Institute Economic Review*, February, pp. 57–70.

Burawoy, M. (1979) *Manufacturing Consent: Changes in the Labour Process under Monopoly Capitalism*. Chicago: University of Chicago Press.

Burawoy, M. (1985) *The Politics of Production*. London: Verso.

CAITS (1988) *Teamworking: Employee Involvement but Worse*. CAITS, April.

Cavendish, R. (1982) *Women on the Line*. London: Routledge and Kegan Paul.

CBI (1991) *Business Success Through Competence: Investors in People*. London: CBI.

Cockburn, C. (1985) *Machinery of Dominance: Women, Men and Technical Know-How*. London: Pluto Press.

Cockburn, C. (1995) *In the Way of Women: Men's Resistance to Sex Equality in Organizations*. Basingstoke: Macmillan.

Conboy, W. (1976) *Pay at Work*. London: Arrow Books.

Conti, R. and Warner, M. (1994) 'Taylorism, Teams and Technology in "Reengineering" Work-organization'. *New Technology, Work and Employment*, **9**, 2, 93–102.

Cooley, M. (1987) *Architect or Bee?: The Human Price of Technology*. London: Hogarth Press.

Cumbers, A. (1996) 'Continuity or Change in Employment Relations'. *Capital and Class*, 58 (Spring 1996), 33–57.

Cusumano, M. (1985) *The Japanese Automobile Industry: Technology and Management at Nissan and Toyota*. Cambridge, Mass.: Harvard University Press.

Delbridge, R. (1995) 'Surviving JIT: Control and Resistance in a Japanese Transplant'. *Journal of Management Studies*, **32**, 6, 803–17.

Delbridge, R., Turnbull, P. and Wilkinson, B. (1992) 'Pushing Back the

Frontiers: Management Control and Work Intensification under JIT/TQM Factory Regimes'. *New Technology, Work and Employment*, **17**, 2, 97–106.

Dohse, K., Jurgens, U. and Malsch, T. (1985) "From "Fordism" to "Toyotism"? The Social Organization of the Labour Process in the Japanese Automobile Industry'. *Politics and Society*, **14**, 2, 115–46.

Done, K. (1990) 'Focus on Suppliers – Components. Survey of World Industrial Review', *Financial Times*, 8.1.90.

Done, K. (1993) 'Rocky Road Ahead for EC Motor Parts Sector'. *Financial Times*, 18.10.93.

Edwardes, M. (1983) *Back from the Brink: An Apocalyptic Experience*. London: Collins.

Edwards, P.K. (1992) 'Industrial Conflict: Themes and Issues in Recent Research'. *British Journal of Industrial Relations*, **30**, 3, 359–404.

Edwards, P.K. and Whitston, C. (1991) 'Workers Are Working Harder: Effort and Shop-floor Relations in the 1980s'. *British Journal of Industrial Relations*, **29**, 4, 595–601.

Edwards, P.K. and Whitston, C. (1993) *Attending to Work*. Oxford: Blackwell.

Elger, T. (1990a) 'Technical Innovation and Work Reorganization in British Manufacturing in the 1980s: Continuity, Intensification or Transformation?' *Work, Employment and Society*, Special Issue (May 1990), 67–101.

Elger, T. (1990b) 'Not the Polyvalent Worker: The Restructuring of Work Relations and Flexible Intensification in British Manufacturing'. Unpublished paper, Department of Sociology, University of Warwick, April 1990.

Elger, T. and Smith C. (1994a) 'Introduction', in Elger, T. and Smith, C. (eds), *Global Japanization? The Transnational Transformation of the Labour Process*. London: Routledge.

Elger, T. and Smith, C. (1994b) 'Global Japanization? Convergence and Competition in the Organization of the Labour Process', in Elger, T. and Smith, C. (eds), *Global Japanization? The Transnational Transformation of the Labour Process*. London: Routledge.

Endo, K. (1991) 'Working Hours in Japan'. Unpublished paper for the Department of Economics, Yamagata University, Japan.

Endo, K. (1994) 'Satei (Personal Assessment) and Interworker Competition in Japanese Firms'. *Industrial Relations Journal*, **33**, 1, 70–82.

Fevre, R. (1989) *Wales Is Closed*. Nottingham: Spokesman.

Fowler, C. and Bresnen, M. (1991) 'Flexible Employment Patterns in South Wales'. *Welsh Economic Review*, **4**, 2, 50–8.

Fox, A. (1974) *Beyond Contract: Work, Power and Trust Relations*. London: Faber and Faber.

Fox, A. (1985) *Man Mismanagement*. London: Hutchinson.

Friedman, A. (1977) *Industry and Labour: Class Struggle at Work and Monopoly Capitalism*. London: Macmillan.

Fucini, J. and Fucini, S. (1990) *Working for the Japanese: Inside Mazda's American Auto Plant*. New York: Free Press.

Fukuyama, F. (1995) *Trust: The Social Virtues and the Creation of Prosperity*. New York: The Free Press.

Garrahan, P. and Stewart, P. (1992) *The Nissan Enigma: Flexibility at Work in a Local Economy*. London: Mansell.

Geary, J. (1994) 'Task Participation: Employees' Participation Enabled or Constrained?', in Sissons, K. (ed.), *Personnel Management*. Oxford: Blackwell.

Geary, J. (1995) 'Work Practices: The Structure of Work', in Edwards, P. (ed.), *Industrial Relations: Theory and Practice in Britain*. Oxford: Blackwell.

Graham, L. (1994) 'How Does the Japanese Model Transfer to the United States? A View from the Line', in Elger, T. and Smith, C. (eds), *Global Japanization? The Transnational Transformation of the Labour Process*. London: Routledge.

Graham, L. (1995) *On the Line at Subaru-Isuzu: The Japanese Model and the American Worker*. Ithaca, N.Y.: ILR Press.

Gramsci, A. (1971) *Selections from the Prison Notebooks of Antonio Gramsci*. London: Lawrence and Wishart.

Grant, D. (1996) 'Japanization and the New Industrial Relations', in Beardwell, I. (ed.), *Contemporary Industrial Relations: A Critical Analysis*. Oxford: Oxford University Press.

Greenhalgh, C. and Kilminster, A. (1993) 'The British Economy, the State and the Motor Industry', in Hayter, T. and Harvey, D. (eds), *The Factory and the City*. London: Mansell.

Gregg, P. and Wadsworth, J. (1997) 'The Changing Nature of Entry Jobs in Britain', in Gregg, P. (ed.), *Jobs, Wages and Poverty: Patterns of Persistence and Mobility in the New Flexible Labour Market*. London: Centre for Economic Performance, LSE.

Griffiths, J. (1992) 'Hostile Attitude is Fading – Japanese Transplants Drive UK Component Supplier Standards'. Survey of World Automotive Components, *Financial Times*, 14.7.92.

Guest, D. (1987) 'Human Resource Management and Industrial Relations'. *Journal of Management Studies*, **24**, No.5, 503–21.

Guest, D. (1991) 'Human Resource Management: Its Implications for Industrial Relations and Trade Unions', in Storey, J. (ed.) *New Perspectives on Human Resource Management*. London: Routledge.

Hammer, M. and Champy, J. (1995) *Reengineering the Corporation: A Manifesto for Business Revolution*. London: Nicholas Brealey.

Harris, C. (1987) *Redundancy and Recession in South Wales*. Oxford: Blackwell.

Hayter, T. (1993) 'New Management Techniques', in Hayter, T. and Harvey, D. (eds), *The Factory and the City*. London: Mansell.

Hendy, J. (1991) *The Conservative Employment Laws: A National and International Assessment*. Institute of Employment Rights.

Hetherington, P. (1994) 'Earnings of 32pc below Poverty Line'. *The Guardian*, 22.11.94.

Holloway, J. (1987) 'The Red Rose of Nissan'. *Capital and Class*, 32 (Summer), 142–64.

Hughes, J. (1994) 'How Deregulation Kills Jobs'. *European Labour Forum*, 12, 29–35.

Humphrey, J. (1994) 'Japanese Methods and the Changing Position of Direct Production Workers: Evidence from Brazil', in Elger, T. and Smith, C. (eds), *Global Japanization? The Transnational Transformation of the Labour Process*. London: Routledge.

Hutton, W. (1995) *The State We're In*. London: Jonathan Cape.

Hyman, R. (1972) *Strikes*. Glasgow: Fontana/Collins.

Hyman, R. (1975) *Industrial Relations: A Marxist Introduction*. Basingstoke: Macmillan.

Hyman, R. (1988) 'Flexible Specialisation: Miracle or Myth?', in Hyman, R. and Streeck, W. (eds), *New Technology and Industrial Relations*, Oxford: Blackwell.

IDS (1990a) *Flexibility at Work*. IDS Study 454 (March).

IDS (1990b) *Total Quality Management*. IDS Study 457 (May).

IDS (1992a) *Team Briefing*. IDS Study 507 (June).

IDS (1992b) *Teamworking*. IDS Study 516 (October).

IDS (1994a) *Absence and Sick Pay Policies*. IDS Study 556 (June).

IDS (1994b) *Multiskilling*. IDS Study 558 (July).

IDS, Employment Law Handbook, Series 2, No. 7: *Industrial Action*.

Imai, M. (1986) *Kaizen*. New York: Random House.

IRS (1990) 'The Japanese in Britain: Employment Policies and Practice'. *Industrial Relations Review Report*, 470 (August).

Jenkins, A. (1994) 'Just-In-Time, "Regimes" and Reductionism'. *Sociology*, **28**, 1, 21–30.

Jones, O. (1994) 'Professionalism and Work Study: An Alternative Perspective on Subjectivity and the Labour Process'. Paper presented to the 12th Annual Labour Process Conference, Aston University, 23–25 March.

Jurgens, U., Malsch, M. and Dohse, K. (1993) *Breaking from Taylorism: Changing Forms of Work in the Automobile Industry*. Cambridge: Cambridge University Press.

Kawamura, T. (1994) 'Characteristics of the Japanese Production System and its International Transfer Model', in Abo, T. (ed.) *Hybrid Factory: The Japanese Production System in the United States*. Oxford: Oxford University Press.

Keep, E. (1991) 'Corporate Training Strategies: The Vital Component?', in Storey, J. (ed.), *New Perspectives on Human Resource Management*. London: Routledge.

Kenney, M. and Florida, R. (1993) *Beyond Mass Production: The Japanese System and its Transfer to the U.S.* Oxford: Oxford University Press.

Kumazawa, M. and Yamada, J. (1988) 'Job and Skill under the Life-long Nenko Employment Practice', in Wood, S. (ed.), *The Transformation of Work.*, London: Hutchinson.

Kumon, H., Kamiyama, K., Itagaki, H. and Kawamura, T. (1994) 'Types of Japanese Factories Located Overseas', in Abo, T. (ed.), *Hybrid Factory: The Japanese Production System in the United States*. Oxford: Oxford University Press.

The Labour Party (1997) *New Labour – Because Britain Deserves Better*. General Election Manifesto. London: The Labour Party.

Labour Research (1990) Wales – an Economy Undermined. (April).

Labour Research (1993a) The Tories' Union-Ballot Mania. (February).

Labour Research (1993b) Union Bashing – the Latest Chapter. (August).

Labour Research (1993c) Are Unions Ditching Check-Off? (August).

Labour Research (1996) Vibration White Finger. (March).

Labour Research Department (1994) UK Tops EU Hours League. *Fact Service*, **56**, 39, 29.9.94.

Labour Research Department (1995) *Human Resource Management: A Trade Unionists' Guide*. LRD Publications (May).

Lash, S. and Urry, J. (1994) *Economies of Signs and Space*. London: Sage.

Lichtenstein, N. (1988) 'The Union's Early Days: Shop Stewards and Seniority Rights', in Parker, M. and Slaughter, J. (eds), *Choosing Sides: Unions and the Team Concept*, A Labor Notes Book. Boston: South End Press.

Lincoln, J. and Kalleberg, A. (1990) *Culture, Control and Commitment: A Study of Work Organization and Work Attitudes in the United States and Japan*. Cambridge: Cambridge University Press.

Littler, C. (1982) *The Development of the Labour Process in Capitalist Societies*. London: Heinemann Educational Books.

Lovering, J. (1983) 'Uneven Development in Wales: The Changing Role of the British State', in Williams, G. (ed.), *Crisis of Economy and Ideology: Essays on Welsh Society 1840–1980*. SSRC/BSA Sociology of Wales Study Group.

Lovering, J. and Hayter, T. (1993) 'British Aerospace: The Ugly Duckling that Never Turned Into a Swan', in Hayter, T. and Harvey, D. (eds), *The Factory and the City*. London: Mansell.

Lowe, J. (1993) 'Manufacturing Reform and the Changing Role of the Production Supervisor: The Case of the Automobile Industry'. *Journal of Management Studies*, **30**, 5, 739–58.

Lucio, M. and Weston, S. (1992) 'HRM and Trade Union Responses: Bringing the Politics of the Workplace Back Into the Debate', in Blyton, P. and Turnbull, P. (eds), *Reassessing Human Resource Management*. London: Sage.

McIlroy, J. (1988) *Trade Unions in Britain Today*. Manchester: Manchester University Press.

Marchington, M., Goodman, J., Wilkinson, A. and Ackers, P. (1992) *New*

Developments in Employee Involvement. Department of Employment Research Series No. 2.

Marginson, P. (1989) 'Employment Flexibility in Large Companies: Change and Continuity'. *Industrial Relations Journal*, **20**, 101–9.

Marsden, D., Morris, T., Willman, P. and Wood, S. (1985) *The Car Industry: Labour Relations and Industrial Adjustment*. London: Tavistock.

Marsh, D. (1992*) The New Politics of British Trade Unionism: Union Power and the Thatcher Legacy*. Basingstoke: Macmillan.

Marx, K. (1976) *Capital*, vol. 1. London: Penguin Books.

Milkman, R. (1991) *Japan's California Factories: Labor Relations and Economic Globalization*. Los Angeles: University of California.

Millward, N. (1994) *The New Industrial Relations*. London: Policy Studies Institute.

Millward, N., Stevens, M., Smart, D. and Hawes, W. (1992) *Workplace Industrial Relations in Transition*. Aldershot: Dartmouth Publishing.

Milsome, S. (1993) *The Impact of Japanese Firms on Working and Employment Practices in British Manufacturing Industry*. Industrial Relations Services.

Mitsui, I. (1987) 'The Japanese Subcontracting System'. Paper presented to the Workshop on Unemployment and Labour, University of Cambridge, 3 March.

Monden, Y. (1983) *Toyota Production System*. Georgia: Industrial Engineering and Management Press.

Moreton, A. (1990) 'On the Crest of a Wave: The Swansea Bay Partnership'. *Financial Times*, 17.9.90.

Morgan, K. and Sayer, A. (1988) 'A "Modern" Industry in a "Mature" Region: The Remaking of Management–Labour Relations', in Massey, D. and Allen, J. (eds), *Uneven Development*. London: Hodder and Stoughton.

Morris, J. (1987) 'Industrial Restructuring, Foreign Direct Investment, and Uneven Development: The Case of Wales'. *Environment and Planning A*, 19, 205–24.

Morris, J., and Hill, S. (1991) *Wales in the 1990s: A European Investment Region*, Special Report No. 2143. London: The Economist Intelligence Unit and Business International.

Morris, J., Munday, M. and Wilkinson, B. (1994) *Working for the Japanese: The Economic and Social Consequences of Japanese Investment in Wales*. London: Athlone Press.

Munday, M. (1990) *Japanese Manufacturing Investment in Wales*. Cardiff: University of Wales Press.

Newsome, K. (1996) '"Beyond the confines": Just-in-time, New Buyer–Supplier Relations and Change in the Labour Process of Suppliers'. Paper presented to the 14th Annual Labour Process Conference, Aston University, March.

Nichols, T. (1986) *The British Worker Question*. London: Routledge and Kegan Paul.

Nichols, T. (1990) 'Thatcherism, Industrial Relations and British Manufacturing'. *Bulletin of Comparative Industrial Relations*, Bulletin 20, 39–61.

Nichols, T. (1991) 'Labour Intensification, Work Injuries and the Measurement of Percentage Utilization of Labour (PUL)'. *British Journal of Industrial Relations*, **29**, 4, 569–92.

Nichols, T. and Beynon, H. (1977) *Living with Capitalism: Class Relations and the Modern Factory*. London: Routledge and Kegan Paul.

Nichols, T. and O'Connell Davidson, J. (1993) 'Privatization and Economism: An Investigation amongst "Producers" in Two Privatized Public Utilities in Britain'. *Sociological Review*, **41**, 4 (November).

NVQ Monitor (Spring/Summer 1994). London: NVQ.

O'Connell Davidson, J. (1993) *Privatization and Employment Relations: The Case of the Water Industry*. London: Mansell.

Ohno, T. (1988) *Toyota Production System: Beyond Large Scale Production*. Cambridge, Mass.: Productivity Press.

Oliver, N. and Wilkinson, B. (1992) *The Japanization of British Industry*. Oxford: Blackwell.

Palmer, G. (1996) 'Reviving Resistance: The Japanese Factory Floor in Britain'. *Industrial Relations Journal*, **27**, 2, 129–42.

Pang, K. and Oliver, N. (1988) 'Personnel Strategy in Eleven Japanese Manufacturing Companies in the UK'. *Personnel Review*, **17**, 3, 16–21.

Parker, M. and Slaughter, J. (1988) *Choosing Sides: Unions and the Team Concept*, A Labor Notes Book. Boston: South End Press.

Parkes, C. (1993) 'German Producers in Turmoil: A Rough Ride for Even the Most Progressive Suppliers'. Survey of World Automotive Suppliers, *Financial Times*, 28.6.93.

Peck, F. and Stone, I. (1992) *New Inward Investment and the Northern Region Labour Market*. Employment Department Research Series No. 6 (October).

Pignon, D. and Querzola, J. (1976) 'Dictatorship and Democracy in Production', in Gorz, A. (ed.), *The Division of Labour: The Labour Process and Class Struggle in Modern Capitalism*. Brighton: Harvester Press.

Piore, M. and Sabel, C. (1984) *The Second Industrial Divide: Possibilities for Prosperity*. New York: Basic Books.

Pollert, A. (1988) 'Dismantling Flexibility'. *Capital and Class*, 38, 42–75.

Pollert, A. (1992) 'The Orthodoxy of Flexibility', in Pollert, A. (ed.), *Farewell to Flexibility?* Oxford: Blackwell.

Price, A., Morgan, K. and Cooke, P. (1994) *The Welsh Renaissance: Inward Investment and Industrial Innovation*. Regional Industrial Research Report No. 14, Cardiff. Regional Industrial Research Centre for Advanced Studies, University of Wales College of Cardiff.

Ramsay, H. (1985) 'What Is Participation For? A Critical Evaluation of Labour Process Analyses of Job Reform', in Knights, D., Willmott, H. and

Collinson, D. (eds), *Job Redesign: Critical Perspectives on the Labour Process*. Aldershot: Gower.

Ramsay, H. (1992) 'Swedish and Japanese Work Methods: Comparisons and Contrasts'. *European Participation Monitor*, 3, 37–40.

Rinehart, J., Robertson, D., Huxley, C. and Wareham, J. (1994) 'Reunifying Conception and Execution of Work Under Japanese Production Management? A Canadian Case Study', in Elger, T. and Smith, C. (eds), *Global Japanization? The Transformation of the Labour Process*. London: Routledge.

Ritzer, G. (1993) *The McDonaldization of Society*. California: Pine Forge Press.

Roberts, I. (1993) *Craft, Class and Control: The Sociology of a Shipbuilding Community*. Edinburgh: Edinburgh University Press.

Roper, I., Prabhu, V. and Van Zwanenberg, N. (1997) '(Only) Just-In-Time: Japanization and the "Non-Learning" Firm'. *Work, Employment and Society*, 11, 1, 27–46.

Roy, D. (1980) 'Fear Stuff, Sweet Stuff and Evil Stuff: Management's Defenses Against Unionisation in the South', in Nichols, T. (ed.), *Capital and Labour*. London: Athlone Press.

Sakai, K. (1990) 'The Feudal World of Japanese Manufacturing'. *Harvard Business Review* (November/December), 38–48.

Saso, M. (1990) *Women in the Japanese Workplace*. London: Hilary Shipman.

Schonberger, R. (1982) *Japanese Manufacturing Techniques*. New York: Free Press.

Schonberger, R. (1986) *World Class Manufacturing*. New York: Free Press.

Scott, A. (1994) *Willing Slaves? British Workers Under Human Resource Management*. Cambridge: Cambridge University Press.

Shingo, S. (1985) *A Revolution in Manufacturing: The SMED System*. Cambridge, Mass.: Productivity Press.

Smith, C. (1991) 'Engineers and the Labour Process' in Smith, C., Knights, D. and Willmott, H. (eds), *Whitecollar Work: The Non-Manual Labour Process*. London: Macmillan.

Smith, D. (1988) 'The Japanese Example in South West Birmingham'. *Industrial Relations Journal*, 19, 1, 41–50.

Smith, P. and Morton, G. (1993) 'Union Exclusion and the Decollectivization of Industrial Relations in Britain'. *British Journal of Industrial Relations*, 31, 1, 97–114.

Spencer, B. (1989) *Remaking the Working Class? An Examination of Shop Stewards' Experiences*. Nottingham: Spokesmen.

Starkey, K. and McKinlay, A. (1989) 'Beyond Fordism? Strategic Choice and Labour Relations in Ford UK'. *Industrial Relations Journal*, 20, 93–100.

Stewart, P. (1996) 'Introduction: Beyond Japan, Beyond Consensus? From Japanese Management to Lean Production', in Stewart, P. (ed.), *Beyond Japanese Management: The End of Modern Times?* London: Frank Cass.

Stone, K. (1974) 'The Origins of Job Structures in the Steel Industry'. *Review of Radical Political Economics*, **6**, 2 (Summer).

Storey, J. (1992) *Developments in the Management of Human Resources*. Oxford: Blackwell.

Taylor, F.W. (1947) *Scientific Management*. New York: Harper and Brothers.

Taylor, R. (1994) 'Matter of Years, not Weeks'. *Financial Times*, 23.9.94.

Taylor, W., Elger, T. and Fairbrother, P. (1991) 'Work Relations in Electronics: What has Become of Japanization in Britain?' Paper presented to the Ninth International Labour Process Conference, UMIST, Manchester, April.

Taylor, W., Elger, T. and Fairbrother, P. (1994) 'Transplants and Emulators: The Fate of the Japanese Model in British Electronics', in Elger, T. and Smith, C. (eds), *Global Japanization? The Transnational Transformation of the Labour Process*. London: Routledge.

Thompson, P. (1989) *The Nature of Work: An Introduction to Debates on the Labour Process*. Basingstoke: Macmillan.

Thompson, P. and Ackroyd, S. (1995) 'All Quiet on the Workplace Front? A Critique of Recent Trends in British Industrial Sociology'. *Sociology*, **29**, 4, 615–33.

Thompson, P. and McHugh, D. (1990) *Work Organizations*. Basingstoke: Macmillan.

Thompson, P. and Sederblad, P. (1994) 'The Swedish Model of Work Organization in Transition', in Elger, T. and Smith, C. (eds), *Global Japanization? The Transformation of the Labour Process*. London: Routledge.

Thornett, A. (1987) *From Militancy to Marxism: A Personal Account of Organising Car Workers*. London: Left View Books.

Thornett, A. (1993) 'History of the Trade Unions in Cowley', in Hayter, T. and Harvey, D. (eds), *The Factory and the City*. London: Mansell.

Tolliday, S. and Zeitlin, J. (1986) 'Shop-Floor Bargaining, Contract Unionism and Job Control: An Anglo-American Comparison', in Tolliday, S. and Zeitlin, J. (eds), *The Automobile Industry and its Workers*. Oxford: Polity Press.

Tomaney, J. (1990) 'The Reality of Workplace Flexibility'. *Capital and Class*, 40 (Spring), 31–55.

Townley, B. (1989) 'Employee Communications Programmes', in Sisson, K. (ed.), *Personnel Management in Britain*. London: Blackwell.

Townley, B. (1991) 'Selection and Appraisal: Reconstituting Social Relations?', in Storey, J. (ed.), *New Perspectives on Human Resource Management*. London: Routledge.

Toyota Motor Corporation (1992) *The Toyota Production System*. Operations Management Consulting Division: Toyota City.

Trevor, M. (1988) *Toshiba's New British Company*. London: Policy Studies Institute.

TUC (1997) 'Underworked and Underpaid: Young People's Labour Market

Experiences in the 1990s'. TUC Case Study. http://www.bizednet.bris.a-c.uk.

Turnbull, P. (1986) 'The "Japanization" of Production and Industrial Relations at Lucas Electrical'. *Industrial Relations Journal*, **17**, 3, 193–206.

Welch, R. (1991) *The Right to Strike? A Trade Union View*. London: Institute of Employment Rights.

Welfare At Work (1996) 'Sick Employers' (Campaign News). http://www.tecc.co.uk/workers/work.html.

Williams, K., Haslam, C., Williams, J., Adcroft, A. and Sukhdev, J. (1992) 'Factories or Warehouses: Japanese Manufacturing Foreign Direct Investment in Britain and the United States'. Polytechnic of East London Discussion Paper No. 6.

Williams, K., Haslam, C., Sukhdev, J. and Williams, J. (1994a) *Cars: Analysis, History, Cases*. Oxford: Berghahn Books.

Williams, K., Mitsui, I. and Haslam, C. (1994b) 'How Far from Japan? A Case Study of Japanese Press Shop Practice and Management Calculation', in Elger, T. and Smith, C. (eds), *Global Japanization? The Transformation of the Labour Process*. London: Routledge.

Willman, P. and Winch, G. (1985) *Innovation and Management Control: Labour Relations at BL Cars*. Cambridge: Cambridge University Press.

Womack, J.P., Jones, D.T. and Roos, D. (1990) *The Machine that Changed the World: The Triumph of Lean Production*. New York: Rawson Macmillan.

Wood, S. (1989) 'The Japanese Management Model: Tacit Skills in Shop Floor Participation'. *Work and Occupations*, **16**, 4, 446–60.

Wood, S. (1991) 'Japanization and/or Toyotaism?' *Work, Employment and Society*, **5**, 4, 567–600.

INDEX

For Product Safety Concerns and Information please contact our EU
representative GPSR@taylorandfrancis.com Taylor & Francis Verlag GmbH,
Kaufingerstraße 24, 80331 München, Germany

Batch number: 08158361

Printed by Printforce, the Netherlands